Auto Electrics

DIY Service Manual

by

Rodney Jacques
& Lindsay Porter

First published in 1996 by Porter Publishing Ltd.

Porter Publishing Ltd.
The Storehouse
Little Hereford Street
Bromyard
Hereford HR7 4DE
England

© Copyright Lindsay Porter and Porter Publishing Ltd, 1996.

British Library Cataloguing in Publication Data.

A catalogue record for this book is available from the British Library.

ISBN 1-899238-18-2

Series Editor: Lindsay Porter
Design: Martin Driscoll, Lindsay Porter and Lyndsay Berryman
Layout and Typesetting: Pineapple Publishing, Worcester
Printed in England by The Trinity Press, Worcester.

Every care has been taken to ensure that the material contained in this Service Guide is correct. However, no liability can be accepted by the authors or publishers for damage, loss, accidents, or injury resulting from any omissions or errors in the information given.

Titles in this Series:
Absolute Beginners' Service Guide
Auto Electrics - DIY Service Manual
Caravan Owner's Manual & Service Guide
Classic 'Bike Service Guide
Diesel Car Engines Service Guide
Ford Escort (Front Wheel Drive) & Orion Service Guide
Ford Fiesta (All models to 1995) Service Guide
Ford Sierra (All models) Service Guide
Land Rover Series I, II, III Service Guide
Land Rover Discovery & Range Rover Service Guide
Land Rover Defender, 90 & 110 Service Guide
Metro (1980-1990) Service Guide
MG Midget & Austin-Healey Sprite Service Guide
Mini (all models 1959-1994) Service Guide
MGB (including MGC, MGB GT V8 and MG RV8) Service Guide
Peugeot 205 Service Guide
Vauxhall Astra & Belmont (All models-1995) Service Guide
Vauxhall Cavalier Service Guide
Vauxhall Nova Service Guide
VW Beetle Service Guide

- With more titles in production -

CONTENTS

000210

Introduction

As everyone who has enjoyed working on their own vehicle will know, there is only one sure way of doing a job properly while saving money at the same time - and that's by doing it yourself!

That's why we, at Porter Manuals, have set about creating this series of how-to books. We know, from our own experience, how satisfying it is to 'get it right'. We also know how difficult it can be to find all the information you need in a form that's 'Making It Easy' to understand. So, we've done our level best, as enthusiastic DIY-ers and car owners, to provide you with the sort of book that we would like to pick up and use. With the information contained in this book, you will be able to:

- carry out your own repairs, using the step-by-step instructions given here.

- gain a clear understanding of what you're doing and why!

- enjoy what you're doing! We enjoy cars, working on cars and producing these manuals, and we hope it shows - and that you can share our enjoyment.

We hope you get a kick out of keeping your in good condition while saving money and knowing that you've carried out the work to a great standard, with the help of this book.

Happy Motoring!

Lindsay Porter
Porter Manuals

Lindsay Porter

Rodney Jacques

Acknowledgements

The one person I would most like to thank for putting me in the position to write this book is, or rather was, a used car salesman who, many years ago, convinced me that the transport I most needed was a 1957 Ford Anglia. An absolutely super car, which he just happened to have available and, just for me, at a bargain price as well.

Electrically speaking, the car was a mobile disaster area. Unknown to me, it had, at some time in the past, suffered from a short circuit behind the dash which, as this particular example was a bit short on fuses, had resulted in a burnt out, and subsequently bodged, wiring loom. The dynamo didn't produce enough power for the headlamps (when they were working) which meant that, after about thirty miles in the dark, the lights grew ever dimmer. The starter worked intermittently and the battery gave up completely after about three months.

Basically, the car was a wreck, but it gave me a good grounding in basic auto-electrics - I replaced virtually everything on the vehicle except the windscreen wipers, and they were vacuum operated.

Moving on to current issues, many people have helped with the actual production of the book and it would be invidious of me to mention any particular individual by name without listing them all. As one who avoids confrontation at almost any cost, I therefore refrain from naming any. But nearly all either work for, or are associated with, the firms listed at the back of the book.

Finally, the major reason for writing this book (other than the obvious one of money) is to try and take some of the mystique out of automobile electrics. It is, fundamentally, a practical book for practical people and if you're looking for an in-depth scientific analysis on matters such as the movement of electrons, then keep on looking, because this book is not for you. But if a down-to-earth guide is what you want, please read on!

Rodney Jacques

SPECIAL NOTE:
*Thanks are also due to Dave Pollard for supplying the information on **ICE: Eliminating Interference.***

CHAPTER 1 - SAFETY FIRST!

You must always ensure that safety is the first consideration in any job you carry out. A slight lack of concentration, or a rush to finish the job quickly can easily result in an accident, as can failure to follow the precautions outlined in this Chapter. Whereas skilled motor mechanics are trained in safe working practices you, the home mechanic, must find them out for yourself and act upon them.

Remember, accidents don't just happen, they are caused, and some of those causes are contained in the following list. Above all, ensure that whenever you work on your car you adopt a safety-minded approach at all times, and remain aware of the dangers that might be encountered.

Be sure to consult the suppliers of any materials and equipment you may use, and to obtain and read carefully any operating and health and safety instructions that may be available on packaging or from manufacturers and suppliers.

PART I: IMPORTANT POINTS

Vehicle Off Ground

ALWAYS ensure that the vehicle is properly supported when raised off the ground. Don't work on, around, or underneath a raised vehicle unless axle stands are positioned under secure, load bearing underbody areas, or the vehicle is driven onto ramps, with the wheels remaining on the ground securely chocked to prevent movement.

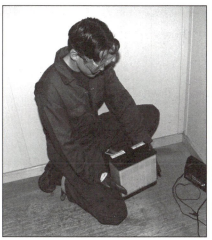

ALWAYS ensure that the safe working load rating of any jacks, hoists or lifting gear used is sufficient for the job, and that lifting gear is used only as recommended by the manufacturer.

NEVER attempt to loosen or tighten nuts that require a lot of force to turn (e.g. a tight oil drain plug) with the vehicle raised, unless it is safely supported. Take care not to pull the vehicle off its supports when applying force to a spanner. Wherever possible, initially slacken tight fastenings before raising the car off the ground.

ALWAYS wear eye protection when working under the vehicle and when using power tools.

Working On The Vehicle

ALWAYS seek specialist advice unless you are justifiably confident about carrying out each job. The safety of your vehicle affects you, your passengers and other road users.

DON'T lean over, or work on, a running engine unless it is strictly necessary, and keep long hair and loose clothing well out of the way of moving mechanical parts. Note that it is theoretically possible for fluorescent striplighting to make an engine fan appear to be stationary - double check whether it is spinning or not! This is the sort of error that happens when you're really tired and not thinking straight. So...

...DON'T work on your car when you're over tired.

ALWAYS work in a well ventilated area and don't inhale dust - it may contain asbestos or other harmful substances.

REMOVE your wrist watch, rings and all other jewellery before doing any work on the vehicle - and especially when working on the electrical system.

DON'T remove the radiator or expansion tank filler cap when the cooling system is hot, or you may get scalded by escaping coolant or steam. Let the system cool down first and even then, if the engine is not completely cold, cover the cap with a cloth and gradually release the pressure.

NEVER drain oil, coolant or automatic transmission fluid when the engine is hot. Allow time for it to cool sufficiently to avoid scalding you.

ALWAYS keep antifreeze, brake and clutch fluid away from vehicle paintwork. Wash off any spills immediately.

TAKE CARE to avoid touching any engine or exhaust system component unless it is cool enough not to burn you.

Running The Vehicle

NEVER start the engine unless the gearbox is in neutral (or 'Park' in the case of automatic transmission) and the hand brake is fully applied.

NEVER run catalytic converter equipped vehicles without the exhaust system heat shields in place.

TAKE CARE when parking vehicles fitted with catalytic

converters. The 'cat' reaches extremely high temperatures and any combustible materials under the car, such as long dry grass, could be ignited.

Personal Safety

NEVER siphon fuel, antifreeze, brake fluid or other such toxic liquids by mouth, or allow contact with your skin. There is an increasing awareness that they can damage your health. Best of all, use a suitable hand pump and wear gloves.

BEFORE undertaking dirty jobs, use a barrier cream on your hands as a protection against infection. Preferably, wear thin gloves, available from DIY outlets.

WEAR GLOVES for sure when there is a risk of used engine oil coming into contact with your skin. It can cause cancer.

WIPE UP any spilt oil, grease or water off the floor immediately, before there is an accident.

MAKE SURE that spanners and all other tools are the right size for the job and are not likely to slip. Never try to 'double-up' spanners to gain more leverage.

SEEK HELP if you need to lift something heavy which may be beyond your capability. Don't forget that when lifting a heavy weight, you should keep your back straight and bend your knees to avoid injuring your back.

NEVER take risky short-cuts or rush to finish a job. Plan ahead and allow plenty of time.

BE METICULOUS and keep the work area tidy - you'll avoid frustration, work better and lose less.

KEEP children and animals right-away from the work area and from unattended vehicles.

ALWAYS tell someone what you're doing and have them regularly check that all is well, especially when working alone on, or under, the vehicle.

PART II: HAZARDS

Fire!

Petrol (gasoline) is a dangerous and highly flammable liquid requiring special precautions. When working on the fuel system, disconnect the vehicle battery earth (ground) terminal whenever possible and always work outside, or in a very well ventilated area. Any form of spark, such as that caused by an electrical fault, by two metal surfaces striking against each other, by a central heating boiler in the garage 'firing up', or even by static electricity built up in your clothing can, in a confined space, ignite petrol vapour causing an explosion. Take great care not to spill petrol on to the engine or exhaust system, never allow any naked flame anywhere near the work area and, above all, don't smoke.

Invest in a workshop-sized fire extinguisher. Choose the carbon dioxide type or preferably, dry powder but never a water type extinguisher for workshop use. Water conducts electricity and can make worse an oil or petrol-based fire, in certain circumstances.

DON'T disconnect any fuel pipes on a fuel injected engine while the ignition is switched on. The fuel in the line is under very high pressure - sufficient to cause serious injury. Remember that many injection systems have residual pressure in the pipes for days after switching off. Consult the workshop manual or seek specialist advice before carrying out any work.

Fumes

In addition to the fire dangers described previously, petrol (gasoline) vapour and the types of vapour given off by many solvents, thinners, and adhesives are highly toxic and under certain conditions can lead to unconsciousness or even death, if inhaled. The

risks are increased if such fluids are used in a confined space so always ensure adequate ventilation when handling materials of this nature. Treat all such substances with care, always read the instructions and follow them with care.

Always ensure that the car is out of doors and not in an enclosed space when the engine is running. Exhaust fumes contain poisonous carbon monoxide, even when the car is fitted with a catalytic converter, since 'cats' sometimes fail and don't function when the engine is cold.

Never drain petrol (gasoline) or use solvents, thinners adhesives or other toxic substances in an inspection pit as the extremely confined space allows the highly toxic fumes to concentrate. Running the engine with the vehicle over the pit can have the same results. It is also dangerous to park a vehicle for any length of time over an inspection pit. The fumes from even a slight fuel leak can cause an explosion when the engine is started. Petrol fumes are heavier than air and will accumulate in the pit.

Mains Electricity

Best of all, avoid the use of mains electricity when working on the vehicle, whenever possible. For instance, you could use rechargeable tools and a DC inspection lamp, powered from a remote 12V battery - both are much safer. However, if you do use mains-powered equipment, ensure that the appliance is wired correctly to its plug, that where necessary it is properly earthed (grounded), and that the fuse is of the correct rating for the appliance is fitted. For instance, a 13 amp fuse in lead lamp's plug will not provide adequate protection. Do not use any mains powered equipment in damp conditions or in the vicinity of fuel, fuel vapour or the vehicle battery.

CHAPTER 2
DOING THE KNOWLEDGE

For many years, London cabbies have had to prove that they know every inch of the Capital's road network before being granted a cabbies' licence. The test and the months of studying required are known as "doing the knowledge". Fortunately, it won't take you months of study to begin using this Manual, but a bit of preliminary "knowledge" will prove invaluable. Part I deals with the basic tools you will require, while Parts II and III lead on to some basic - and easy to follow! - electrical theory. Hope you enjoy finding your way around!

PART I - TOOL TALK

We are living in the age of the specialist. The television engineer doesn't install aerials, the central heating expert won't fix a leaking tap and, in the automotive world, there are those who only fit exhausts or shock absorbers. Even in most car repair workshops, the ordinary mechanics won't touch automatic transmissions or get involved in electrical problems. Instead they call in the specialist - in this (latter) instance, an auto-electrician.

Obviously, it's good to be able to rely on an expert, but many electrical problems on cars can be sorted out quite easily with a few basic tools, a little common sense and a simple explanation of what it's all about. The main purpose of this book is to assist with that latter requirement, but we'll start off by looking at some of those basic (and not so basic) tool requirements.

By far the majority of us already have the most important tools of all: our eyes, ears, nose and hands. For even though we can't see, hear, smell or feel electricity - or at least, not in low voltage form, we can often use these senses to detect its presence as detailed in *Chapter 14, Fault Finding*.

Many of us will also have the basic mechanical tools such as standard pliers, assorted screwdrivers and a range of spanners including a socket set - useful because some electrical jobs, such as a starter motor repair, can involve some relatively heavy dismantling work.

That may be so, but most work of an electrical nature on cars does call for a more lightweight range of tools and it would be advisable to have a pair of thin nosed pliers, a good set of cross-head (Phillips) and straight bladed screwdrivers (all with insulated handles), a range of smaller spanners/sockets and a crimping tool for making connections. For some jobs, you may also need a soldering iron, preferably mains powered and, of

at least 150-watt capacity. If you use anything lighter, you'll wait forever for wires and components to get up to temperature and probably end up making a faulty 'dry' joint.

Most socket sets include a spark plug spanner but if not, one will be needed, and you'll also need a set of feeler gauges.

When it comes to test equipment, an essential 'beginners' item is a simple test light. These are available quite cheaply from most accessory shops and most are something like a small screwdriver in appearance, with a bulb in the handle and a lead with a crocodile clip extending from the handle end. Some actually double-up as a screwdriver, but those with a sharp probe in place of a blade are preferable - these can be used to prick through cable insulation and make contact with the actual wire, without causing any damage.

making it easy! Alternatively, a home made test light is even cheaper. All that's needed is a bulb holder (one from an old side or tail light is ideal), a couple of lengths of cable (each about 50cm long), a couple of crocodile clips and, of course a bulb. In practice, it's best to use something like a 5-watt (sidelight) bulb, but if you fit a 21-watt stoplight bulb, you can also use the light as an inspection or lead light as well - in this role you might also find it advantageous to make the leads a little longer. Admittedly, this light doesn't have the 'probe' facility, but you can always use a pin to prick through cable insulation and then connect one of the light leads to it.

Although a test light may be an extremely useful and convenient piece of equipment, it is basically just an ON/OFF indicator and therefore limited in scope. A voltmeter does almost everything a test light will and much more besides, and although it might be a little more expensive the additional capability will more than justify the extra cost.

However, stand-alone voltmeters are pretty thin on the ground and, in the majority of cases a voltmeter will be just one mode in a multi-range instrument generally referred to as a multi-meter.

Multi-meters come in all shapes and sizes and generally with prices to match. Most incorporate a voltmeter, a tachometer and a dwell facility (for setting contact breaker points) whereas the more expensive versions may have three, or more, voltage ranges, an ohm-meter, an ammeter, a diode checking facility and much more. Both digital and analogue versions are available with the former being the more expensive.

Basically, as with most things in life, you get what you pay for and, in general, the more expensive the tool, then the better it is, but do you need it? Remember, you can start off, and achieve a great deal, with just the bare minimum - a pair of pliers, a couple of screwdrivers and a simple test light. Then, as you become more competent, and more ambitious, you can buy the other items as the need arises.

2/1 There's nothing more frustrating than getting part way through a job only to find you can go no further because you don't have the right tool. In some cases there are ways of overcoming the problem, but even

then, the right tool, at the right time, would have made the job easier.

There are a number of variations in the design of fasteners (screws/bolts etc.) used on modern cars, and without the corresponding tool it can be difficult, or even impossible, to release them without damage. For some cars a metric range of spanners will be needed and for some an Imperial or inch (AF) set. Indeed, there are a few models where both may be needed.

It's much the same with screwdrivers. In a modern car's electrical system you may come across slotted-head screws, cross-head (commonly called Phillips) screws, star pattern (often referred to as Pozidriv) versions and various forms of splined head types, all requiring a compatible driver.

It therefore makes sense to buy a screwdriver/socket set similar to that shown here containing a selection of small sockets and various screwdriver bits.

2/2 The three most common types of screw head - slotted, cross (Phillips) and star shaped (Pozidriv). Obviously, only a flat

Screw head types

Slotted   Cross-head   Starred

2

bladed screwdriver can be used in a slotted-head screw, but while you can use a Phillips driver in a Pozidriv screw with some degree of success, you can't, or shouldn't, try doing it the other way round - using a Pozidriv driver in a Phillips headed screw.

2/3 If you intend adding electrical accessories, you're almost certain to need a range of connectors and some form of crimping tool. While it's true that most accessories come with all the connectors required to complete the job, it's wise to have a few spares available - or even a box full of them!

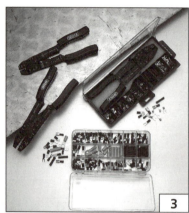

2/4 Although soldered connections on modern cars are far less common than they were some years ago, they haven't been completely eliminated and, with some repair jobs, a soldered joint is still the preferred option. For most applications, a mains powered soldering iron would be best although, for more intricate work the re-chargeable versions could be of more use.

2/5 Most socket sets contain a spark plug spanner, but if not (and unless your car's a diesel), it's one tool you will be sure to need. It's not uncommon now for the plugs to be deeply recessed in the cam

cover and the long tubular type spanner will be required.

INSIDE INFORMATION: One advantage with using a purpose built spanner is that there is far less danger of overtightening the plug in the head - the handle won't give that much leverage.

6

2/6 While on the subject of spark plugs, it is sometimes desirable to check that the HT current is reaching the plug. The old method of holding the plug lead about 6mm (1/4in) away from an earth point and watching for the spark can now be both dangerous to the operator and harmful to many modern ignition systems. Using a set of HT testers like these will overcome both hazards.

2/7 A selection of test lights, some with a 'prick-through' pointer and others with a screwdriver blade. Under normal circumstances one of the 'prick-through' variety would be of more use as a diagnostic tool, but it's a matter of personal preference.

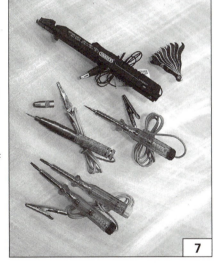

7

SAFETY FIRST!
Note that these testers are not designed for use on the domestic mains supply.

2/8 There are a wide selection of multi-meters available, some with only a volts, an ignition dwell and an engine speed (tachometer) measuring capability, whereas other, more sophisticated versions such as that shown here may have more than ten different functions. While the limited range (and lower priced) models are adequate for basic electrical work and fault finding, those with more facilities are obviously more useful.

8

2/9 One question that's often asked about multi-meters is, "Which is the most accurate - analogue (with a needle and scale) or digital (with a numeric display)?" The answer has to be, the digital versions, but in reality it's very seldom that such a high degree of accuracy is required and, perhaps of even more importance, the scale of an analogue meter can be designed to provide much more information than a digital display. The analogue versions are, in general, less expensive but, as explained later on in the relevant chapter, should not be used when carrying some checks on electronic equipment.

9

2/10 Kits such as this, with a wide selection of tools and test equipment *are* really intended for the professional auto-electrician. But they are generally available and usually at a price somewhat less than the cost of the individual items. One major advantage of such a kit is that everything is contained in one box and is well protected.

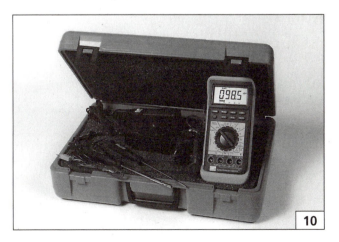

10

11

12

2/11 To some people, the only connection an exhaust gas analyser has with a car's electrical system is its (12 volt) power supply. That may be so, but when working on electronic ignition or fuel injection systems, it's often desirable to run a check on the exhaust CO (Carbon Monoxide) levels and the only way of doing so is with an analyser. It's also extremely useful for pre-MoT checks.

2/12 Extra lights may help lighten up the darkness, but the additional load on the electrical system and wiring could result in an overload leading to burnt out wiring and switches. But, it doesn't have to if you work out what the additional load is (in amps) and then re-wire accordingly. See *Chapter 3, Electrical Circuits.*

PART II: CURRENT VALUES

Just as in a subway or underground transport system, the wiring layout in a car is basically a distribution network, delivering power from a central supply base (the battery) to various consumer units (lights, windscreen wipers and so on) spread throughout the car. As a complete system it looks very complicated and difficult to follow but, taken on its own, each individual circuit is quite simple, especially when, as with an Underground or Subway map, each one is a different colour.

Any circuit, by its very nature, must have a beginning and an end. And for anything to move around that circuit, there must be some primary force or difference in potential between one end and the other.

Perhaps, the easiest method of showing how an electrical current flows through a simple circuit is to compare it with a similar hydraulic (water) version.

2/13 In this, the two tanks contain water at different levels and, when the tap is opened, water will flow from the left hand tank to that on the right until the two are equal. The reason it does so is the pressure applied by the extra weight of water in the left hand tank.

2/14 In our simple electrical circuit, the battery has a 'high pressure' terminal generally referred to as the positive (+) and a 'low pressure' one called the negative (-). When the switch is closed, electricity will flow from positive to negative until both are equal - the battery is then considered flat. In electrical terms, the 'pressure' that causes the flow is measured in Volts and is dependant on the size and capacity of the battery - on most cars it will be 12 volts. In some text books this pressure may be referred to as the potential difference or electro-motive force (emf).

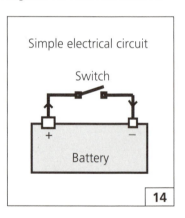

Simple electrical circuit

14

How quickly water flows through our hydraulic circuit is dependant upon a number of factors covered in the next paragraph, but it can be measured in litres per minute. In an electrical circuit the rate of current flow is normally measured in Amperes or, as it is generally known, Amps.

Going back to the hydraulic circuit - it is pretty obvious that the rate of flow from one tank to the other is primarily dependant on the resistance to movement created by the tap, the size (length and bore) of the pipe and the finish of its internal surface. It's much the same with the electrical circuit where a resistance can be created at the switch and along the cable, again depending upon its length/width and, in this case the material from which it is made. To a lesser extent its temperature will also have an effect. The unit of electrical resistance is the Ohm, (named after the German physicist

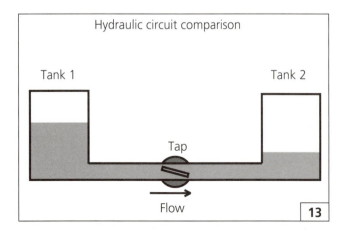

Hydraulic circuit comparison

Tank 1

Tank 2

Tap

Flow

13

Georg Simon Ohm). One Kilo-ohm (KΩ) = 1,000 ohms and one Megohm (MΩ) = 1,000 Kilo-ohms.

Obviously the three factors (volts, amps and ohms) are related, but it was the aforementioned German physicist who defined the relationship in what is considered the most fundamental rule in electrical engineering - Ohm's Law.

The strength of an electrical current is equal to the voltage applied, divided by the resistance of the conductor.

In formal symbols, if V is the voltage, I is the current in amperes and R the resistance in ohms, the law may be expressed as:

$$I = V/R \quad \text{or} \quad R = V/I \quad \text{or} \quad V = I \times R$$

These formulae can be of use in more advanced fault finding techniques when, if two values are known the third can be easily calculated.

WATT POWER?

Another formula which is perhaps of even more use is that relating to power.

With two exceptions, all electrical components in our cars are power consuming items - the exceptions being the battery which acts as an electrical storage pot and the generator which converts mechanical power into electricity.

Exactly how much power each component consumes depends upon the type of unit and the work it does. For example, a headlight will consume more power than a sidelight simply because it's bigger and brighter; a windscreen wiper motor will need more power to wipe a dry screen than it would a wet one because the wiper blade will be more difficult to move; a starter motor will make considerable demands on the power supply when starting a cold engine, but much less when it is warm.

Electrical power is generally measured in Watts and is, of course, related to both the voltage in a circuit and the current consumed, and again, by using the following formula, the value of any one can be calculated when the other two are known. (W = Watts):

$$I = W/V \quad \text{or} \quad V = W/I \quad \text{or} \quad W = V \times I$$

Calculations of this nature are often used when fitting additional components into the electrical system, a typical example of which would be a set of fog or spot (driving) lights. Although it would be quite an easy operation to add these to the existing wiring set-up, there could be a danger of creating an overload with burnt out cables and/or switches.

Cables and switches are rated by their current carrying capacity and, in this particular situation, it would be useful to know exactly how much (extra) current the fog lights would draw. This could then be added to the existing load and if the total was higher than that specified, the new lights could be wired independently of any existing circuits.

Assuming, for convenience, that the lights were fitted with 60 watt bulbs, their current consumption could be worked out as follows (bearing in mind that there are two of them):

$$I = W/V \quad \text{or } I = 60 \times 2 \div 12 = 10 \text{ amps}$$

*INSIDE INFORMATION: If your car is one of the old-timers such as earlier VW Beetles or cheaper '50s Fords with a six volt electrical system, the current consumption would be doubled (**not** halved!) and therefore heavier gauge cable may be required.*

The watt is a relatively small unit of power and in some domestic (and industrial) situations the kilo-watt (kW) or 1,000 watt unit is used. For example, an electric fire may be rated at 1, 2 or 3 kW. Indeed, in some industrial situations (power stations) the mega-watt (MW) or 1,000 kW unit is quoted.

Whereas, in the past, it was general practice to quote engine power in BHP (brake horse-power) or the German PS-DIN equivalent, in the interests of standardisation, it is now often given in kilo-watts. However, these factors can be easily converted:

1 PS-DIN = 0.736kW or 736 W
1 kW = 1.359 PS-DIN

A 65 horsepower engine will therefore be described as a 48kW unit (65 x 0.736). The correct answer should be 47.84kW, but the figures are always rounded off (up or down) to the nearest whole number.

Typical power consumption figures:

Continuous loads	Prolonged loads	Brief loads
Ignition 20W	Headlights (each) 60W	Stop lights (each) 21W
Electric fuel pump 55W	Sidelights (each) 5W	Indicator lights (each) 21W
Fuel Injection 90W	Rear lights (each) 5W	Radiator fan 200W
	Number plate light 10W	Horn 40W
	Panel lights (each) 2W	Starter motor 800-2500W
	Windscreen wiper 30-100W	Power windows 150W
	Heated rear window 130W	Rear wiper 60W
	Auxiliary lights (each) 55W	Cigarette lighter 100W
	Heater motor 60W	Interior light 5W
	Radio/cassette 15W	Headlight wash/wipe 60W

The Simple Circuit

As we've already seen, any circuit must have a beginning and an end, and in automotive situations these are the positive and negative terminals on the battery.

2/15 In the most basic of circuits (Fig 1/15), we have the battery as the power source, the item that's being powered - or as it's often called, the consumer unit (bulb, electric motor, heater or whatever), a switch to turn it on or off, and the necessary cable runs to link them all together.

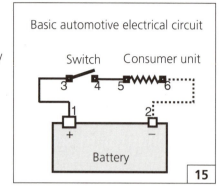

Basic automotive electrical circuit

15

When the switch is closed, current flows from the battery (+) terminal, through the switch to the consumer unit and either lighting the bulb or causing the motor to turn. But, as in our hydraulic circuit, it doesn't stop there for the circuit has to be complete and the current flow continues, albeit at a reduced pressure, back to the negative terminal on the battery. This state of affairs will then continue until the switch is opened again or the battery runs down, or indeed, until a fault develops in the circuit.

If closing the switch doesn't have the expected result - that of lighting the bulb or driving the motor - there is a fault. This may be visually obvious - a disconnected cable, for instance - or it may be that you will need either a test light or voltmeter (multimeter) to locate the problem. If so, it makes sense to follow a logical test sequence and, with this circuit, the procedure would be as shown in Figs. **2/16 - 2/21**.

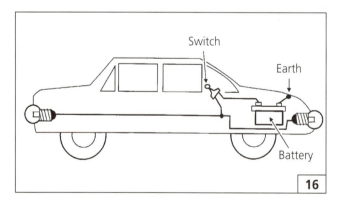

16

2/16 In practice, there is rarely an earth, or 'return' cable as such (other than on plastic bodied cars.). The metal body of the vehicle acts as if it is the earth 'wire' and the battery earth connection is strapped to the car's body.

2/17 The first step would be to check the power source - in this case the battery. Do so, by connecting the testlight or voltmeter across the two battery terminals (1 & 2), remembering that the voltmeter red

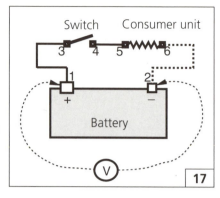

17

lead should go to battery positive (1) and the black lead to the negative terminal (2). The test light can be connected either way. Should there be no reaction (no light or reading on the voltmeter), either the battery is (very) flat or your test instrument is defective.

2/18 If the test proves positive (light or reading), leave the negative terminal connection (2) intact, but move the other lead (or probe in the case of a test light) to the switch input terminal (3). A positive result here, proves that circuit between points 1 & 3 is intact.

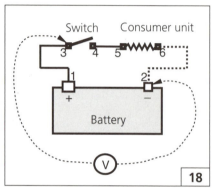

18

2/19 Next, move the lead from the switch input (3) to the output terminal (4), which will test the switch (which must be closed). A good reading proves that the switch is satis-

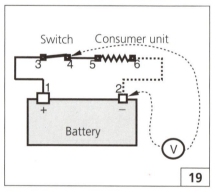

19

factory whereas no reading indicates a faulty switch.

INSIDE INFORMATION: Try operating it a few times to see if there's an intermittent fault.

2/20 If the switch is in order move the 'floating' lead to the consumer unit input terminal (5) in order to check the remainder of the supply circuit - the switch should be left in the On position.

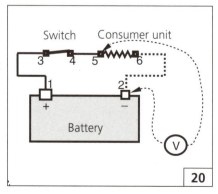

20

2/21 No reading at this point would obviously indicate a wiring fault between (4) and (5), whereas a good reading most likely means a faulty consumer unit.

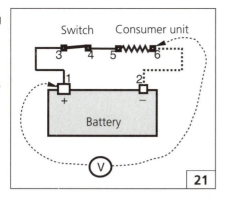

21

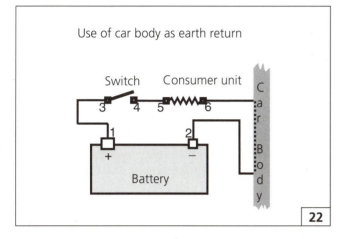

Use of car body as earth return

22

2/22 In practice this will normally be as far as you can go with a test light simply because there will be no consumer output terminal as such. The remainder of the circuit (6 back to 2) will be what is known as an earth return (Fig. 2/22) through the consumer unit mounting arrangement and the body of the car. However, even this can usually be checked out by moving the test light (voltmeter) 'fixed' lead from the battery negative (2) to battery positive (1) and then touching the 'floating' lead on to terminal (6) or the body of the consumer unit. A good reading here would normally indicate that the 'earth-return' part of the circuit is satisfactory.

There are other methods of checking this section of the circuit as detailed in *Chapter 14, Fault Finding*.

Obviously, in practice, it does get more complicated than the procedure shown here and access to some points may be difficult, but it's always possible to skip one or more checks and then work backwards. For example, after ensuring that the power supply (battery) was performing as it should, you could go straight to the consumer input. A reading here (with the switch closed) would indicate that the circuit was in order and the consumer unit faulty.

Of course, not all circuits are quite as basic as these shown here. In fact very few are! But neither are they that much more difficult to follow. Some may have more than one consumer unit along the line and these may be wired differently (in parallel) and, of course, with an earth return, but the general check sequence will be much the same.

making it easy! Don't try to be too clever. Many's the time that hours have been spent tracing a fault that doesn't exist - check in the car handbook for any peculiar switching sequence (you may even have forgotten something simple, such as switching the ignition on first - we've all done it!) and, if it's a lighting fault, check the bulb first!

Combined Circuits

Unfortunately, as already stated, very few of the electrical circuits in a car are quite as basic as our example, simply because such layouts just wouldn't be practical. For instance, we have shown just one consumer unit in the circuit, whereas in practice there may be four or even more and to give each its own separate cable and switch would be both extremely expensive and complex.

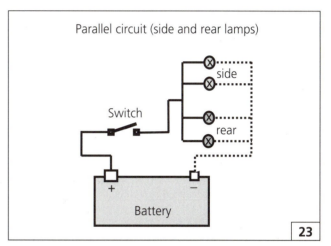

Parallel circuit (side and rear lamps)

23

2/23 A typical example would be the side and rear lights, all of which need to be switched on and off at the same time. It would therefore be logical to wire them all through one switch and our basic side and rear light circuit diagram (Fig. **2/23**) shows how this is done. In this layout, each light is wired in parallel with the others and each is, in effect, an individual circuit with the voltage across each being the same (12 volts).

Circuits of this nature may seem more complex than our basic example, but in reality they are nothing more than a number of those simple layouts joined into one and, as such, are almost as easy to check through should a fault occur. Indeed, in some cases, where only one light has failed, they can be easier on the assumption that, if all the other lights are working, everything must be satisfactory up to the connection for that particular light.

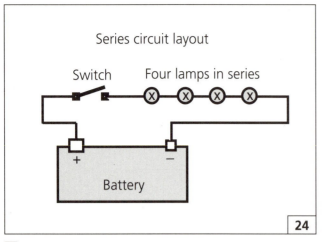

Series circuit layout

Switch   Four lamps in series

+   −

Battery

24

☐ **2/24** Although not very often used in automotive applications, there is another method of wiring, whereby the lights, or any other consumer units, are connected in series - one behind the other as shown in Fig. **2/24**. In this, there is only one circuit and the applied voltage would be shared between the four lights. Assuming they were all the same, each would therefore need a 3 volt bulb (in a 12 volt electrical system):

Although rarely used in automotive wiring, in the domestic field, some 240 volt Christmas Tree lighting sets use this arrangement with, perhaps, 40 x 6 volt bulbs all wired up one after the other which, of course, brings about the famous drawback, that if one bulb blows, they all go out!

Current Types

The two main types of electric current are direct current (DC) and alternating current (AC) and both are used in automotive applications, although AC is only used to a very limited extent.

It is easier to generate and transmit AC current, hence its widespread use in domestic and industrial applications but, unlike DC, it can't be stored in a battery, hence its limited appeal for automotive use. However, in most modern cars the alternator produces an AC current which is then converted to DC for battery storage purposes.

INSIDE INFORMATION: Direct current flows continuously in much the same way as a fluid would do in our hydraulic circuit - that is, in a steady flow or stream. Conventionally, it is said to flow from positive to negative and - despite the fact that, as a matter of fact, electron flow flows from negative to positive - for all practical purposes the conventional 'myth' (positive to negative) can be used and is so throughout this book.

As its name implies, alternating current undergoes rhythmic changes of direction in very rapid cycles. There are no positive and negative poles as such, just continuous forward and backward movements, each combination of which is one cycle. The number of cycles per second is known as the frequency or, in more modern terms, Hertz (Hz). In the UK and most of Europe, the household mains frequency is 50Hz, whereas in the United States it is 60Hz.

For all practical purposes on the car, the difference between the two types of electricity can be ignored and even though the alternator generates an AC current, it is, in by far the majority of cases, converted to DC within the unit itself. In other words, the actual *output* from the alternator is DC.

PART III: ELECTRICITY & MAGNETISM

There's a very close relationship between electricity and magnetism. In a car electricity is used to create magnetic forces and conversely magnetic forces are used to generate electricity.

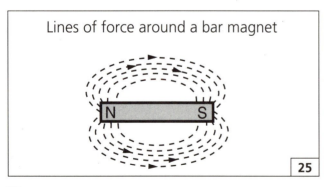

Lines of force around a bar magnet

N   S

25

☐ **2/25** As any school girl and boy knows, a bar of steel that has been magnetised develops a North pole at one end and a South pole at the other. Neither of these are readily apparent, but in a standard scientific demonstration involving a magnetised bar, a sheet of paper and some iron filings, the magnetic field surrounding the bar can be made obvious, with the lines of force making up the field clearly visible and showing up as tracks between the two poles.
Furthermore, it's also a widely known fact that 'like' poles repel one another, whereas opposite poles attract. In other words, if the North poles of two magnets were brought into close proximity with one another, they would try to push themselves apart, whereas if it were two different poles (one North, the other South), they would try and pull themselves into contact with one another. Both poles would attract a non-magnetised material, assuming of course it was a material that could be magnetised - this would exclude some metals such as brass or copper which are non-magnetic.

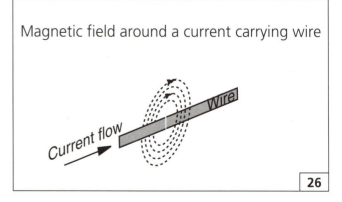

Magnetic field around a current carrying wire

Current flow   Wire

26

☐ **2/26** The interesting thing as far as auto-electrics are concerned is that, when an electric current flows through a wire, a similar effect occurs and a magnetic field is set up around that wire. However, in this case, the lines of force are in the form of concentric circles around the wire, travelling in a clockwise direction when viewed in line with the current flow (see diagram).

If the wire carrying the current is wound in the form of a coil, the lines of force will form a magnetic field around the coil, very similar to that around a bar magnet. Indeed if a steel bar were inserted into the coil, it would become magnetised with North and South poles identical to those shown in **2/25**. This steel bar would then remain magnetised, even if the power supply to the coil was switched off or the bar removed from the coil. It would, in effect, become a permanent magnet.

Mind you, as already stated, not all materials *can* be magnetised - and of those that can, not all retain their magnetism when the 'power' source is removed. Soft iron is one such material. When enclosed within a coil of wire it will become magnetised when a current flows through that wire - in fact it will help create a stronger magnetic field than that produced by the coil alone. But immediately the current is switched off, it loses its magnetism.

By using this effect, a temporary magnet is produced which can be switched on and off at will, and devices of this type are used in a variety of ways throughout the car. In by far the majority of cases, such devices are used to attract a piece of iron (when switched on) which, in turn, is linked to (and operates) either a switch or some mechanical device. These devices are known as solenoids or relays, depending on their exact function.

Solenoids and Relays

Quite a lot of the car's equipment carries an electrical load which is greater than the capacity of a regular dash-mounted switch. For example, both the starter motor and the headlights come into this category. To overcome this difficulty, the ignition key switch operates a solenoid, which *does* have the capacity to operate the starter motor, and the solenoid operates the starter. Your lighting switch operates the headlights in the same way, but via a relay. Devilish cunning, these auto-electricians!

☐ **2/27** A solenoid is made up of a coil of wire (windings) with a Spring loaded, soft iron rod floating in its centre, the rod being attached to one pole of a heavy-duty switch. When the solenoid is energised, by passing a relatively small electrical current through the windings, the magnetic field set up around the windings attracts the iron rod (or plunger) and pulls it in towards the centre of the coil, against the pressure of a spring. In doing so it moves one pole of the (heavy-duty) switch into contact with another and in this case, provides a path for (i.e. 'switches on') the high amperage current needed by the starter motor.

Once the power to the solenoid windings is switched off, the magnetic field collapses and the plunger is forced back by the spring, so separating the heavy-duty switch contacts and interrupting the circuit to the starter motor. One of the most obvious uses of this kind of arrangement is the starter solenoid. Depending upon the type of starter motor fitted, this may be either a relatively simple magnetic switch, or the same kind of switch combined with a mechanical lever arrangement. This latter type is more fully described in *Chapter 6, Starter Systems*.

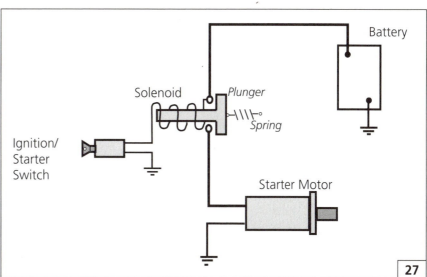

27

☐ **2/28** Located in the heavy-duty cable between the battery and starter motor, the solenoid is operated by an electrical current supplied through the ignition/starter switch. Its purpose is twofold. In the first place it provides a more positive switching arrangement (less arcing between the switch contacts) than could be achieved with manual operation, and second it obviates the need for a heavy-duty switch at the dash, along with the use of thick, high current-carrying cables to and from it.

Other, more lightweight solenoids are used throughout the car. Many carburettors and diesel fuel injection pumps are fitted with solenoid fuel cut-off valves, the vast majority of petrol injection systems employ solenoid operated injectors. Most central locking systems, anti-lock braking systems and even some interior heater controls feature solenoids at some point

28

in their circuit layout. However, despite this solenoids are outnumbered on most modern cars by their close relation, the relay.

2/29 In most cases a relay is used as a remote control switch, and often for the very same reasons a solenoid is used in the starter circuit - the ability to switch a heavy current by means of a much smaller, control current. Typical applications include a switching arrangement for headlights, heated rear window elements,

horns and other high current consuming items. Relays, in one form or another are often used for intermittent operation of the windscreen wipers, as a safety measure in some fuel pump circuits and sometimes as flasher units for direction indicators - and that's not counting those used in advanced electronic control functions - engine management, anti-lock braking and transmission systems.

In theory a relay is very much like the solenoid, but instead of a moving central rod or plunger, the windings surround a fixed central soft iron core (armature) which, when energised attracts a spring loaded, hinged 'clapper' plate. Depending on the type of relay, this movement either makes of breaks two (or more) contacts.

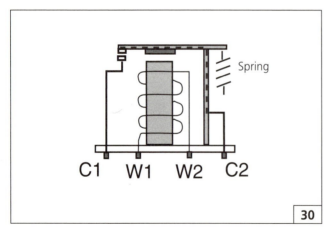

2/30 A simple relay will normally have four terminals, two for the winding and two for the contacts carrying the heavy current. In this illustration these are shown as C1 and C2. When a (small) current is passed through the winding (terminals W1 and W2) the central core becomes magnetised and attracts the clapper plate, so closing the two contacts and providing a circuit between C1 and C2 for the heavy current. Some form of spring is used to open the contacts when the winding current is interrupted.

FACT FILE: RELAY MARKINGS.

Unfortunately there is no common standard for terminal markings, but the following table shows some of the most common equivalents:

C1	87	88a	H
C2	30	88	B
W1	85	85	P or S
W2	86	86	Unmarked

Induction Coils

With all the above devices (solenoids, relays and the like) electricity is used to produce magnetism, but there are also a number of components on the car where magnetism is used to produce electricity and one such component is the ignition coil. It is, in fact, a form of induction coil used to produce a high voltage current from a low voltage input.

Just as passing an electrical current through a wire produces a magnetic field around that wire, then passing a wire through a magnetic field produces an electrical current within the wire.

Think of two wires laid side by side, with an electrical current flowing through just one of them and the other lying within the magnetic field created by the first. If the current is suddenly interrupted, the magnetic field will collapse inwards and, as it does so, its lines of force will be cut by the second wire. In this scenario, the magnetic field moves in relation to the wire, but it has the same effect as a wire moving through a magnetic field and induces a momentary surge of current in the second wire.

In an induction coil, the two wires are wound around an iron core with one forming what is known as the primary or low-tension (LT) winding and the other making up the secondary, or high-tension (HT) winding.

2/31 The ignition coil is made up of two windings wrapped around a soft iron core. The primary winding consists of around 300 turns of relatively thick wire connected through some form of 'make-and-break' switching arrangement to the ignition switch, while the secondary winding could be up to around 12,000 turns of a much finer wire connected ultimately to each of the sparking plugs.

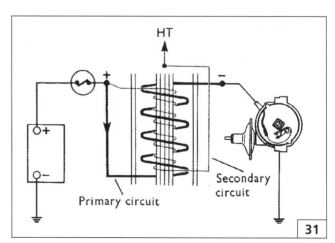

When the ignition is switched on and normal battery voltage is applied to the primary winding, the magnetic field created around the soft iron core encompasses the secondary winding. Once the (primary) power supply is interrupted, the magnetic field collapses and its lines of force are cut by the thousands of turn of wire making up the secondary winding. This induces a high voltage pulse of around 15,000 volts or so into the secondary winding which is then used to produce a spark at the designated plug.

In this instance, there are a number of factors affecting both the voltage (pressure) and strength of the current so generated. These include the size of the magnetic field (the more lines of force, the greater the induced current), the speed with which any movement takes place, the number of wires involved and their relative positions.

In a typical ignition coil the strength of the magnetic field is determined by the size of the primary winding and the low voltage current (12 volts). How fast things happen is largely dependant on the engine concerned (number of cylinders) and engine speed but, on a four-cylinder engine, would normally be in the region of 6-8,000 cycles per minute. However, it is the number of wires, or rather the number of coils in each winding, that has the greatest bearing on the output - a ratio of about 40:1 with a few hundred in the primary winding as opposed to thousands in the secondary.

32

☐ **2/32** Ignition coils can be checked for condition by measuring the resistance of both the primary and secondary windings and comparing the results with the manufacturers specifications.

Generators

It is this principle of moving a wire through a magnetic field that is the basis of generator theory, whether it is in a power station or on a simple bicycle. By far the majority of energy producing (or rather, *converting*) machines are rotary, whether they are a water wheel, a gas turbine or a typical car engine, so it naturally follows that any electricity generating device being coupled to them should also have a rotating action. And so it is, with either the dynamo or alternator on a car almost always belt driven from a pulley on the front end of the engine crankshaft.

33

☐ **2/33** Compared with the dynamo used on older cars, the modern alternator is very reliable, compact and long lasting. But most are still belt driven from the engine crankshaft.

☐ **2/34** Fundamentally, any vehicle's generator is made up of a horseshoe shaped permanent magnet with a loop of wire mounted on a rotating spindle within its two legs. Then, as the spindle (and wire loop) rotate, the wire cuts the magnetic lines

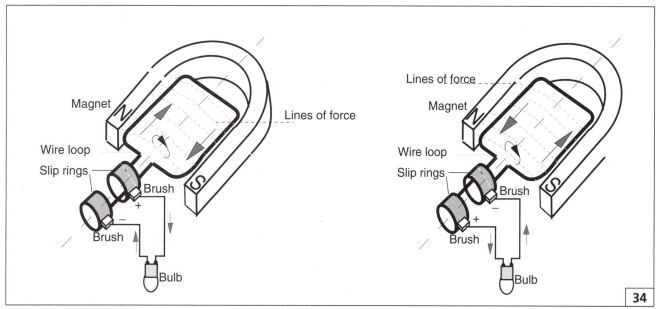

34

of force set up between the North and South poles of the magnet, and a small electric current will be generated in the wire. If each end of the wire terminates in a slip ring, each of which is insulated from the other, this current can be picked up by static brushes rubbing on the slip rings and used to power any electrical device.

As the central spindle (and wire loop) rotate, the wire will cut the lines of force making up the magnetic field, generating a small surge of current within the wire. However, when the loop turns through 180° the section of wire that cut the magnetic field at the North pole will now do so at the South pole and the current flow will be reversed. This is known as alternating current and while perfectly adequate for lighting a bulb, and for many domestic applications, it isn't of much use on the car.

Unfortunately, due to this changing current flow in the rotating loop, the electricity so generated is totally unsuitable for battery charging. Consequently, before it can be used, it has to be converted into direct current, which is acceptable to the battery. How this is done is explained in *Chapter 5, Charging Systems*.

In practice, other than on some motor-cycles, most automotive generators use an electro-magnet rather than the permanent one shown in the illustration. The major reason for this is that generator output can be controlled by varying the strength of the magnetic field - virtually impossible with a permanent magnet, but relatively easy with an electro-magnet.

Motors

The primary difference between a generator and a motor is that instead of physically rotating the wire loop so that the wire cuts the lines of force, an electrical current is passed through it. This sets up a magnetic field around the wire which is opposed by that from the permanent magnet, so forcing the wire loop to turn.

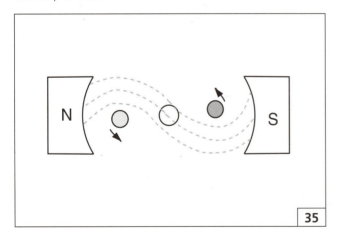

2/35 In one sense, magnetic lines of force can be likened to elastic bands in that they always try to pull themselves straight. In an electric motor those between the N and S poles of the permanent magnet would normally be more or less straight, but when an electrical current is passed through the wire loop, the resultant magnetic field set up around the wire distorts those (permanent magnet) lines of force and, in trying

to resume their normal path, they reject the wire, so turning the loop.

With an alternating current and its continual reversal in current flow (see Fig. **2/34**), the loop keeps turning. But not so with direct current: Having turned through 180 degrees, the polarity of the wire and that of the permanent magnet would be such that they would attract one another. The loop would be held enthralled by the opposing poles of the magnet and the result would be a very rigid 'motor' - which is why direct current can't be used in this way.

As with generators this is overcome on DC machines by dispensing with one of the slip rings and dividing the other into two (half- round) segments, each being connected to one side of the loop and also in contact with one of the brushes. This split type of slip ring is known as a commutator. In practice, there are a number of loops (possibly 30 or more) and each is connected across two segments of the commutator.

The operation of the commutator is explained in more detail in *Chapter 5, Charging System*s.

Now that you've 'Done The Knowledge' and know something of your way around, it's time to get out there into the big, busy, real world of your car's electrical system!

CHAPTER 3
ELECTRICAL CIRCUITS

If the sight of the knitting bag of wires in your cars loom, or the hyroglyphics of a wiring diagram give you daytime nightmares, don't worry; you're not alone! But things aren't as bad as they seem, and with the aid of this Chapter, you'll be able to find your way through the maze.

SAFETY FIRST!
Always remove the battery earth lead before tinkering with your car's electrical system. The only exception is when you need to find a live/earth lead before you commence the fitting and wiring procedure. In this case, you should use your 12v tester to ascertain which wires are which and then remove the earth lead.

Almost every part of the car is connected in some way with the electrical system. Those long coloured tentacles of cable wind and loop into every corner and link to every electrical component. Fortunately, tracing wiring is not too difficult, thanks to the systems used by (almost!) all manufacturers.

3/1 Although a mass of cables like this might seem confusing to begin with, tracing any particular one isn't all that difficult. Unfortunately, there is no standard method of illustrating a wiring diagram and no international agreement on cable colouring. What this means is that wiring diagram layouts vary considerably, with some much easier to read and follow than others and the system of coloured cables in, for example, a German built car will often not be the same as one made in America or Japan - and not all of the cars built in the same country will always follow the same system.

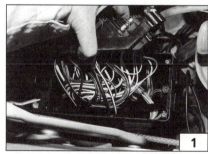

FACT FILE: MODULAR WIRING

Because of the increasing amount of vehicle electronics, many manufacturers are going over to a modular type of wiring system, as commonly used on American cars, along with the American colour coding system.

With the modular wiring system, each vehicle contains a number of smaller wiring looms and, as a result, the same colour might be used for different systems in different parts of the car. This means that, in order to know which cable you are looking at, you need to be sure which system (i.e. which wiring loom) it relates to. For this, you will need access to the manufacturers wiring diagram for your car. You may have no option but to pay a visit to your local main dealer and find out there the information you need.

In addition, some manufacturers, such as Ford, have changed what were traditionally regarded as their regular colour codes. As a result, European Fords - at least the ones that are part of Ford's World Cars program - have changed from using Brown (BN) as their earth/ground colour, to using Black (BK). Once again, the moral is - check your manual or main dealer!

Take note also, that with the modular system in use, manufacturers are taking the opportunity to give more information on their wiring diagrams. Until you crack the codes, this can seem somewhat daunting - but in fact, its a great opportunity to understand more about the system, if you check it out carefully! Here's an example, from Ford again:

31S-AC3A | 1.5 BK/RD

The Ford Key will explain that all these symbols provide really useful information! 31 = Ground; S = Additionally switched circuit; AC = Headlight levelling; 3 = Switch connection; A = Branch; 1.5 = 1.5 sq. mm cable; BK/RD = Black basic colour, Red identification colour.

As a result of all this World Car stuff, cars from what were once thought of as different manufacturers from different parts of the world now have the same system in use. For example, all Jaguars from the XK8 model-on have adopted the Ford (i.e., largely the American) coding system.

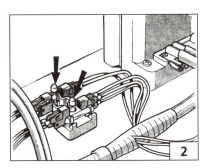

2

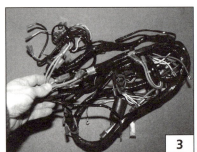

3

☐ **3/2** Years ago, things were superficially simpler. Cars had fewer cables but most were the same colour and were poorly insulated by today's standards - so there were down-sides too. But the good news about today's wiring systems is that, despite the differences, there is a rational basis to it all and once you know how to sort your way through, it's not nearly as complicated as it seems.

Obviously, it is not possible to cover all the various colour alternatives in these pages, but if we go through the standard British (Lucas) system, it should give some idea of what it's all

making it easy! **3/3** The colours used in a wiring loom, for instance, do have some sort of logic behind them. In most cases, a single principal colour is used for each main area of the system, with trace colours (stripes) being used for the sub-circuits. For example, the main feed for the lights may be blue, with the sub-circuit from the dipswitch to the dipped headlights being blue with a red trace and that to the main beams being blue/white. Once you get to know the system on your particular car, tracing any individual circuit becomes fairly straightforward. The other thing to realise right at the beginning is that, though the whole system may look like a single great tangle of wiring, it is not just one enormous circuit, but a lot of smaller, simpler circuits, linked together.

about and the table of colour equivalents shown in **FACT FILE: CABLE COLOUR CODING** will be of assistance if your car originates from elsewhere.

The place to start is the point where all the power comes from - the battery. There are usually two main cables running from

FACT FILE: TRADITIONAL COLOUR CODING

This is a guide to what have been traditionally the most commonly used cable colours. Bear in mind that World cars are increasingly using the American system - see **FACT FILE - MODULAR WIRING**. In addition, some manufacturers simply refuse to play the game at all! Some Citroens, for instance, don't colour code their cables at all. They use a dab of what appears to be paint on each end of each (identically coloured) cable, trusting to luck that the paint doesn't get worn off. When (not if!) it does, there's nothing for it but to trace each individual cable through the loom with a circuit tester. Some mechanics have even been known to resort to cutting entire sections of loom open so that cables can be physically traced - a horrifying thought!

However, in the vast majority of cases, consult your workshop manual for specific information on the colours used on your car and take a look at the typical examples used below - but do bear in mind that not all manufacturers stick to them!

Circuit	British	French	German	Japanese
Battery or solenoid to alternator	Brown	Black/blue	Red	White/red
Alternator to ignition warning light	Brown/yellow	Grey/black	Blue	White/red
Ignition switch to coil	White	Red	Black	Black/white
Ignition coil to distributor	White/black	Black	Green	Black
Ignition switch to warning light	White	Black/red	Black	Green
Ignition switch to starter solenoid	White/red	Black	Red/black	Black/yellow
Ignition fuse to wiper motor	Orange	Red	Green	Blue/red
Ignition fuse to flasher	Green	Grey/red	Black	Green
Ignition fuse to stop-light switch	Green	Grey/red	Black/red	Green/yellow
Light switch to side/tail lights	Red	Red/maroon	Grey	Green/blue
Light switch to dipswitch	Blue	Blue	White/black	Red/yellow
Dipswitch to dip beam	Blue/red	Grey/green	Yellow	Red/black
Light switch to main beam	Blue/white	Grey/pink	White	Red/white
Wiper switch to wiper motor	Orange/blue	Red	Black/yellow	Blue/white
Stop-light switch to stop lights	Green/purple	Salmon/pink	Black/red	Green/yellow
Flasher unit to indicator switch	L/green/brown	Black/blue	Black/white	Yellow
Indicator switch to L/H flashers	Green/red	Grey/violet (front) black violet (rear)	Blue/black	Green /red
Indicator switch to R/H flashers	Green/white Green/black	Yellow/maroon (front) Black/maroon (rear)		Black/green
Petrol gauge to tank unit	Green/black	Red/yellow	Brown	Yellow
Horn push to horn	Purple/black	Red/white	Brown	Green
Earth	Black	Black	Brown	Black

the two battery terminals. One is connected straight to the metal bodywork or chassis. This is the earth cable and it provides the return to the battery for every circuit in the car. It is via the other cable that power is distributed throughout the vehicle. It is thick and heavily insulated and it connects initially directly to the starter solenoid.

Wiring Diagrams

3/4 These are the basics of a (British) colour coded wiring diagram with one predominant cable colour for each specific area such as the ignition (white) or lighting (blue). The diagram is not supposed to represent the layout on any particular car and neither is it strictly correct. For instance, the stop lights and in some cases the indicators may not be wired through the ignition or even through the fuse box and, in such cases the colour coding will be different.

Nearly all wiring diagrams are printed in black and white only, so the colours are identified by a letter code (but note that different manufacturers may use different codes - see your manual):

B Black	U Blue	N Brown	G Green	O Orange
P Purple	R Red	S Slate	W white	Y Yellow

NB Where a cable has a trace colour it will be shown by a two letter code. For example, a green cable with a red trace (L/H flasher lights) will be shown as GR or G/R.

So as to keep things fairly simple, we haven't included some circuits, such as those for the windscreen wipers (orange coloured cables) or instrument panel, and neither have we incorporated all the components in the circuits we have shown

- relays in the headlight circuits for instance, or the flasher unit for the indicators. You'll need your manual for those. Furthermore on some cars, the headlights may be fused individually requiring four fuses for the headlights alone, whereas other cars may have just two fuses for the complete system.

Cable Sizes

So as to provide greater flexibility, motor vehicle cables have a number of thin strands rather than a single thicker core wire. For example, 14/0.30 cable has 14 strands of 0.30 mm diameter wire. Obviously, the more strands, the thicker the overall cable size and the greater its current carrying capability, but one with relatively thick strands will still be more flexible than an equivalent sized single core cable as you can envisage when you think of the rigidity of fixed household wiring.

5

3/5 It's possible to buy cable by the meter and in mini- reels as shown here. But before making any decision work out what quantity you want in what size and in which colour.

It is important that the different sizes of cable are recognised, and if any extra wiring is installed the correct type is used. If any doubt exists about which size cable to use, check on similar cable runs to existing components with broadly the same power usage. However, always bear in mind that the cable itself provides a resistance, (particularly on long runs), creating both a volt drop along the cable and a power loss (heating effect). Should there be any doubt about cable size, it's always best to err on the side of caution and go for the next size up.

Excluding those used in starter circuits, the following are the most common cables used in automotive applications:

4

Number & diameter of strands, in mm	Current rating (Amps)	Typical applications
65/0.30	35.00	Alternator and ammeter circuits
44/0.30	25.50	Dynamo and control box circuits
28/0.30	17.50	Heavy duty general purpose cable. Headlights, horns etc.
14/0.30	8.75	Popular general purpose cable. Side/stop lights, indicators etc.
9/0.30	5.75	Lightly loaded circuits such as instrument panel and interior lights.

FACT FILE: CLASSIC CAR CABLE SIZES

Although metric sizes have been used in Britain for the last twenty years or so, there are still a number of cars around whose manuals refer to the old Imperial (inch) sizes. These follow the same 'labelling' principles as metric except that the equivalent wire diameter to 0.30 mm, for instance is given as 0.012 in. . The most commonly used cable would therefore be 14/.012 - virtually identical to 14/0.30 and with no appreciable difference in current capacity.

WIRE SIZES AND CURRENT RATINGS

IMPERIAL SIZE	CURRENT RATINGS (amps)
9/0.012	5.75
14/0.010	6.00
36/0.0076	8.75
14/0.012	8.75
28/0.012	17.50

Starters

Starter cables vary considerably with much depending upon the size of the starter motor and battery location, but the following should give some idea of what may be used.

Number & diameter of strands (mm)	Current rating (Amps)
37/0.71	105.00
266/0.30	135.00
37/0.90	170.00

Working on Wiring

MAINTENANCE

The wiring loom is one part of the car that is almost always left alone until something goes wrong. In any case, there is little that can be done in the way of maintenance except to keep an eye on it.

It's important that all elements of the wiring should stay where the manufacturer put them and that means all the harness clips and straps being in position. Normally, they only get misplaced when work is done on the car but loose, hanging wiring can be dangerous, particularly under the bonnet. If it strays into the path of the cooling fan and gets chopped up or onto the exhaust manifold and is burnt, it can create all kinds of problems including the incineration of the whole car!

Other typical problems arise when rubber grommets in the bulkhead, through which the wiring passes, slip out of position. Vibration will then soon help the sharp edges of metal to chafe through the cable insulation. The result of this, if you're lucky, will only be a blown fuse. If you're not lucky, you might have a wiring fire.

It's as well to know where any multi-pin connectors in the wiring harness are in your car. They often join sections of the loom at the bulkhead, or perhaps separate the steering column switch wiring from the rest. If a large part of the electrics suddenly fail, it might not be anything more serious than a loose multi-pin plug!

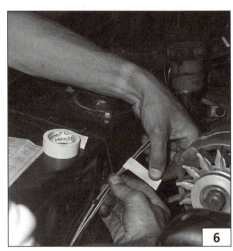

3/6 INSIDE INFORMATION: When adding accessories or renewing any wiring, it's generally best to run the new cables alongside existing ones, taping them together where necessary.

6

CONNECTORS AND TERMINALS

However you choose to make your electrical connections, one thing is certain; wrapping a piece of electrician's tape around a couple of bare bits of bared wire is not an electrical connection! Apart from being stunningly unprofessional, it can lead to all manner of problems, from a non-functioning (or sporadically functioning) piece of equipment to a possible fire risk. Fitting the right connector to a wire is so simple that it's just not worth the hassle of doing it wrong.

3/7 These are used right through the wiring loom and a selection of the various types can be seen here. It is essential that all the existing ones should be kept clean and tight

and if any new wiring is installed, the proper connections should be used throughout.

A selection of the more common cable terminals (from left to right): Eyelet, Bullet, Lucar and Fork. In most cases the insulation colour indicates the size, with red being the smallest (9 or 14/0.30 cable), yellow the largest (44 or 65/0.30 cable) with blue, the most popular, in between (21, 28 or 35/0.30 cable.

3/8 The most common cable terminals are the flat bladed, snap-on variety, known as Lucar connectors. Nearly all electrical accessories (relays/lights etc.) now have this kind of terminal.

Two ways of fixing connectors to cables are possible - soldering and crimping, the latter being a method that has grown in popularity in recent years. Soldering, however, is still acknowledged as the best and it is not the difficult task people sometimes imagine.

SOLDERING

3/9 The first essential is a soldering iron that is adequate for the job. That means an electrical iron of about 150 watts rating or a good heavy gas-heated type of at least 4

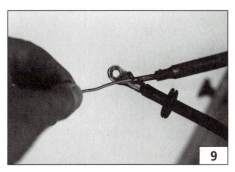

oz weight. The little radio-type electric irons aren't really man enough for this type of work. In fact the soldering iron shown here is only just about adequate for this kind of work - on a battery cable, where a soldered joint is far preferable to anything else. Note the grommet, pushed on to the cable for use where it passes through a body panel.

When the terminal concerned is the blade type, strip about 5mm (¼ in.) of wire first. Slide the appropriate plastic insulating sleeve back away down the wire, push the stripped end of the

making it easy! Cleanliness is the next essential, both of the soldering iron bit and the parts being soldered. It's been said that all parts should be both 'physically' clean and 'chemically' clean. Brown oxidation on copper and brass must be fine-sanded back to bright metal (while with rusty steel, you've got virtually no chance!) and there must be no grease or other contaminants. (Ensure that your hands are grease-free and clean.) Use methylated spirits (industrial alcohol) to remove any grease that may be present.

wire through the hole in the connector (give it a twist first to keep all the strands in place) and then clamp the cable insulation using the little clips and a pair of pliers. Spread the wire over the back of the connector, apply the solder and the tip of the iron until the solder flows. Don't overdo it - you don't want an ungainly blob, just enough to colour the joint silver. When soldering blade type connectors, keep the blade pointing upwards. The solder won't the run into the grooves and prevent you fitting it on its tag. Finally, slide back the insulating sleeve.

INSIDE INFORMATION: The second you heat metal, it oxidises, which prevents solder from 'sticking'. All electrical solder contains a core of flux, which shields the metal for as long as it takes the solder to 'flush'. 'Dab' the end of the solder onto the job at an early stage - before the solder will melt - to make sure there's some flux in place. And be sure to use ONLY proper 'electrical' solder.

3/10 In reality, circumstances often dictate the actual soldering procedure. But, in cases like this, it's best to put an old rubber mat or something similar beneath the job to catch any excess solder.

INSIDE INFORMATION: The art of soldering is to heat the joint before you apply the solder - NOT at the same time. When the heat has been applied, the solder will flow willingly through the joint. At this point, remove the iron and let the joint cool naturally. Don't blow on a joint to cool it quicker, otherwise you could end-up with a 'dry joint' - a joint which looks as if it is solid from the outside but that is bad beneath the solder. The intermittent faults which often result could send you potty!

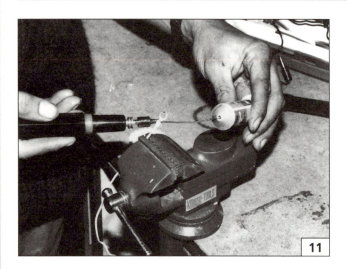

11

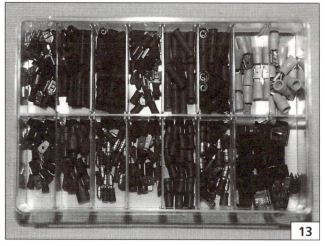

13

3/13 For those who already own the tools, additional connectors are available in small packs of five or so, but larger packs like this could work out cheaper in the long term.

3/11 To solder a bullet or other terminal, first bare the end of the wire to about 13 mm (1/in.). In the case of a bullet connector, slide it onto the wire so that the end of it protrudes through. Hold the cable in the vice so that the bullet rests vertically on top of the jaws. Apply solder and hot iron to the tip of the bullet so that the solder runs inside. Let it cool, remove it and trim off the spare wire with pliers.

The idea of the vice is to stop the bullet sliding down the wire as the insulation softens with the heat. You can use heavier pliers or a self gripping wrench if you're working on the car and there isn't a vice handy. Bear in mind that if you grip the connector in the vice or clamp, the surrounding metal will act as a heat sink, so the connector will never heat up enough to melt the solder.

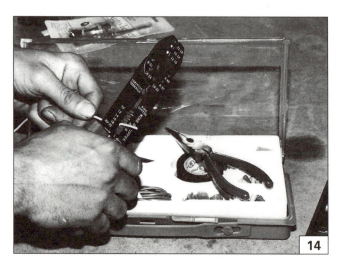

14

3/14 Here's how to fit crimped terminals. Strip off the appropriate amount of insulation...

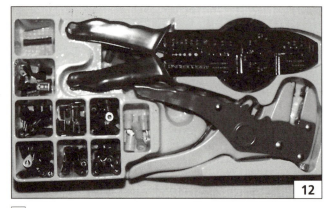

12

3/12 Crimped terminals, of course, do not employ solder, and normally they are fitted with the aid of a special crimping tool. If you favour this method, it is best to buy a kit from the local accessory shop. Many crimping kits come complete with a crimping tool, wire strippers and a range of connectors.

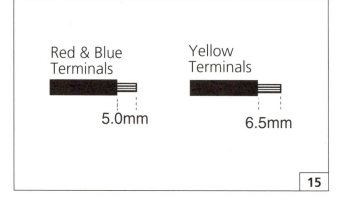

Red & Blue Terminals

5.0mm

Yellow Terminals

6.5mm

15

3/15 ...less for the smaller wires, more for the larger sizes.

3/16 Make sure the insulation butts firmly against the terminal barrel.

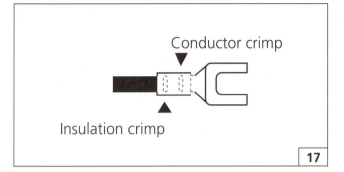

16

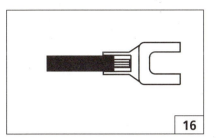

Conductor crimp

Insulation crimp

17

3/17 Make sure both the conductor and insulation are crimped, using the crimping tool or pliers. (Be careful not to cut through with the latter!)

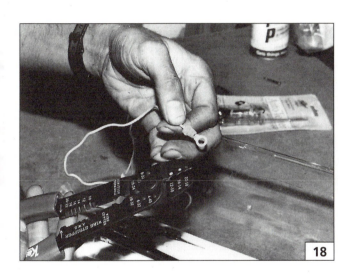

18

3/18 Note that there are two crimps; one secures the bared wire to the terminal and the other secures the lead by its outer sheathing - what you don't want is a terminal physically held by its electrical connection.

SCOTCHLOK CONNECTORS

3/19 There is another type of 'self-stripping' connector known as the Scotchlok. It's a plastic insulating cover which incorporates a small sharp plate designed to cut through cable

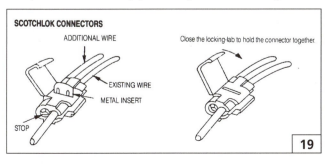

SCOTCHLOK CONNECTORS

ADDITIONAL WIRE

Close the locking-lab to hold the connector together.

EXISTING WIRE

METAL INSERT

STOP

19

insulation without breaking the wire. It's mainly used for adding accessories, but should not be used to carry a large current, nor where there will be a need to disconnect again later on. Nor should it be used in damp conditions because the steel components will then corrode, causing a breakdown in the current.

When fitting, the original supply cable goes into one half of the Scotchlok while the feed cable for the new accessory goes into the other. Locking the device up with pliers drives the sharp blade through the insulation and provides an electrical connection between the two wires.

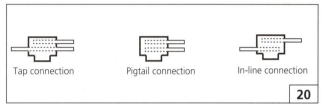

Tap connection

Pigtail connection

In-line connection

20

3/20 Self-stripping Scotchlok connectors can be used in a variety of ways, as shown. In use, the cables are positioned as required in the connector, the sharp plate is then forced down with a pair of pliers and the hinged cover clipped over.

JOINING CABLES

Wherever possible, cables should be joined using bullet connectors - it's by far the most secure method. The only exception to this is where a repair has to be made in a 'wrapped' section of the wiring harness, where perhaps overheating (following a short circuit perhaps) has caused damage.

In these circumstances, because any other type of repair would be too bulky, the wires can be twisted together, soldered and insulated.

3/21 INSIDE INFORMATION: When making a soldered cable joint, it's sometimes convenient to slide a short length of plastic tube over one of the cables, then use it as an insulator afterwards.

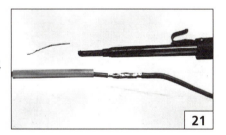

21

The first step is to carefully cut away the insulating tape wrapping, to expose the individual wires. Check that the cable colours are the same on both side of the damaged area and if there is any doubt, label both sides.

Cut out all of the wires in the damaged section of the loom using wire cutters, but don't make all the cuts dead in line. Stagger them as much as possible, so that the repair does not 'bulk up' in one spot. The cable used to make the repair should be exactly the same type and size as that which has been damaged - even the same colours if you can get them. Strip back insulation for about ¾in. twist the wires together and tin them lightly with solder so they won't pull apart. Tape up each joint with insulation tape, but before reinstalling the

ELECTRICAL CIRCUITS

harness, try out all the electrical circuits involved to ensure they are working. Use a test light to check continuity before binding the whole bunch of repaired cables. Wrap the cables in a spiral pattern with tape and re-clip the loom back into the correct position in the car.

If you have to repair damaged cables in an open position, where there is plenty of space, equip all the wire ends with bullets and join with snap connectors.

INSIDE INFORMATION: Buy a section of wiring loom from a similar car in a breaker's yard so that the cable sizes and colours will match.

Know Your Fuses

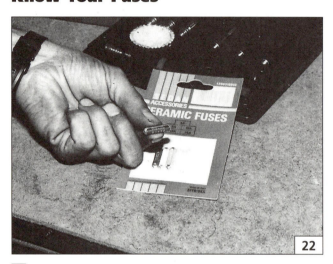

22

☐ **3/22** Every modern car has fuses - probably a whole bank of them. They are installed to protect the electrical circuits. When something goes wrong - a short circuit or an overload - it's better that a small, inexpensive fuse should blow, than that the wiring should catch fire.

☐ **3/23** A comprehensive fuse box, complete with spare fuses. Any blank spaces are usually from missing fuses, but are for different applications on other models.

☐ **3/24** The first important point about fuses is to know where they are on your car. Some manufacturers site them prominently and sensibly under the bonnet or another obvious position...

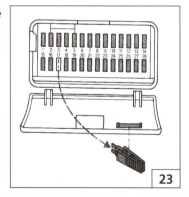

23

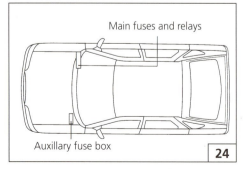

Main fuses and relays

Auxillary fuse box

24

☐ **3/25** ...others hide them under the dash or somewhere equally obscure. Many modern cars, those with modular wiring systems in

25

particular (see **FACT FILE: MODULAR WIRING**) have more than one fuse box. See your handbook or Porter Manual for your car.

When you find the fusebox you will see one of the three mains types of fuse. The older glass type may have either a thin wire or a thin metal strip running through. When the fuse 'blows' this thin central line melts, breaking the circuit and protecting components and wiring against damage.

The second type is a similar metal strip and end caps mounted on the outside of a cylindrical shaped ceramic body. It's exactly the same in principle. The third type is the most recently introduced and its use is becoming increasingly widespread. Known as a blade fuse, it has thin fuse wire inside its plastic body.

☐ **3/26** These are the three main types of fuse: glass on the left, ceramic in the middle and the blade fuse on the right. There are

26

two types of glass fuse, one with square ends as shown here and the other with cone-shaped ends - similar to the ceramic type.

Changing a fuse is a simple operation. All three types are a push fit into some sort of spring clip. The difficult part may be knowing which one has blown. Normally the circuits protected by each fuse will be listed in the handbook and in some cases marked on the fusebox. It's a useful exercise not only to know where the box is sited, but what fuses are in it and what circuits they protect. Check the values of each fuse and make sure that you have replacements in the spares kit.

INSIDE INFORMATION: If you're not able to tell exactly which fuse protects which component, switch on all the relevant electrical components and extract each fuse one at a time until you find out which one affects the component you are looking for.

3/27
Usually, it's possible to see if a fuse has blown simply by looking at it, but sometimes, if the break is slight and the glass or plastic

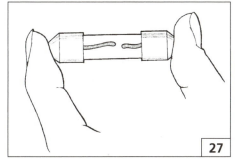

envelope is dirty, it may not be so easy. A new substitute fuse will remove any doubts.

If replacing the fuse completely cures the trouble, it may well have been the fuse that was at fault. If the new fuse blows immediately, suspect some other problem in that circuit and check it out.

Don't forget that the contacts on the fuse itself can be suspect. Clean the end contacts on the fuse with fine sand paper (not emery cloth, because the grit can conduct electricity) and get rid of any signs of corrosion from the spring holders.

INSIDE INFORMATION: If one fuse protects a number of different circuits, turn all of them off and fit a new fuse. Switch on each of the components one at a time. The one that has the problem will blow the fuse and will obviously have to be checked out.

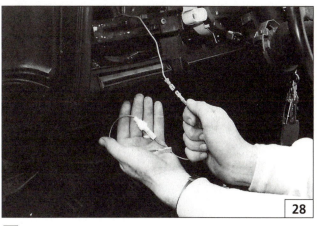

3/28 Apart from the fusebox there may be other separate fuses in the car. The most likely is a line fuse protecting the radio/cassette player. The fuse itself is a low value, conventional type, but it's usually mounted between spring loaded contacts inside a two part plastic case - although with some makes, it can be in the head unit itself.

Yet another type of fuse used in some cars is a 'thermostatic interrupter'. An overload in the circuit heats up a metal contact which bends and breaks the circuit. When it cools, power is restored again. It's ideal for a headlight circuit, where the interrupted circuit can continue to operate on reduced power, instead of all the lights being extinguished, which could obviously be very dangerous.

SAFETY FIRST!
*Do not be tempted to replace a blown fuse with one of a higher rating and **never** bridge the fuse holder contacts with anything solid like a nail or an old fuse covered in silver paper - that's a sure way to cause a wiring fire!*

Fuse Ratings

There is often some confusion about fuse values. They are all rated in amps and the modern system is to indicate the continuous current the fuse can carry. If it's marked **10A CR**, this means it can carry 10 amps continuously and can cope with surges up to twice that. The older system rated fuses (mostly the glass type) at the maximum they could carry. A fuse marked **10A** under this system could only carry 5 amps continuous current. To help eliminate this confusion, some fuses are now marked with both ratings.

FUSE VALUES (Continuous rating other than where shown as 'Max.'

Type	Colour	Rating (amps)
Glass fuses (cone end)	Blue	3 Max.
	Yellow	4.5 Max.
	Nut brown	8 Max.
	Red on Green	10 Max.
	White	35 Max.
Glass type (flat end)	Red on Blue	2
	Red	5
	Blue on Green	8
	Black on Blue	10
	Light brown	15
	Blue on Yellow	20
	Pink	25
	White	35
	Yellow	50
Ceramic	Yellow	5
	White	8
	Red	16
	Blue	25
Flat blade	Purple	3
	Pink	4
	Orange	5
	Brown	7.5
	Red	10
	Blue	15
	Yellow	20
	White	25
	Green	30

One last device fitted to some modern cars is the 'fusible link'. This is a series of cables between two plugs and is fitted into the main battery lead. It protects all the circuits in the car except the starter, and the only time it will melt is under a massive overload, such as might occur in a crash. The main purpose is to protect the vehicle against fire. Needless to say, this must never be supplemented or replaced by a different type of cable or additional wiring.

Printed Circuits

29

3/29 These are often used, principally because they speed up assembly at the factory, but they don't do anything to help you to carry out repair work! Connections are made by means of thin foil links 'printed' onto the panel. The problem is that the flimsy links can easily burn out if there's a short circuit or overload. On rare occasions, it is possible to 'repair' the damage by soldering in a piece of 5 amp fuse wire, but generally, a damaged board will need to be replaced.

Many rear light units incorporate a form of printed board circuit and some frequently cause trouble both at individual bulb connections or, more often, at the board earth connection both or which can be improved by cleaning up with fine sandpaper.

The board is linked to the rest of the car's wiring by means of a plug and socket, make sure they are making good electrical contact and the plug is pushed home properly. Check also that anything that plugs into the board makes good contact - a typical example of this would be the bulbs in a rear light cluster printed board already mentioned.

FACT FILE: TERMINAL NUMBERS

There is an increasing tendency towards easing the identification of various electrical circuits by numbering the terminals. These numbers are cast, moulded or otherwise marked on the components being connected, with each having the same terminal numbers. For example, in the German DIN system, if an electrical supply only works with the ignition switched on, the power supply terminal at the switch (or motor) is numbered 15, as is the supply source (such as the ignition switch). The same numbering system has been adopted by Ford, for instance, for their World cars - but you would be wise to check your manual to be certain that the regular conventions have been followed on your car. The following guide shows many of the most popular terminal numbers and is based on the German DIN system.

	Ignition coil to distributor
1	LT (low voltage)
4	HT (high voltage)
15	**Ignition controlled feed**
15 a	**Ballast resistor to ignition coil**
	Glow plug and starter switch
17	Start
19	Pre-heat
30	**Feed from positive battery terminal, direct**
31	**Earth or battery negative**
	Electric motors
32	Return
33	Main terminal
	Flasher unit
49	Feed
49 a	Output
50	**Starter feed (direct)**

	Wiper motor
53	Feed
53 a	Wiper (+), self-parking switch
53 b	Wiper (shunt winding)
53 c	Windscreen washer pump
53 e	Wiper (brake winding
53 i	Permanent magnet motor third brush (2-speed)
	Lighting
55	Fog lights
56	Headlights
56 a	Main-beam and main-beam indicator
56 b	Dip-beam
56 d	Headlight flash contact
58	Sidelights, tail lights, number plate lights instrument panel lights
61	**Charge-warning light**
75	**Radio, cigar lighter**
76	**Loudspeakers**
	Normally-closed and changeover switches
81	Feed
81 a	First output
81 b	Second output
	Normally-open switches
82	Feed
82 a	First output
82 b	Second output
82 z	First input
82 y	Second input

(Continued on page 31)

ELECTRICAL CIRCUITS

Multi-position switches

83	Feed
83 a	Output, position 1
83 b	Output, position 2 83 L Output, left-hand
83 R	Output, right-hand

Current relays

84	Feed, winding and relay contact
84 a	Finish of winding (negative)
84 b	Output, relay contact

Switching relays

85	Finish of winding (negative)
86	Start of winding
86 a	Start of winding or first winding
86 b	Winding tap or second winding

Normally-closed and changeover contacts

87	Input
87 a	First output (break side)
87 b	Second output
87 c	Third output
87 z	First input
87 y	Second input
87 x	Third input

Normally-open and changeover contacts

88	Input
88 a	First output (break side)
88 b	Second output
88 c	Third output
88 z	First input
88 y	Second input
88 x	Third input

Generator and generator regulator (i.e. dynamo, alternator)

B +	Battery positive, generator output
B -	Battery negative
D +	Generator positive
D -	Generator negative
EX, EX	Generator field
IND	Warning light

FACT FILE: TERMINAL NUMBERS (continued)

☐ **3/30** According to these standards a typical relay used, for example, when wiring in a set of auxiliary lights, would have markings as follows: Terminals 85 & 86 are the start and finish of the winding, with 88 (and 87) being the (contact) inputs and 88 a (and 87 a) being the outputs.

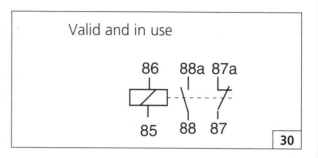

Valid and in use

86   88a 87a

85   88   87

30

☐ **3/31** However, there are still many relays being supplied with what are termed 'invalid' designations - these are as shown, with 85 & 86 still being the start and finish of the winding, but with 30 being the contact inputs and 87 (and 87 a) the outputs. Once again, check your manual!

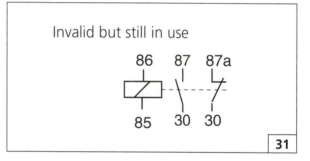

Invalid but still in use

86   87   87a

85   30   30

31

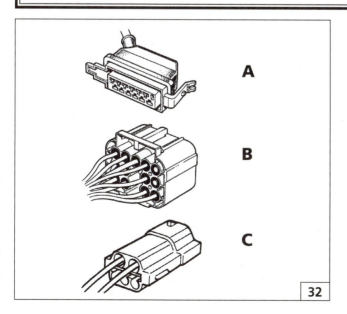

A

B

C

32

☐ **3/32** Although there are different appearances and colours, there are basically three types of integral connectors. Those with a moulded cover (A) are designed to be completely sealed and it is generally impossible to remove the rubber without destroying the plug's sealing qualities. Other connectors (B) have individually sealed wires, while a third type, used at the rear of dashboards, for example (C) are non-sealed connectors. For the first two types, connections will have to be tested at the cable where it exits from the connector, but it is possible to insert a probe into the rear of the third type. DON'T attempt to fit a connector upside down or damage the pins in any way. Connectors are usually shaped, or there is a key-way so that the connectors can only go together one way round. **SPECIALIST SERVICE:** If damaged, these connectors will have to be replaced by an auto. electrician. Only the type of connector block (not shown here) which contains separate spade connectors can be dismantled and repaired.

CHAPTER 4
THE BATTERY

Batteries are electrical storage pots. Some, such as most torch batteries, can be traditionally filled just once and, when all the stored power has been used up, are thrown away or, preferably, disposed of properly (although there are special battery chargers for these batteries...). Others, like those we use in our cars, can be and indeed are, topped up (electrically) all the time by the car's own power station - the generator.

But, sometimes things go wrong, with either the battery becoming a less efficient store or the generator delivering less than is being taken out. In both cases the battery will become weaker and weaker until such time as it is incapable of producing what is required.

All electrical components on the car such as the lights, windscreen wipers and starter motor, consume power (when they are operated) and of these, the starter motor is the biggest consumer. So it is, that when a battery is down on power, the first indication is usually that the starter doesn't work or does so very slowly.

On some, comparatively rare occasions, the battery will get weaker as you drive, in which case it will become noticeable that the lights get dimmer and dimmer (if switched on) or that the indicators get slower or stop working, or perhaps, that the engine stops when you press the brake pedal and apply the brake lights.

But, troubles with the starter motor are generally the first signs of impending battery failure and if action isn't taken to sort out the problem immediately, complete failure will come all the sooner. Continued use of the starter motor with the battery in this condition will also hasten its demise. However, starter troubles can arise from a number of other faults, a selection of which are shown in *Chapter 6, Starter Systems*.

A battery down on power is reckoned as being 'flat' or discharged, whereas one that does what it should, is fully charged, and obviously, if the one on your car falls into the first category, the major priority is to get it into the second - see the *Battery Charging* section on page 35.

Most of today's cars are fitted with a 12 volt lead acid battery. There are exceptions - older Volkswagens (and motor cycles), for instance, which have a 6 volt system, and some commercial vehicles which have a 24 volt system, often comprising two 12 volt batteries connected in series.

Battery Construction

☐ **4/1** Car batteries are made up of a number of separate cells, each of which consists of a series of positive plates connected to the positive terminal of the battery, and interleaved with a series of negative plates connected to the negative terminal. This is often referred to as a plate group.

☐ **4/2** Each cell has a nominal voltage of two volts so there are six cells in a 12 volt battery, arranged so that the positive and negative plates alternate right across the battery and are further interleaved by ceramic separators. The whole plate assembly is immersed in a dilute solution of sulphuric acid called the electrolyte.

The positive plates are formed from an oxide of lead and the negative plates are a spongy form of lead.

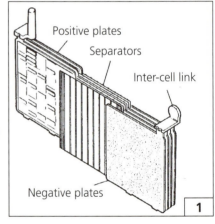

Positive plates
Separators
Inter-cell link
Negative plates
1

When the plates are connected, as they are when the battery is in circuit in the car, and a load is imposed (the lights are switched on, for instance), the plates turn slowly to lead sulphate, while the acid of the electrolyte turns slowly to water. In this condition, the battery is discharged. The action just described, however, can be reversed and when the battery is charged, the plates change back to lead oxide and the electrolyte reverts to dilute sulphuric acid. The battery cell is then charged and ready to supply power again for the car's circuits.

Over a period of time some of the lead in the plates falls off and drops to the bottom of the battery and will, eventually build up to such an extent that it will short out the positive and negative

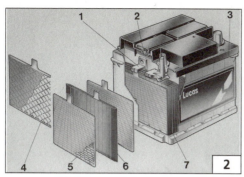

1. Inter cell link
2. Maintenance-free type vents.
3. Polypropylene container
4. Negative plate
5. Positive plate
6. Plate envelope
7. Ribbed base

plates so rendering that cell unserviceable. This can be avoided to some extent by the manufacturer creating a larger and deeper (ribbed) well below the plates and/or by enclosing each of the plates in its own self-contained envelope. However, both options add to the initial cost, but should mean a longer life battery.

Battery Maintenance

This is something that, according to some battery manufacturers, is no longer necessary. There are a lot of 'maintenance free' batteries around now, but what this means in effect is that the unit is sealed and therefore needs no topping up with electrolyte. In most cases, it is still necessary to keep it clean and to check the terminals.

How much cleaning your battery needs will depend largely on where the manufacturers in their wisdom have sited it. Normally it's under the bonnet somewhere, so keeping an eye on it is not difficult - nor is cleaning it.

Generally it's simply a matter of keeping the terminals clean and wiping off any accumulations of oil film and gunge. If a coating of muck is left there it is possible for current to leak across between the terminals. The other time when cleaning is needed is before topping up, so that no dirt gets into the cells, and after topping up, when it's a matter of mopping up any spilt de-ionised water.

☐ **4/3** Clean battery terminals are an essential part of a trouble free electrical system. Careful use of a wire brush or emery cloth is the most favoured method of cleaning them.

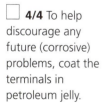

☐ **4/4** To help discourage any future (corrosive) problems, coat the terminals in petroleum jelly.

TOPPING UP

With a sealed maintenance-free battery this should not normally be needed, but many still have provision for checking the electrolyte level and topping up. For the older type of battery this is a regular requirement.

☐ **4/5** Start by cleaning the top of the battery thoroughly and then undo the cap or take out the one-piece filler cover.

making it easy! Use only distilled water or de-ionised water for topping up and the sensible thing is to buy the stuff in the sort of bottle you can most easily use in your car. If there's practically no clearance between battery top and bonnet lid, a big bottle is not a lot of use!

You may also in these circumstances have a lot of trouble seeing inside the cells to find out what the level is. A mirror and a torch can help here. The alternative is to use a battery filler bottle of the type you can poke into the top of the cell which correctly regulates the electrolyte depth above the plates and separators inside. The level to which the electrolyte should be filled may be marked on the battery case where this is the transparent type. Otherwise, just covering the separators inside each cell is the usual recommendation.

Give each cap a quick wipe before refitting and then wipe off any surplus water from the battery top. It's also not a bad idea to have the battery out occasionally. Releasing the battery locating bar and nuts or butterfly nuts enables these to be cleaned of rust and the thread greased before refitting. It also ensures that the bottom of the battery does not become firmly welded to a badly corroded battery tray.

If your battery terminals are coated with a nasty white crystalline growth (sulphation), wash it off with warm water and soda. One possible cause is that the battery is not being correctly charged for some reason and a check of the charging system is advised. This is covered in C*hapter 6, Starter Systems*.

☐ **4/6** Sulphation does not just occur on the battery terminals as this picture shows - the battery clamp is almost fully encrusted.

THE BATTERY

4/7 Wash it away with warm water or a solution of bicarbonate of soda and warm water.

If you discover that your battery case is cracked, check if it's still under guarantee, and if it is, take the matter up with the shop you bought it from. If it isn't, it is possible to repair the case with a special sealant, but consider carefully whether a new battery might be the best solution.

SAFETY FIRST!
A fully charged battery can produce a very hefty spark so to avoid a nasty burn or worse, there are one or two sensible precautions to observe:
• When disconnecting a battery, always remove the earth lead first before the 'live' one and replace it last.
*• Don't lodge tools on top of the battery or near it. If a spanner drops and bridges the 'live' terminal then the car's body, and you grab it at the same time, a nasty burn and shock could result. For the same reason, never wear a metal wrist watch strap or identity bracelet. Also see **Chapter 1, Safety First!***
• When charging a battery, the cells will be giving off hydrogen, a highly explosive gas. Don't go near it with naked lights or with a lighted cigarette. Also take care when disconnecting the battery charger. Turn the mains off first and avoid creating a spark when pulling the crocodile clips off the terminals.

Battery Testing

It is possible to check the battery's state of charge in two different ways. The time-honoured method is to use a hydrometer to check the specific gravity of each cell. The hydrometer is a graduated glass tube with a rubber bulb on top. In use it's dipped into the electrolyte in each cell in turn and acid siphoned up into the tube by means of the bulb. Inside the tube is a float and the position of this against the scale indicates the specific gravity reading. Once the reading has been made, the acid in the hydrometer is squirted back into the same cell from which it was siphoned.

The reading for a fully charged battery in good condition should be between 1.260 and 1.290. Partially discharged but still OK will produce readings between 1.230 and 1.260. Between 1.200 and 1.230 it needs charging. Below that, the battery is totally flat.

These readings are all for a battery tested at a temperature of 60 degree F. If it's a warm day and ten degrees hotter than that, add four points. If it is ten degrees colder, subtract four points.

4/8 Some hydrometers incorporate three coloured balls (green, yellow and red). In use if just the green ball rises the battery is satisfactorily charged.

If the green and yellow rise, the battery is low but probably adequate whereas when the red ball rises, it needs charging.

The readings for all the cells should be close to one another. If one is wildly below the others, it's an indication of a failed cell and the need for a new battery.

4/9 An alternative method of testing a battery's state of charge is to use a volt meter (or a multi-meter used in the volts mode) connected across the battery

terminals - in most cases the red lead of the instrument will be connected to the battery positive (+) terminal and the black lead to the battery negative (-).

Normal battery voltage should be 12.6 volts. It might be up to 0.5 volts more than this if it has been recently charged, but should not be lower than 12.2 volts. That would mean either a faulty battery or one that's in a low state of charge. Some multi-meters may have a special 'battery-charge' indicator scale with coloured sections to show battery condition - with the needle in the green, it's fully charged. In the white it's part charged and in the red, low or flat.

If the battery is one of the now-rare older types where it is possible to reach the individual cell terminals, it should be possible to read off the voltage of each cell using the low voltage scale. For a cell in good condition and fully charged, the reading should be more than 2.10 volts. Partially charged, the reading would be between 2.08 and 2.10 volts. Below that, the cell is faulty, particularly if the other readings were all higher.

The starting capacity of a fully charged battery can also be checked using a voltmeter. First, disable the ignition to prevent the engine from starting (but check with your handbook or dealer - this should *not* be done with some electronic ignition cars. It can be dangerous, or it can damage the ignition components.) Then, with the multi-meter connected across the battery as before, crank over the engine on the starter. If the battery is sound and fully charged, the voltage should remain in the region of around 9.5 to 11 volts and remain there (while cranking) for a minute or more, even when it's freezing weather. A minute, while operating the starter, is a very long time, but if the needle falls back after only a few seconds, the battery is probably faulty.

If the engine only turns slowly and the voltage stays higher than 11 volts, it would probably mean a 'high resistance' - probably a poor connection, either on the battery terminals or between battery and starter - checking out this kind of problem is covered in *Chapter 6, Starter Systems*.

Buying New

When finally convinced you need a new battery, you're faced with the problem of deciding what to buy, and there are plenty of alternatives.

One factor to consider is how long you intend keeping the car. If it's only for a short term, a cheap type might be good enough. If you want several years' use, a more expensive model with a long guarantee is a better answer. To some extent, you can base your decision on price, working on the assumption that you get what you pay for, bearing in mind what we said earlier on coping with falling debris from the battery plates. Generally, the standard 'old fashioned' type is cheapest, followed by low-maintenance and maintenance-free types which do have the facility for topping up if necessary. At the top come the sealed for life types.

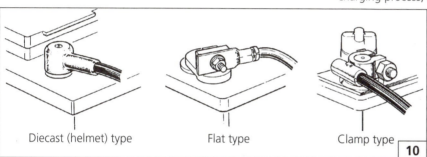

Diecast (helmet) type   Flat type   Clamp type **10**

☐ **4/10** When buying a new battery always ensure the lugs (terminal posts) on the replacement are the same as those on the old unit. The three most common types are shown in the illustration.

Capacity should also be considered. At one time batteries were rated in amp/hours (Ah). If you see one marked say 48 Ah, it means the battery when fully charged will deliver a current of one amp for 48 hours, or eight amps for six hours. The modern battery's capacity is more likely to be defined by its cold cranking performance. That's how well it can spin the starter motor in very cold weather conditions. There's a standard test to establish this carried out at -18 degrees C, a temperature at which any battery's performance must be at its lowest. There's no need to go into technicalities of the test, but the cold start performance figure can be used to compare one battery with another. The higher the figure, the better the performance, so that 330A would be better than 240A, for instance.

There's yet another parameter battery manufacturers use nowadays - Reserve Capacity. That's the time taken in minutes for a 12 volt battery to drop to 10.5 volts when discharged at a running load of 25 amps at 25 degrees C. Effectively, it indicates how long you can go on running after the car's charging system has failed.

It should be noted incidentally, that cold start figures used by British manufacturers are to a BS standard. You can't compare them directly to (American) SAE or (German) DIN.

The simplest way is to go to a well known local supplier. Buy a new battery of a recognised make and make sure it is the one specified for your car. That way it should be the right physical size and shape, have the right capacity rating and capable of being simply exchanged for the old one.

Battery Charging

You would think that charging a flat, or partially flat battery is simply a matter of hooking up a battery charger, then leaving it to do its own thing and, in essence, you would be right. But there's a little more to it than that! In fact, there are a few points to consider before getting to that stage.

In the first place, to avoid the possibility of causing damage to any electronic components (including those in the alternator) it's generally advisable to first disconnect the battery from the car circuits. In an ideal situation it's also best to remove the battery from the car.

☐ **4/11** If the battery has filler/breather caps at each cell or a single cap over all the cells, they/it should be either removed or loosened to allow the escape of gases generated during the charging process; normally this would be most likely during the latter stages. In extreme cases, droplets of corrosive electrolyte may also be ejected, hence the advice to remove the battery from the car. If your battery is one of the so-called 'maintenance free' types with no removable breather caps, see the section on charging sealed batteries.

Most battery charger leads are coloured red and black. Red is the 'positive' lead, which should first be connected to the positive (+) terminal on the battery, followed by the black lead to the battery 'negative' terminal. After this, check that the battery charger

11

SAFETY FIRST!
The gases given off by the battery are explosive, so make sure the area is well ventilated and, as most battery chargers are equipped with an overload/thermal cut-out, internal sparking may occur. So don't place the charger on or alongside the battery. On a similar theme don't attempt charging a battery outside in wet weather. If water finds its way into the charger through any vent holes, it could result in damage to the charger, the battery and to you, personally.

Before making any connections to the battery, ensure that the charger is disconnected from the mains supply - and, once charging is complete, switch off at the mains before disconnecting the battery leads. This cuts down the risk of sparking.

switches are in the correct positions - for example, if there is a 6/12 volt changeover switch, make sure it's providing the required supply for your battery. Any HI/LO or FAST/NORMAL switch can be changed over during the charging process, although it's best not to and in any case better for the battery if left in the LO/NORMAL position, especially during the initial stages.

When switched on, the charger will now (or should) begin charging the battery. Initially this will normally start off at a fairly high rate, decreasing as the battery becomes charged. However, if the battery is fully discharged, it may create a high resistance to current flow, in which case the charging rate will be low or even appear non-existent but should then increase as the internal resistance is overcome - this could take up to an hour or so.

INSIDE INFORMATION: If your charger shows a zero reading at first, therefore, don't assume it's bust!

It's difficult to be specific upon the charge duration since it depends both on the capacity of the battery and its existing state of charge along with the rated output from the charger, but it could take up to around 18 hours to bring an average sized car battery from the completely flat to the fully charged position using a standard 4-6 amp battery charger.

Battery chargers range from the simple (plug-in) 1-amp units to the fully automatic versions, best suited for charging sealed batteries.

Other than checking with a hydrometer, voltmeter or other instrument, a good indication that the battery is reaching the fully charged state is when the chargers ammeter shows a constant low rate of charge in the region of 0.5 to 1 amp, or when the battery is freely 'gassing' - that is, continuous bubbling of gas observed in the individual cells of the battery. Further charging will then reduce the water content of the electrolyte and is best avoided. Excessive gassing in some cells but not others most probably means that those cells are faulty and that the battery is approaching the end of its useful life.

CHARGING SEALED BATTERIES

☐ **4/12** Most maintenance free or low maintenance batteries have no filler caps as such, and consequently no apparent facility for topping up the electrolyte. However, with some it may be possible, even though a little difficult, to prise off what may appear as permanently sealed caps (or strips) and top up the electrolyte as normal.

Even so, it's always best to ensure that these batteries are not allowed to gas when being charged. Ideally they should only be charged with a voltage controlled or automatic charger. These are designed to deliver a maximum of 14.1 volts (7.05 volts in the case of 6 volt

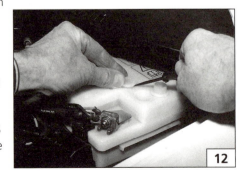

12

chargers) - below this point virtually no gassing takes place. However, it is possible to use an ordinary charger if care is taken not to exceed this voltage.

To this end a voltmeter should be connected across the battery terminals, so that the voltage can be monitored during the charging process. So long as the voltage remains below the 14.1 (7.05) point all is well, but once it reaches that figure, charging should be discontinued and the battery left standing for around 30 minutes. After this period charging can again be resumed, until once again the 14.1 volt point is reached, when again the charger should be switched off.

This cycle should be repeated until the battery voltage rises to 14.1 volts shortly after the charger is switched on, when the battery can be deemed to be fully charged.

Any battery, maintenance free or otherwise, should be kept in a fully charged state if maximum life is to be achieved. This is particularly important in the winter months, when the electrolyte in a discharged battery could freeze solid.

FACT FILE:
DISCONNECTING THE BATTERY

Many vehicles depend on a constant power supply from the battery and you can find yourself in all sorts of trouble if you simply disconnect the battery on those vehicles. You might find that the car alarm will go off, you could find that the engine management forgets all it has ever 'learned' and the car will feel very strange to drive until it has re-programmed itself, and you could find that your radio refuses to operate again unless you key in the correct code. And if you've bought the car second-hand and don't know the code, you would have to send the set back to the manufacturer for re-programming. So, on later cars with engine management systems you must ensure that the vehicle has a constant power supply even though the battery is removed. To do so, you will need a separate 12 volt battery supply. You could put a self tapping screw into the positive lead near the battery terminal before disconnecting it, and put a positive connection to your other battery via this screw. But you would have to be EXTREMELY CAREFUL to wrap insulation tape around the connection so that no short is caused. The negative terminal on the other battery has to be connected to the car's bodywork.

☐ **4/13** A better way is to use something like the Sykes- Pickavant Computer Saver shown here. Clip the cables to your spare battery and plug it into your cigarette lighter. (You may have to turn the ignition switch to the 'Auxiliary' setting to allow the cigarette lighter to function.)

13

You have to hold in the red button on the Computer Saver while inserting it into the cigarette lighter, and if two green lights still show after the button is released, you have a good connection and your battery can now be disconnected and removed.

Be sure not to turn on any of the car's equipment while the auxiliary battery is connected.

CHAPTER 5
CHARGING SYSTEMS

The heart of practically any vehicle's electrical system is the generator - the machine that converts mechanical power into electrical energy. Its purpose is to keeps the battery fully charged and to power most of the consumer units once the engine is running.

Twenty-five, or so, years ago, many cars were fitted with a DC (Direct Current) type generator, commonly referred to as a dynamo, a machine that even then was becoming incapable of fulfilling its intended role, simply because of the increasing number of electrical accessories being fitted as standard equipment.

The answer to the problem was the alternator, an AC generator both smaller and more powerful than the dynamo. The alternator has also proved more reliable, longer lasting and virtually maintenance free - but it can still go wrong!

Dynamo

In its basic form, a dynamo consists of a looped coil of wire which is made to rotate between the North and South poles of a magnet. As it does so, it cuts the lines of force between the two poles.

The major problem with this simple layout is that as one side of the loop passes the North pole, an electro-magnetic field (emf) is induced which is reversed half a rotation later when it passes the South pole. In fact if a voltmeter were connected between either end it would give an alternating positive/negative reading as the loop turned.

This, as stated in *Chapter 2, Doing the Knowledge*, is a form of alternating current (AC) which cannot charge the battery. Therefore it has to be converted into a non-reversing direct (DC) supply.

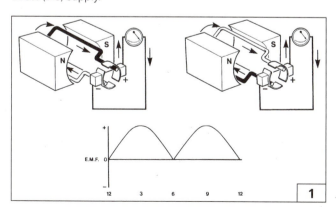

1

☐ **5/1** In a dynamo, this is achieved by connecting the ends of the loop to either side of a divided slip ring and arranging a couple of collectors (brushes) to contact, one on each side as the loop (and slip-ring) rotates. This provides a one-directional

flow, but one that peaks as each loop passes the pole position and then fades off again as shown in the graph at the bottom of **figure 5/1**.

☐ **5/2** To overcome this peaking effect, a series of looped coils are used, the ends of which are connected to opposing bars of a segmented ring known as the commutator, the whole assembly being called the armature. In this arrangement as one loop 'peaks' the next is moving towards its peak position, giving a smooth, one-directional flow of current.

In this simple layout, for any given number of looped coils, the output would be purely dependent upon the rotational speed of the armature. However, if instead of a permanent magnet, an electro-magnet (coil of wire around a soft iron core) is used, the strength of the magnetic field could be varied by regulating the current passing through the coils. In effect, this provides a form of output control.

In practice there are usually two coils (known as the field windings) wrapped around soft iron pole shoes and securely attached to the inside of the dynamo housing, with the armature rotating between them. Furthermore, these pole shoes always retain a small residual magnetism, even if there is no current flow through the field windings.

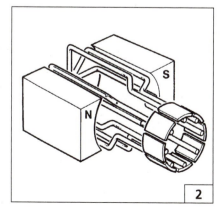

2

DYNAMO CONTROL

5/3 It is a characteristic of the normal two-brush dynamo, that its output rises as the armature speed increases. As the armature is driven by the engine, a dynamo that designed to

operate satisfactorily at low engine speeds would overcharge the batter and possibly burn-out at higher speeds.

For this reason, some form of control is required to regulate output at these higher speeds and this is achieved by inserting a resistance in the circuit to the field winding, so decreasing the strength of the magnetic field.

Most dynamos are considerably larger than alternators, incidentally, but produce less power.

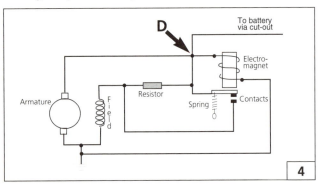

5/4 The basic layout of such a control is as shown in this illustration and consists of a coil around a soft iron core (a form of relay) which, when energised attracts a spring loaded armature and opens a set of points. In operation, when the dynamo armature begins to turn, there is no current flowing through the field windings but, due to the residual magnetism, a small emf is induced into the armature. As the points are spring loaded into the closed position, there is a circuit which runs from the armature to the output terminal (D), on through the points and field windings to the negative side of the dynamo.

This small electro-magnetic force means that there will be a small current flow through the field windings, increasing the strength of the magnetic field. Then, as the engine speed increase, the dynamo output will go up, more current will flow through the field windings increasing, even more, the magnetic field strength and so it goes on.

However, a circuit also exists through the winding of the regulator coil and as the dynamo output increase, so will the magnetic effect of its iron core. Eventually, this will be enough to attract the armature and open the points against spring pressure.

The circuit to the field windings is now directed through the resistor, thereby reducing the current flow and strength of the magnetic field. As dynamo output consequently falls, the spring of the regulator contact reasserts itself and closes the points. Output then begins to rise again and the whole cycle is

repeated. In practice, the whole sequence takes many times a second, rather like an electric buzzer.

The regulator contacts spring is adjustable, so that the regulator voltage setting can be varied.

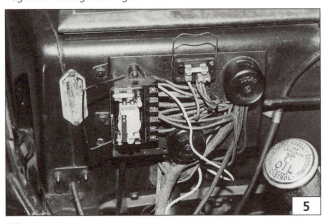

5/5 How it used to be, back in 1937. The control box from a Standard 14 with a cut-out, two fuses and two junction boxes. Basic principles remained unchanged throughout the life of the dynamo.

CUT-OUT

If the dynamo and battery were permanently connected, it would result in the battery discharging back through the dynamo whenever it wasn't being charged. This could be at low engine revs or when the engine was switched off. In fact the battery would try to treat the dynamo as a motor, which not being powerful enough to turn the engine, would be held static by the fan belt and burn out.

To prevent this from happening, an automatic switch is provided which opens when these conditions exist. Termed the cut-out, it's basically something like a relay, with the coil being powered through the dynamo output terminal. When energised, the electro- magnet attracts a spring loaded armature, closing a set of contacts and completing the circuit from dynamo to battery. if the dynamo output falls below that of the battery, the spring opens the contacts, breaking the circuit.

5/6 These are the contacts in a typical control box cut-out unit. When in place on the car, on no account close these contacts (or allow them to close) when the engine is either stopped or idling.

Both the regulator and the cut-out are incorporated into a single unit, generally referred to as the control box.

Alternator

1. Pulley
2. Front bearing
3. Rotor
4. Rotor windings
5. Stator
6. Stator windings
7. Rear bearing
8. Rectifier and brush box/ regulator
9. Slip rings

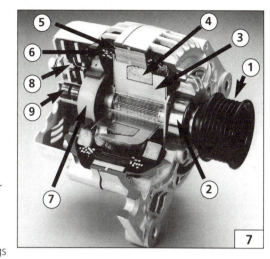

5/7 Unlike the cut-away of the Bosch Compact alternator shown here, the dynamo has certain inherent disadvantages. In the first place, its entire output is transmitted through the commutator and brush gear, invariably resulting in arcing and burning of the commutator segments. Secondly, the large number of (thick) looped coils in the armature give it a heavy rotational mass.

Both these factors limit the speed at which the dynamo can be driven which, in effect, limits its output - the only other alternative would be to increase the number of coils in the armature windings making the whole assembly both larger and heavier with consequential further restrictions on speed. Modern motor cars, with their ever growing use of electrical gadgetry, need more power, but not at the expense of a dynamo nearly one third the size of the engine! - hence the absolute necessity for the alternator.

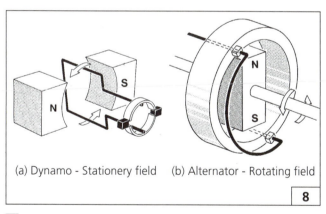

(a) Dynamo - Stationery field (b) Alternator - Rotating field

5/8 The alternator can be considered as a dynamo turned inside out where, instead of a mass of looped coils rotating in a magnetic field, the magnetic field rotates within a series of coils.

With this arrangement, the output is generated in the stationary coils (called the stator) and only a relatively small current is passed through the brushes and slip rings to the much finer (field) windings in the rotating section - the rotor.

The stator coils, being static, can be made larger than in a dynamo and, with improved air passages between them, are more easily cooled. In addition the lower weight of the rotating

section and lack of a commutator also means that an alternator can be run at considerably higher speeds than a dynamo. This is achieved by the simple expedient of fitting the alternator with a smaller drive pulley, so giving the additional advantage of a greater charge at low engine speeds - even at idling.

The alternator slip rings are continuous and not, as in the dynamo commutator, segmented. This greatly reduces wear and, together with the low current passed through the rotor windings virtually eliminates arcing. However, it does mean that since there is no commutator to reverse the current flow at each half revolution, the alternator (as its name implies) generates alternating current.

In practice, modern car alternators operate on the three-phase principle where, instead of a simple two coil stator arrangement (set 180° apart), three coils are used each being 120° from its neighbour. Although more expensive to produce, this layout makes better use of the (stator) space within the alternator casing and therefore, for any given unit size, produces more power. All modern alternators use semi-conductors (diodes) to convert the alternating current to direct. These diodes can be considered as electrical one-way valves, passing current in one direction only. In effect, the alternating current which flows first in one direction and then the other, has the reverse pulse blocked by the diode.

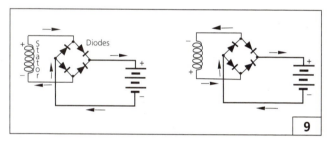

5/9 Using only one diode would result in a one directional flow in a series of distinct pulses, but this can be overcome by employing what is termed a bridge circuit with four diodes. In effect this changes the direction of the reverse pulse as show in here, giving a, more or less continuous, one-directional flow of current.

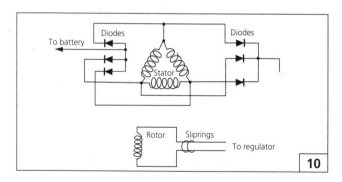

5/10 In practice, on most three-phase alternators a star-connected stator winding layout is used, employing six diodes. Older, battery-excited alternators (where battery power was used to energise the field winding) also often used some form of external cut-out or field isolating relay. Modern units are chiefly self-excited where, once the initial excitation has taken place, some of the alternator output current is directed through the rotor. These units will have an additional diode in each of the stator winding circuits, making a total of nine diodes in all. Exciting, isn't it?

All the diodes (regardless of how many) are usually contained within one assembly, often referred to as either the diode pack or, more correctly, as the rectifier and, with most modern units, this assembly is located within the alternator body. Output control of the alternator is virtually the same as with the dynamo in that it is achieved by regulating the field current. However, with most, it's much more sophisticated than the old coil-and-contacts arrangement, being a solid-state electronic unit employing transistors and usually located (along with the rectifier) within the unit housing.

Ignition Warning Light

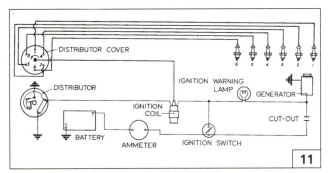

11

The ignition warning light, as it is called, has very little to do with the ignition. It is, in fact, wired into the charging system.

5/11 In a dynamo equipped system, the light is wired in parallel, across the cut-out contacts - but see this Opel/Vauxhall diagram of how the light fits into the circuit in practice. When the contacts are open and the ignition switched on, a circuit is made from the battery through the light and dynamo armature. The light will then light up.

Once the engine has started and generator output rises, the voltage across the light will get less and less until the generator output equals that of the battery when, with no current flow, the light will go out. As generator output rises further, the cut-out contacts will close but there will still be virtually no voltage across the light and it will remain extinguished.

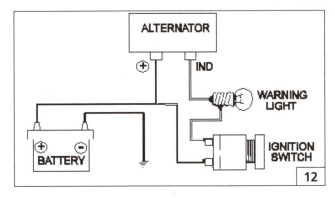

12

5/12 Various methods have been used to wire in an ignition light into the alternator circuit, but the modern trend is to wire it in series (one behind the other) with the rotor field windings which, in turn are connected in parallel (and through diodes) with the stator windings. When the ignition is switched on, there will be a circuit from the battery through the brushes and rotor, but not through the stator windings.

Once the engine starts, alternator output (from the stator) passes through the diodes to the rotor, with the same voltage being applied to the other side of the warning light. As the engine speed increases (in practice at tickover speed) the same voltage will be applied to either side of the warning light and it will go out.

Alternator Fixes

5/13 If the ignition warning light doesn't come on at all, the reason may be nothing more than a

13

defective bulb, in which case the alternator may not work, or may only do so at high speed.

If this still leaves the alternator not charging, it's probably due to a problem at the brushes. However, if neither the test light nor warning light came on in the test, check the ignition warning light bulb and circuit.

making it easy! To check, disconnect the alternator, switch on the ignition and check with a test light at the smaller (IND - see **Fig. 5/12**) cable connection. If both the test light and ignition warning light glow dimly (they are connected in series), then the warning light circuit is in order.

If the ignition warning light doesn't go out in normal use, the fault is most likely to be in the alternator, although a short in the light to alternator circuit could produce similar symptoms.

Also check with your test light at the thicker cable connection at the alternator. This should be live at all times - if not check the circuit back to the battery.

INSIDE INFORMATION: If the alternator on your car has a separate (external) regulator, then this could be faulty - it's always a wise move to replace both regulator and alternator, if one is defective. Other than that, SPECIALIST SERVICE: have a good auto-electrician check it out.

making it easy! **5/14** A simple test of generator output is to switch on your car's headlights and then start the engine. If the lights don't get brighter when the engine is running at a fast tickover, it's a pretty safe bet that your generator isn't charging.

If you own a voltmeter, connect it across the battery terminals (that is, between the positive and negative terminals). The normal reading would be similar to

14

that shown here (12.63 volts) but rise to around 14 volts once the engine is started and running at a fast idle - if it is more than about one volt away from this, there is either an alternator or a regulator problem.

COMMON FAILURES

Some of the more common alternator problems and possible reasons for failure are:

Poor brush contact
Caused by;
Sticking brushes (dirt). Worn brushes. Dirty slip rings.

Rectifier (Diode) failure
Caused by:
Dirty or loose battery connections or earth leads. Battery being connected incorrectly (wrong polarity). Alternator or battery terminals being disconnected while the engine is running. Vehicle jump started incorrectly. Electric arc welding on the vehicle without disconnecting the alternator. Dirty, loose or corroded terminals at the alternator.

5/15 Rectifier units, or diode packs, as they are sometimes called, come in various forms and may be quite difficult to remove. But once this is achieved most can be checked quite easily using nothing more than a test light and power source (12 volt battery). Check one way, then reverse the connections. The light should light up in one direction only.

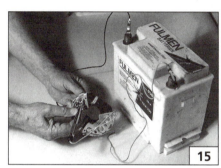

5/16 A far better method of checking the diodes is to use a multi-meter and especially one with a special diode testing facility. For those without this facility, set the meter to the 'ohms' mode and carry out a normal continuity test. Once again there should be a reading in one direction, but nothing of any consequence in the other. Do not use the generator type ohmmeters commonly called 'Megger' meters.

Bearing failure
Caused by:
More often than not, an overtightened drive belt. A slipping belt generally squeals, especially if there is a load on the alternator. However, this may not mean that it is loose - a worn drive belt, for instance, will tend to bottom on the Vee in the pulley, instead of gripping on the sides, it will then slip and squeal. Misaligned pulleys (crankshaft, alternator, water pump, idler) may also result in both eventual bearing failure and a squealing belt.

5/17 In general the generator drive belt tension can be considered correct when moderate thumb pressure, at a point midway along the belt's longest straight stretch should deflect it by about 1/2in (13mm).

Alternator Fault Finding

For most drivers, the first indication of a problem with the alternator is that the ignition warning light stops doing what it should. It may be that it doesn't come on at all when the key is turned, it may be that it does come on but then doesn't go out when the engine starts or perhaps doesn't do so until the engine is turning over at a very fast idle. It may be that it glows dimly when the engine is running, perhaps getting a little brighter as the engine speeds up, or indeed, it may flicker on and off, once the engine starts.

While it's true that most of these warning light indicators do point to a fault with the alternator, it's also true that many of them could also result from a problem elsewhere and, para-doxically, needn't necessarily mean that the alternator isn't fulfilling its primary function - that of charging the battery. At the other extreme, the fact that the warning light is functioning normally, doesn't necessarily mean that the alternator is!

Alternator Repair

5/18 There's nothing difficult or complex about an alternator and, probably because of this, they don't often go wrong. But, go wrong they do, if only because, after some time, parts of them wear out.

Cost and age should be the deciding factors when considering a repair or replacement. But if adopting the latter course, it's best to go for a remanufactured unit from a well known supplier such as Bosch or Lucas. Both companies supply alternators (and starter motors) for most applications - mostly with an 'As-New' warranty.

Alternators are basically electro/ mechanical components and in most cases it's the mechanical bits that fail. Indeed, when the electrical or electronic sections stop working, it's generally the result of a failure elsewhere - a short circuit, an open circuit or, sometimes, human error.

That may be so, but in many instances, it's difficult to differentiate between the electrical and mechanical areas.

Most alternators incorporate some means of passing electrical current through a rotating armature (the rotor) which means that at some stage there must be a static component in touch with a moving one - in fact there are two - the brushes. These are not brushes in the sense that they have bristles or anything like that: They are solid chunks of copper, brass or carbon that are held in contact with smooth (rotating) slip rings on the rotor, under spring pressure. Naturally enough they wear down and, in time, will lose touch with the slip ring. The brushes are mechanical, yet once worn to this degree, any electrical contact with the slip ring is lost. So it's a mechanical fault but an electrical failure.

With some alternators, it's possible to replace the brushes without removing the component from the car, whereas with others it not only has to be removed, but also virtually stripped down. The Nippon Denso (ex-Toyota Celica) shown in the

following sequence falls into this, latter, category and is, in many ways, typical of the type. This particular unit doesn't have a built-in regulator, but those that do won't be far different as far as brush replacement is concerned.

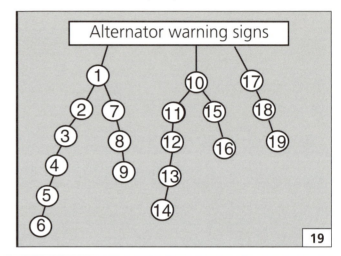

Alternator warning signs

19

1. Warning light doesn't come on.
This assumes that the warning light doesn't light up when ignition has been switched on and that all (or most) other electrical items work as normal. Although unlikely, a break in any of the brush cable leads could have the same effect.

2. Worn/sticking brushes.
Any fault which prevents the brushes from making good rubbing contact with the slip rings can affect the warning light. On occasion, a build up of dust may result in the brushes sticking in the their holders and, if so, it is possible that a light tap on the side of the unit could free them off. But it would probably be only a temporary solution.

3. Worn/glazed slip rings.
Depending upon the make and type of alternator, it may be possible to simply remove the brush box and inspect the slip rings and, if they are just dirty, to wipe them with a cleaning rag. But, again this would probably be a temporary cure. Brush/slip ring problems are also the most likely cause of a flickering ignition warning light.

4. Defective regulator.
Most modern regulators are solid state electronic units and may be incorporated into the brush box assembly - they cannot be adjusted or repaired. Overcharging is almost certainly due a to faulty regulator whereas undercharging could also be due to other factors.

5. Defective rotor windings.
Once the alternator has been dismantled, the rotor windings can be checked for continuity (between the two slip rings) and insulation (between slip rings and rotor core). Any fault will inevitably mean a new rotor.

6. Earthing strap defective/missing (where normally fitted).
Some alternators are mounted on rubber bushes and these, invariably have an earthing

strap between the casing and engine. It's not uncommon for these straps to be left off or disconnected on any alternator removal or repair job.

7. Defective warning light bulb.
Obviously a blown ignition warning light bulb will not light up, but with many alternator systems, the bulb is an integral part of the charging excitation circuit and, if blown, may prevent the system from charging.

8. Poor connection - warning light circuit.
A poor or broken connection in the actual charging circuit is unlikely but, if it does occur could result in complete alternator failure. However, the same thing in the ignition key/warning light circuit, or even in the brush/slip ring circuit within the alternator, would probably just result in a no-charge situation.

9. Wiring problem - warning light circuit.
Virtually the same problems as in number 8 except that a short circuit within the charging system could result in extensive damage to the alternator, the battery, the wiring and a possible fire.

10. Warning light doesn't go out.
This assumes that the warning light comes on with the ignition but then fails to go out once the engine started.

11. Defective rectifier.
In most cases the rectifier is an integral part of the alternator and has to be removed for checking. Although in theory, diodes can be replaced, in practice they are unobtainable and the rectifier unit has to be replaced.

12. Defective stator windings.
The stator windings can be checked for both continuity and insulation but only once the stator has been removed and disconnected from the rectifier. In most cases the cost of any repair would not be justified.

13. Brush wiring problem.
A problem within the alternator allowing the warning light current to short to earth could result in the light burning all the time the ignition was switched on. It could also result in a no-charge situation.

14. Seized bearing (noisy).
In the unlikely event of the alternator rotor not turning due to seized bearing or any other fault, the light would remain on. At the same time, the drive (fan) belt would make a screeching noise.

15. Wiring problem.
A wiring fault external to the alternator could cause the warning light to remain on all the time or just when the ignition was switched on. Depending upon the actual fault it may, or may not, affect the charging rate.

16. Defective fan belt.
Obviously a broken or loose drive belt would result in a no- charge situation and the warning light remaining on with the ignition. Depending upon the layout, it could also result in the cooling fan and water pump not working with consequent overheating problems.

17. Warning light glows dimly when the engine is started.
In some cases the following faults could cause the warning light to glow dimly all the time the engine was running and, in others the light may actually get a little brighter as engine speed increases.

18. Defective rectifier.
See number 11.

19. Resistive connection in warning light circuit.
Because the warning light goes out when there is a balance between battery and alternator output, it follows that any resistance in the light circuit could cause an imbalance.

In some cases, the slip rings may be worn as well, in which case they would also need replacing. Most simply pull off, but it will probably be necessary to use some form of puller on them and, of course, to remove the bearing first. They will also be connected in some way to the rotor windings - often a soldered joint which would need sorting out. This wasn't necessary in this particular instance, but we've shown a similar operation separately on another make of alternator.

ALTERNATOR PROBLEMS

☐ **5/19** Here is an excellent step-by-step checklist to identifying alternator problems. Follow it through in the order shown.

Alternator Brush Replacement

☐ **5/20** There are three, long, cross-headed screws holding the assembly together. These are generally pretty tight.

making it easy! It may be advantageous to soak them in penetrating fluid before trying to release them. It's also advisable to release them initially with an impact screwdriver. Although not strictly essential, we would advise you make some form of alignment marks on the front and rear sections.

☐ **5/21** It's not unknown for those 'through' screws to break and if that happens you might find it better to start looking for a replacement alternator. If it

doesn't, separate the two halves ensuring that the stator (the bit in the middle) comes off with the rearmost portion, even though, as in this picture, the initial movement would indicate otherwise. If you use a screwdriver to prise the bits apart, take care not to damage the stator coils.

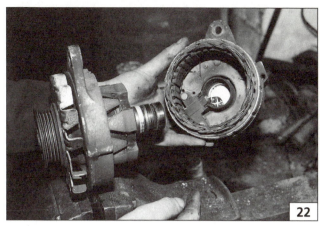

☐ **5/22** This probably gives a better idea of how the two sections come apart - you can also see the stator coils. The section left in the vice incorporates the pulley, fan, rotor and the slip rings which, in most cases, needn't be stripped any further, although (obviously) any defect in the front bearing would mean further dismantling, as may a damaged pulley or fan.

☐ **5/23** These are the slip rings, seen here in more detail and gives a fair idea of why the alternator wasn't charging. The outermost 'ring' is the bearing, with the two innermost being

the actual slip rings and, of these, the one on the inside is glazed, due to poor brush contact.

☐ **5/24** There are four threaded studs protruding through the rear cover with (10 or 11mm) nuts on them and which hold the stator and rectifier assembly in place. One is under the

rubber cover over the end of the capacitor cable.

INSIDE INFORMATION: Undo the nuts while, at the same time, making a note on a piece of paper of the location of any insulating washers. Otherwise, you're bound to forget later! Also don't forget this cable clamp on reassembly.

5/25 Lift off the end cover to expose the rectifier and brush-box assembly. There's no need to worry about any alignment marks for reassembly - it would be difficult to put it together incorrectly.

5/26 INSIDE INFORMATION: These two inverted 'top-hat' insulators are vitally important, as are their two counterparts under the top cover nuts. They all fit over the 'live' terminal posts and if missed out, or fitted incorrectly, could result in a short circuit and extensive damage. The insulating washers of the other two (earthed) posts are less important, but its still better to make sure they stay in place.

5/27 As the brushes wear down they naturally get shorter, but what wears off doesn't just disappear. It gets converted into copper dust and coats the inside of the slip ring housing, which is no great problem. However, it can also coat the slip

rings themselves (see **Ill. 5/23**) forming a conductive path between the two - and if this does happen, the alternator will stop working.

5/28 The brushes, or rather their (braided) leads are soldered into place and their removal/replacement involves the application of heat, preferably with an old (solid-copper) type soldering iron. If you can, do this as shown so that any molten solder falls out, rather than running into the brush-box.

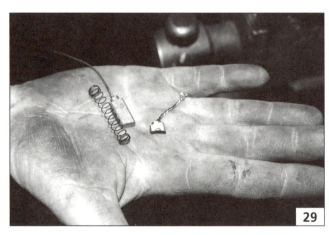

5/29 This shows the old and new brushes - no points for guessing which is which, but it's pretty obvious why the alternator stopped charging!

INSIDE INFORMATION: Note that both the old and new brushes are angled at the end - this is how they sit on the slip ring. Make sure the new ones go in the right way round and don't forget the springs!

5/30 When fitting the new brushes, first feed the braided cable through the brush-box then loop it round the box extension as shown so that it holds the brush in place against the (light) spring pressure. Although we've only shown the operation on one brush, it needs doing on both.

5/31 With the brush held in this position, solder the cable at the top of the brush-box, taking care not to let any excess solder run down into the box where it might restrict brush movement. This is the main reason for using a really hot iron for a very short time and using very little solder. However, make sure it's a really good (soldered) joint. Snip off the spare cable afterwards.

5/32 Unless they are deeply scored, there's nothing very hi-tech about cleaning up the slip rings. Often a simple rub-down with a strip of fine emery cloth will do; sometimes with just a petrol/meths soaked cloth. Either way, clean away any debris

or grease afterwards. If necessary pack a little high melting point grease into the bearing before reassembly.

making it easy! **5/33** It will be impossible to assemble the unit with the brushes poking out of their holders. So push them down and while holding them there insert a length of wire (about a couple of inches or 50mm long and $\frac{1}{16}$ in. or 1.5mm diameter) through the brush box as shown to hold the brushes in the 'fully-in' position.

5/34 When reassembling the unit (which is more or less a reversal of the strip-down operation) ensure that the 'brush-holding' wire protrudes through the end cover - there's a hole in it just for this purpose. The as a final move, slowly pull out the wire, when you should hear two distinct clicks as the (spring-loaded) brushes contact the slip rings.

Slip Ring Replacement

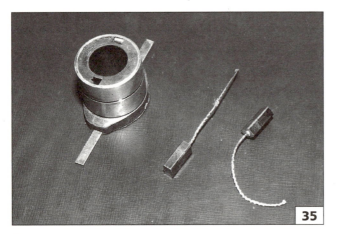

5/35 This shows the spare parts that will be needed: A couple of brushes and a slip ring assembly. They should be available from your local auto electrical specialist - look in Yellow Pages under Car Electrical.

5/36 Lever up the slip ring wings attachment points on the rotor. They may well be soldered in place but, even if not, will probably need soldering on reassembly.

5/37 Pull off the bearing first. It's doubtful if you will have access to this kind of jig, but you can use a two-legged puller or, if absolutely necessary, you could use a couple of screwdrivers. Take *great care* not to damage the bearing!

5/38 Then pull off the slip ring assembly in the same way. The replacement can normally be lightly tapped into place, but it can be a tight fit so take care that it doesn't become distorted. Fit the bearing in the same way and lubricate it before reassembling the unit.

CHAPTER 6
STARTER SYSTEMS

Turning over the relatively high compression engines used in most modern cars, and to spin them at around 100 revolutions a minute, requires a very powerful motor. This, in turn, means a very high current demand - something in the region of 300 to 400 amps to initially get the engine moving (or considerably more in the depths of winter when the oil is turgid and thick) dropping to around 80 amps once it's turning. Normal wiring is obviously inadequate and that's why much heavier cable than normal is used to connect the three basic components in the circuit - battery, solenoid and starter.

☐ **6/1** Current is carried from the battery to the solenoid, then when its contacts are closed, through the other heavy leads (or links) from solenoid output terminal to the motor. The earth return is through the motor's internal connections and casing to the engine via the mounting bolts. The engine itself is usually earthed back to the car body by means of a metal braided strap.

☐ **6/2** The inertia type motor drive was used in older cars and is basically a heavy toothed pinion fitting loosely on a shaft with a spiral thread. When the starter spins, the threaded shaft turns, but the inertia on the heavy pinion means that it initially turns much more slowly and consequently winds itself along the thread and into engagement with the flywheel, so turning the engine.

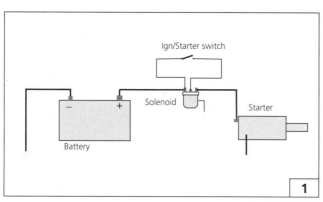

1

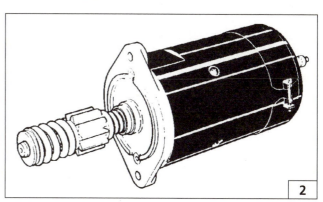

2

Starter Types

The starter is basically a heavy duty electric motor with a gear type drive arrangement which, when energised, is made to engage with corresponding gear teeth on the engine flywheel or, in the case of most automatic transmission cars, on a plate attached to the torque converter.

There are two basic types of starter motor, with the type of drive arrangement being the most significant difference between the two. Indeed, the different starters are generally referred to by the type of drive - inertia (sometimes called Bendix) or pre- engaged.

☐ **6/3** Once the engine starts, the flywheel turns faster than the pinion and in so doing, makes it unwind back along its thread and out of mesh.

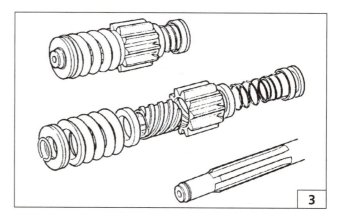

3

6/4 The inertia system is a rather crude arrangement in that the pinion is turning (albeit slowly) as it engages with the flywheel. In effect this means engaging a moving gear with one that is static, creating

both a noise problem and the possibility of damaged gear teeth both on the pinion (**Fig 6/4**) and on the flywheel.

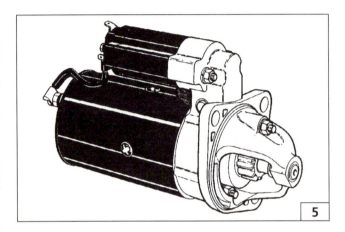

6/5 Because of this most cars produced over the last thirty years or so have been fitted with pre-engaged starter motors in which the pinion engages with the flywheel before it starts turning. These can be easily identified because they have the solenoid mounted directly on the casing as shown this and in the heading pictures.

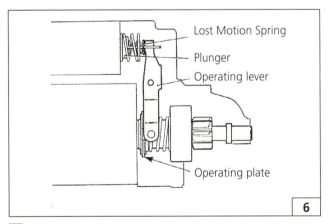

Lost Motion Spring
Plunger
Operating lever
Operating plate

6/6 With the inertia type of starter motor, the separate solenoid acts purely as a heavy duty switch, protecting the contacts on the ignition switch from burning. On the pre-engaged units it has a dual function - again as a switch, but also engaging the starter pinion just before the starter motor begins to turn. This is achieved through an extension lever and fork attached to the (moving) armature of the solenoid at one end and the (sliding) starter pinion at the other. The 'lost motion' spring helps ensure that the solenoid contacts separate before the pinion is retracted.

A further (operational) difference is that the pinion is not automatically thrown out of mesh when the engine starts, but stays engaged until the ignition key is released. A free-wheel clutch is usually incorporated into the drive arrangement to help avoid any problems this might create - mainly that of an inexperienced driver keeping the starter motor engaged after the engine has started.

Starter Motor Checks

WIRING, CONNECTIONS AND CLAMPS

Before assuming that there *is* a problem with the starter, bear in mind that, quite frequently, the problem lies with the heavy duty connections rather than the starter itself.

Having established that the battery is sound and that the terminals to the battery are doing their job, it is now essential to ensure that the power is getting to where it's needed. The biggest drain on the battery occurs when you start the engine, so the biggest cables on the car are those which carry the power directly from one side of the battery to the starter motor, and from the other side of the battery to the car's bodywork which acts as an 'earth cable'.

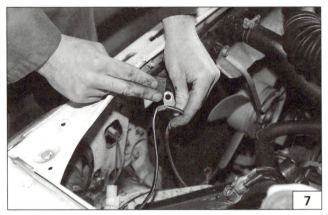

6/7 Unbolt the cable that goes from the battery to the bodywork, clean the metal on the clamp and on the car's body until it is shiny and bright in that area, coat it with copper-impregnated grease to prevent corrosion, then reassemble.

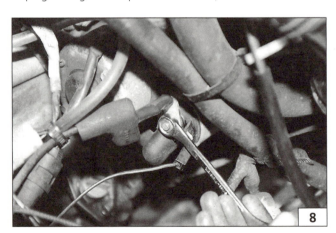

6/8 Do the same with the clamp that is bolted to the starter motor. In this way you will have ensured that the power flowing to and from the battery is getting through. N.B. DISCONNECT THE BATTERY NEGATIVE LEAD FIRST! This terminal leads directly to the battery: if that spanner touches any part of the bodywork a massive short will result!

9

6/9 It is often forgotten that, although the car's bodywork is an effective 'earth', the engine is insulated from the bodywork by the rubber engine mounts. Somewhere, there will be an engine earth/ground strap bolted between engine and body. As with the previous stage, remove both ends, clean until all connections are bright and re-fit with a protective coating such as copper-impregnated grease.

INSIDE INFORMATION: If the throttle or choke cables on your car become hot when you attempt to start the car, it means that the earthing system has broken down and the cables are trying to give the engine the earth connection it needs.

JAMMED STARTER PINION

If when you turn the key the starter motor makes its usual noise but almost instantly stops with a 'clunk', it may be jammed. Wait a couple of seconds, then try again. If the result is a whirring noise with an absence of the normal trying-to-start, engine-turning-over sound, it has almost certainly jammed. The sound emanates from the starter pinion (also known as the starter dog) which is shot along a pinion shaft, turning as it goes, until it comes into contact with a large ring gear, typically 450 mm (18 in.) in diameter, on the engine flywheel. This gear is *supposed* to turn the flywheel and thus the engine until it starts. The trouble is that when the gears wear, the starter dog can stick in the flywheel gears like a piece of celery between the teeth. Unfortunately, a toothbrush is no help...
There are three self-help steps you can take:

10

6/10 Some older (inertia-type) starter motors have a squared pin on the end of the motor housing. Turn this with a spanner and you can wind the stuck dog back down the pinion shaft. Try starting up again - it won't stick every time.

11

6/11 You could hit the starter motor on the side of the casing or on the solenoid with a hammer. This might also help to free a starter dog that has gone 'sticky' on the pinion shaft or a sticking solenoid (but be careful not to crack the starter motor case!).

12

6/12 Alternatively, put the car in a low gear and 'rock' it backwards and forwards (ignition OFF!) until the dog comes free.

The real cure for a starter that regularly sticks is, unfortunately, replacement of the ring gear on the flywheel - an engine-out job.

A starter dog that sticks on the pinion only needs you to remove the starter motor and thoroughly clean the pinion shaft, checking for wear and a broken spring. On the other hand, a scrap-yard or 'exchange' unit will be needed if the motor has become slow and lazy - but do remove, clean and re-fit all electrical connections before leaping to conclusions.

PRELIMINARY CHECKS (WITH TESTLIGHT)

6/13 Start by checking the battery and its terminals (see *Chapter 4, The Battery*) then connect one lead of the test light to the main battery feed (large) terminal of the solenoid (1) and the other to earth. If the light lights, the fault is either the solenoid or the starter motor.

Move the lead from the battery side of the solenoid to the smaller (switch) terminal at the solenoid (2) and operate the starter switch. If the light doesn't light, suspect the starter switch or the switch circuit.

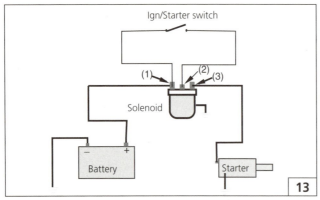

Ign/Starter switch

(1) (2) (3)

Solenoid

Battery

Starter

13

Now move the lead to the other main terminal (starter side) of the solenoid (3) and again operate the starter switch. If the light doesn't light, suspect the solenoid. However, if the light does light, it proves that the solenoid is working, but it still doesn't necessarily mean that the solenoid contacts will pass the starter current.

making it easy! *Try another quick check: Connect one of the light leads to either battery positive or the battery side of the solenoid and the other initially to an earth point on the car body and then to a similar (earth) point on the engine. If the test light lights on the body, but not on the engine, there's likely to be a problem with the engine/body earth strap - assuming it is there and not broken. As mentioned earlier, check it for condition, security and good contact, especially if any work has been carried out which may have disturbed it.*

Although satisfactory as far as they go, these checks with a testlight have their limitations. Far more conclusive results can be obtained using a voltmeter.

Solenoid Checks

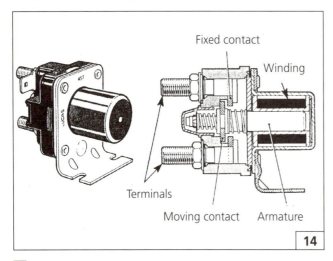

Fixed contact

Winding

Terminals

Moving contact   Armature

14

☐ **6/14** The simplest way to find out if the solenoid is working is to listen to it while a helper operates the starter switch. If it is working, you should be able to hear the click of the contacts closing. If you can't, it may be a faulty solenoid, or alternatively, the fault may be in the wiring to it - this would include the ignition switch and its power supply.

☐ **6/15** It is sometimes possible to effectively by-pass the solenoid by bridging its two big terminals, but be very careful for there could be considerable sparking as you do so. Peel back the rubber covers (if fitted) and wedge a screwdriver (holding its insulated handle)

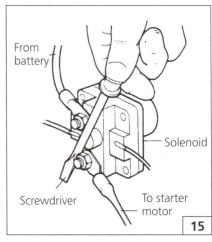

From battery

Solenoid

Screwdriver   To starter motor

15

between the terminal studs - try a pair of pliers if there's an insulating bridge between the two terminals. If the starter now turns, the solenoid is faulty. Most solenoids are one-piece sealed units and cannot be repaired so, if it is faulty, the only solution is to renew it. IMPORTANT NOTE: Put the gearbox in Neutral or Park, turn ignition off, watch out for moving engine parts and keep everything flammable away.

Circuit Checks (with voltmeter)

Despite the fact that this procedure should only be necessary if the starter isn't working, it's quite possible that it could decide to spring to life at any time during the test sequence with potentially dangerous consequences. It is therefore advisable to prevent the engine from starting by disabling the ignition. On most petrol engined cars this can be done by disconnecting the low-tension supply to the coil and on diesels by cutting the supply to the fuel shut-off valve at the injection pump.

The following tests assume that all checks relating to engine condition, a jammed starter pinion and battery condition have been satisfactorily carried out and any faults rectified. In addition, they relate to 12 volt, negative earth electrical systems.

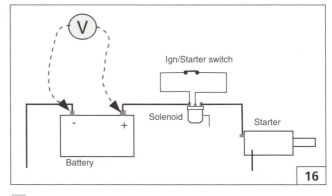

Ign/Starter switch

Solenoid

Starter

Battery

16

☐ **6/16** Test 1 - Battery working voltage

Connect a voltmeter across the battery and note the reading when the starter switch is operated - this should be in the region of 10 to 11 volts for most petrol engines and around 9 to 10 volts for a diesel. A lower voltage would indicate a fault with the starter, whereas no appreciable drop in voltage could mean a defective solenoid or ignition/starter switch, or trouble in their respective circuits.

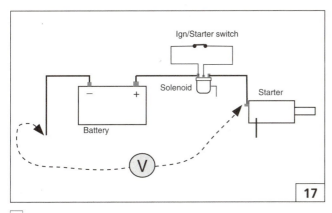

6/17 Test 2 - Starter voltage

Connect the voltmeter between the starter input terminal and earth. When the starter switch is operated the reading should be not more than 0.5 volts below that obtained in Test No. 1. If the reading is within this limit, the starter circuit can be considered satisfactory. However, a low reading would point to a high resistance somewhere in the circuit - probably at one of the connections or at the solenoid contacts.

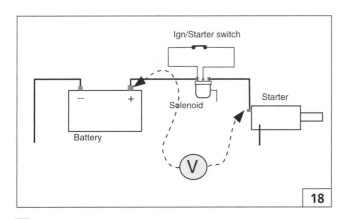

6/18 Test 3 - Supply circuit

To confirm a low reading in Test No. 2, connect the voltmeter between battery positive and the starter input terminal. The meter should now register battery voltage but, when the starter switch is operated the reading should drop to practically zero. Anything higher would again mean a high resistance in the starter circuit.

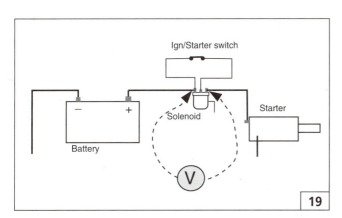

6/19 Test 4 - Solenoid contacts

To check for any resistance at the solenoid contacts, connect the voltmeter across the two main solenoid terminals. The

meter should read battery voltage (12 volts), but when the starter switch is operated it should fall to zero or very, very near it. Anything higher would indicate a problem with the solenoid contacts. If the previous test showed a high reading and this one is satisfactory, the high resistance must be due to fault in the cable or its connections.

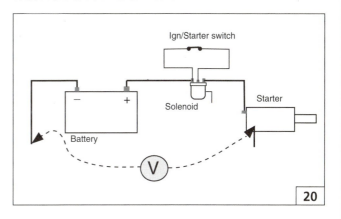

6/20 Test 5 - Earth return

Finally, to check for a high resistance on the earth side of the circuit (between motor body and battery earth), connect the positive lead of the meter to the battery earth terminal and the negative terminal to the starter motor body. Operate the starter and the voltage be around the zero mark and certainly below 0.5 volts. If it isn't, look for a bad connection either on the engine earth strap or the battery earth.

Starter Motor Fault Finding

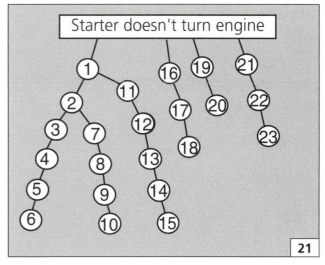

6/21 These faults and their symptoms are intended as a guide only since it would be impossible to list all the possible problems associated with starter motors. For example, it has been known for the motor armature to break up or for the pinion to split in two, but both are very rare events and, along with many other such defects, hardly worth listing.

And neither does it always follow that the symptoms given always apply. A poor connection at the battery, for instance, would probably cause the lights to dim when the starter is operated, but one at the solenoid may or may not. But it all adds to the fun of auto-electrics, doesn't it!

Fault:
Starter will not turn the engine

1. Switch on car headlights and operate starter.

Switch on the car headlights and watch the beams as you operate the starter. If you can't see if the lights dim as the starter switch is turned try switching on the interior light as well and watch that. Do not operate the starter in these conditions for periods of longer than about 5 seconds with at least a 10 second interval between attempts.

2. Lights go dim.

If the lights dim when the starter switch is turned it could be due to either an electrical or a mechanical fault. Just how dim the lights go under these conditions depends on many factors such as the state of the battery and the type and location of the fault.

3. Check battery condition.

One of the most common causes of this condition is a flat battery. This may be due to driver error (leaving the lights on), a fault in the charging system (covered in *Chapter 5, Charging Systems*) or a problem with the battery itself (*Chapter 4, The Battery*). Quite frequently a car in this condition can be push/tow started or 'jump' started from another vehicle - the procedure for this is also covered in *Chapter 4*.

4. Check battery/starter connections.

Another common, so-called starter fault is a poor connection, somewhere within the battery/starter circuit This could be a dirty or loose connection at the battery itself, at the starter solenoid or in the earth return side of the circuit - this usually takes the from of a braided strap between the engine and car chassis/body and the strap can suffer either a partial or complete fracture. In some cases this can result in any other metallic link (choke cable) between the engine and body acting as an earth return and getting very hot when the starter is operated. Incidentally, it's not unknown for the strap to be forgotten during some repair operation - so creating a starting problem.

5. Loose starter motor.

The starter motor mounting bolts are, in many cases, also part of the earth return and, if they are loose it may amount to a poor connection. In some cases the braided earthing strap connection will be under one of the mounting bolts. Depending upon how many (and how loose) the bolts are, the starter could also be noisy in operation.

6. Defective starter motor.

There are a number of defects within the starter motor itself which could cause this kind of situation, but the most common would be trouble with the brushes and commutator. It's also quite possible that problems in this area could also produce a burning smell as the starter is operated - if so,

avoid using the starter until the trouble is sorted out.

7. Engine difficult to rotate by hand.

It's seldom possible to actually turn the engine of a modern car by hand, but with most it would be possible to do much the same thing by engaging gear and moving the car. This should help give an indication of any mechanical problem.

8. Pinion jammed.

A jammed starter motor pinion frequently produces symptoms very similar to a seized engine. The condition is more likely with an inertia starter than with pre-engaged versions and can usually be rectified by engaging a gear (3rd preferred) and rocking the car backwards and forwards. If, for any reason (automatic transmission) this isn't possible, the only solution would be to remove the starter motor.

Alternatively, some starter motors may have a squared off section on the end of the armature shaft which permits it (the starter armature) to be turned with a spanner, so freeing it off. This square section may be hidden under a small tin (top-hat) cover which can usually be prised off quite easily. If the car is an automatic, taking the starter off is the only remedy. (See page 49.)

9. Partially seized engine.

A partially seized engine is unlikely to occur without making itself fairly evident through other (non-electric) factors. However, it's not uncommon for a newly rebuilt engine to be initially somewhat 'tight' and, in exceptional cases, this tightness could be such that the starter won't turn the engine.

10. Seized accessory.

Depending upon their drive arrangements, a seized alternator, water pump, power steering pump or other belt driven accessory would put an additional load on the starter. If such a condition didn't prevent the engine from starting, the slipping belt would probably make a loud screaming noise. An unusual, but cold weather related, fault of this nature would be a frozen water pump.

11. Lights remain bright.

If the headlights remain bright when the ignition key is turned to the start position, but the starter motor remains inoperative the fault could still be either electrical or mechanical, but one which is not related to battery strength.

12. Ignition switch fault.

Any defect in the circuit between the ignition switch and starter solenoid which prevents the solenoid from working is unlikely to affect battery output to any degree. Such defects could include loose/poor connections or a cable break. Any problem with the power supply to the ignition switch would affect other circuits as well.

13. Defective solenoid/starter.

Problems with the solenoid could be with the actual winding or, more likely, with the contacts. These switch the full starter current and, as such, are subject to some degree of arcing which eventually could result in no contact being made. However, in this case, the solenoid should make a clicking noise when energised. An open circuit within the starter motor (most likely in the brush/commutator area) could produce similar symptoms.

14. Sticking pinion.

A sticking pinion could prevent engagement with the flywheel, but the starter motor may still turn and will be heard to do so. This fault is more likely to occur with inertia type starters and can sometimes be (temporarily) rectified by clouting the starter with a hammer handle or chunk of wood.

15. Faulty auto-box isolator.

Most automatic transmission equipped cars are fitted with an isolator switch, preventing the engine from being started other than N (Neutral) or P (Park) is selected. Problems with the switch (or its connections) could affect starter operation at any time with, potentially, the most dangerous situation arising when the engine can be started with the transmission in Drive. If there's no reaction in N or P move the selector through the gears a couple of times and try again.

16. Starter makes a noise when key is turned.

Noise (or lack of it) can help when trying to diagnose various starter motor problems. No noise whatsoever could be due to completely flat battery, a solenoid circuit fault or, with inertia starters, a jammed pinion.

17. Clicking noise.

If the starter makes a clicking noise every time the key is turned it indicates that the solenoid is operating - that's all. The problem could still be with the battery or the battery/starter circuit, or indeed with any of the faults listed here from 1 to 16!

18. Grating noise.

A sharp grating noise is indicative of the pinion gear teeth clashing with those on the flywheel and could be due to the condition of the teeth on either component or problems with the pinion drive arrangement (sticking). It's unlikely to be associated with the electrical system.

19. Low humming noise.

A low humming noise, often following the click of the solenoid operating, indicates that power is reaching the starter motor but, for some reason or other it isn't turning. This could be due to the condition of the commutator or any of those problems making the engine difficult to turn. The starter motor can get very hot in these conditions.

20. Whirring noise.
A whirring noise when the starter is operated probably means that it is turning but that the pinion is not engaging with the flywheel - see Test 14.

21. Engine turns a little then stops.
Discounting any mechanical problem such as a broken con rod or anything equally serious, the most probable causes of the starter motor turning the engine as normal, but only briefly, are those described in numbers 22 and 23

22. Over advanced ignition.
An over advanced ignition firing the mixture in the cylinder well before TDC and forcing the piston back down the wrong way. This is most likely due to sticking advance weights in the distributor.

23. Water in cylinder.
Water in the cylinder preventing the piston from reaching the TDC position. Unless the vehicle has been driven through water, the most probable cause would a leaking head gasket. In either case, continued use of the starter motor could lead to extensive engine damage.

Fault:
Engine turns the engine over slowly:
Possible causes:
Most of the reasons for the starter not turning the engine could also result in it turning over slowly. In addition, the use of an incorrect grade oil can also contribute to slow cranking speeds

Fault:
Starter turns but the engine doesn't.
Possible causes: Battery low on power (3)
Sticking pinion (14)
Defective starter solenoid (13)
Defective starter motor (6)
Loose starter motor (5)

Fault:
Engine fires but stops again when starter switch is released
Possible causes:
Faulty ballast resistor (ignition)
Ignition circuit fault (Low Tension side)

Starter Motor Repair

Other than with Post Office and other short-trip delivery vehicles, where the starter motors are in constant use, by far the majority of so-called starter problems will be down to either the battery or battery/starter circuit connection (including earth return) problems, but occasionally it will be the starter motor at fault and, when it is, it's invariably a solenoid or brush/commutator defect. The starter motor featured here is a Paris Rhone D8E 144 and came from an old Renault 17, but similar units are used on later models and on cars from other (mainly French) manufacturers. Indeed, having said that, most starter motors (other than the old inertia type) are much the same, although many solenoids will be one-piece units and can't be taken apart.

In the picture sequence, we haven't covered removing the starter from the car for the simple reason that it varies from model to model but with most it's fairly easy, even if access can sometimes be a problem. We've also concentrated more on the reassembly process, rather than the strip down, but the individual operations will be similar.

Other than a good soldering iron, preferably the old-fashioned type shown here, you don't need any special tools and it's quite possible you won't need any spare parts either. However, if you do, you might be in trouble, for whereas most outlets, including the main dealers, will quite happily supply a new or reconditioned starter, they won't stock any bits for them. If so, your best bet is to look up any specialist suppliers under the 'Car Electrical Equipment Dealers' heading in your local Yellow Pages directory.

Although we've shown a complete overhaul (other than renewal of the pinion gear) in the picture sequence, we've skipped the odd job, like, for instance, renewing the bush in the end plate. This is much the same as renewing that in the pinion housing and hardly worth repeating.

Of course, it is possible that either the field coils or (more likely) the armature coils are burnt out, but this would normally be pretty obvious. It's also possible that the armature has overheated and its soldered connections at the commutator end have melted. This would normally show as a ring of solder within the outer casing and would not normally be (economically) worth repairing.

On reassembly, insert the brushes into their housings as shown in Pic 36, then use their holding down springs to keep them in the raised position by clamping them on their sides. Once the end cap is fitted, pull the springs up to their normal positions, holding the brushes in contact with the commutator.

Finally, be careful when testing the unit, for it will jerk quite severely when you make contact between the positive and solenoid terminals. You might find it best to put your foot on the body of the motor to hold it in place.

☐ **6/22** After releasing the two terminal clamping screws on the solenoid unit, undo both the 8mm nuts holding the endcap in place.

22

---

making it easy! The field coils in this starter (as in most others) are aluminium and are therefore difficult to solder using normal materials. It is for this reason we advise you cut the existing connecting wire when installing a new brush (Pics 34 and 35) and solder the new brush leads to the wire stump. You may need to cut the leads on both new brushes, but it's easy to determine where, simply by comparing them with the old ones. Don't forget the insulating sleeves and, on the field coil brush, you might find it advantageous to tie the two leads together loosely with insulating tape.

23

6/23 Carefully lift off the end plate to reveal the two main contacts (in the endcap) and the contact plate, along with its spring and plunger.

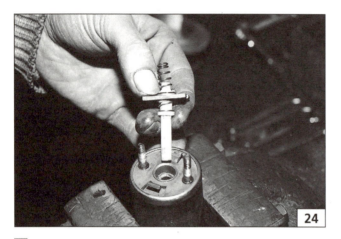

24

6/24 The contact plate and plunger assembly can now be simply withdrawn from the main body of the solenoid.

25

6/25 Depending upon its condition the contacts and the contact plate can now be cleaned up and replaced, or new ones fitted.

26

6/26 The choice is yours, but if you can locate a supplier, it's probably best to renew both components. The cost should be quite reasonable.

6/27 It is, of course, possible that the bushes at both ends of the starter itself are worn, but this one at the drive-end is the prime candidate.

27

6/28 Drive it out as shown (in 6/27) using a 12-13mm drift, then carefully drive in the new one as shown here.

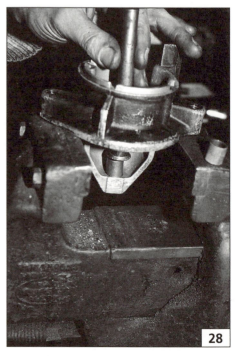

28

6/29 One brush is soldered to a terminal plate in the starter endcap. Either cut it off or de-solder it and clean off the plate.

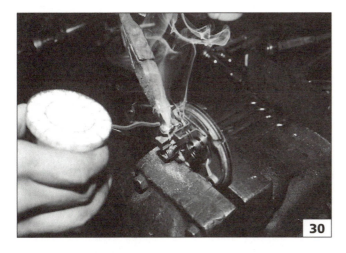

6/30 Then, before soldering the new brushes in place, 'tin' the terminal plate - 'flush' solder on to it. These soldering jobs are all best done with a very hot iron.

6/31 Determine the approximate length of the brush leads from the old ones, or from the distance to the brush holder.

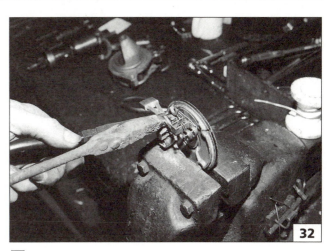

6/32 Tin the wires in the appropriate spot (6/31), then solder the new brush in place, removing any excess (fallen) solder.

6/33 Snip off any extra lead length, making sure no odd strands of wire remain. Check again that the soldered joint is sound.

6/34 The second brush is attached to one of the (aluminium) field-coils. Cut the old brush off leaving a short length of old lead in place.

6/35 After tinning the new brush leads, solder them in place after, again, determining the lead (and insulator) length.

6/36 On re-assembly insert the brushes part-way into their holders, then use their return springs to hold them in place.

6/37 The commutator can often be cleaned up with a strip of emery cloth. At other times it may need skimming in a lathe.

6/38 Using a sharp implement (re-profiled hacksaw blade) clean out between the commutator segments.

6/39 The drive pinion on this unit was satisfactory, but they are easily changed if necessary. Lightly grease the drive.

6/40 Insert the armature into the casing and fit the end plate over the armature shaft, taking care not to disturb the brushes.

6/41 Now using a 'hooked' length of wire, pull up the brush springs, slide the brush down on to the commutator and fit the spring over it.

6/42 When stripping the unit, you will have found a couple of washers under a bolt at the brush end of the unit. Refit them.

6/43 The 10mm bolt has a left-hand thread, so tapping it as shown will be tightening it further.

6/44 At the working end, slide the coupling fork over the pinion and insert the solenoid plunger into the top yoke.

6/45 Fit the drive-end housing. Line-up the coupling fork and insert its pivot pin - it will only go in from one side.

6/46 Make sure the end plate and drive housing are correctly located. Then insert and tighten the 11mm through bolts.

STARTER SYSTEMS

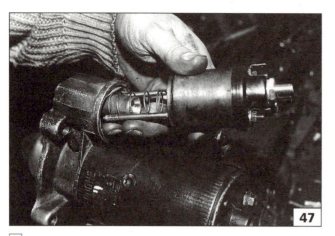

6/47 With its spring in place, insert the solenoid unit. Making sure it is the right way round and that the plunger seats correctly.

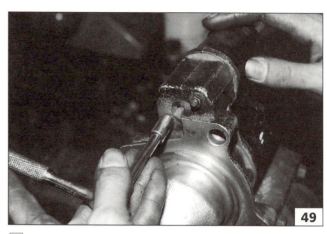

6/49 If everything is in order, tighten the two 8mm nuts holding the unit in place. Then check the whole assembly.

6/48 If you re-fitted this link strip correctly this is how the solenoid should look. That floating cable fits on the lower terminal.

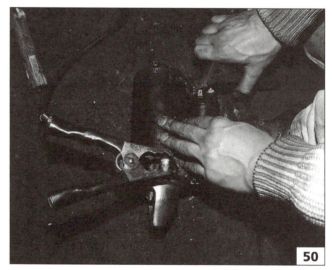

6/50 To test the starter, connect up 12 volt supply and earth leads, then link the positive and solenoid connections.

CHAPTER 7
IGNITION SYSTEMS

The sole aim of any car's ignition system, whether it is called electronic, dynamic, cyclonic or any other fancy name you'd care to give it, is to produce a spark at the right place, at the right time and of sufficient strength to fully ignite the compressed fuel/air mixture in the combustion chamber. However, since the speed at which it all happens is so high, the timing of the event is so critical, and the amount of wear that the components have to withstand is so intense, there's a lot to check and maintain, and, there are some impressive improvements to be made to your engine by getting it right!

☐ **7/1** Until the widespread use of electronically controlled systems during the 1960s and '70s, most ignition systems were very similar to one another and followed this basic layout. As with every other electrical circuit in the car, it starts off with the battery which, in this case, supplies power to the ignition switch. The system from here can be considered as being made up of two separate, but interconnected, circuits.

In the illustration we've shown these by thin and heavy lines, the thin ones being the low tension (LT) or primary circuit operating at battery voltage, and the other, thicker section , being the high tension (HT) or secondary circuit, where voltages can be in the region of 15 to 20,000 volts.

Tracing the primary (thin) circuit through we can see that, when the ignition switch is closed (ON), there will be current path from the battery to one of the low tension terminals of the coil. In most cases this terminal will be marked either as '+' or SW.

From there, the current will flow through the primary winding of the coil to the '-' or CB terminal and then on to the contact breaker. In fact, current will flow only when the contact breakers are closed, completing the circuit to earth and back to the negative side of the battery.

The secondary (thick) circuit of the system begins at the coil, where one end of the winding is connected to the CB side of the primary winding. The other end is taken to the central tower terminal of the coil unit, from where an HT cable, sometimes referred to as the 'King lead', connects the coil to the distributor. The rotor arm within the distributor then directs the high tension current through 'plug leads' to the appropriate sparking plug.

So much for the basic layout of the system, which doesn't explain how it works. Probably the best way to do this is to take the various component parts and see what they do.

Ignition Switch

For our purposes we can regard this as a simple ON/OFF switch, albeit key operated. In practice, the switch is often used for other purposes as well and is combined with the starter switch.

Coil

If you have ever watered your garden or washed your car, you will appreciate that, to get a good strong jet, first and foremost you need high water pressure. In much the same way, to get a good fat spark across the gap in the sparking plug under all operating conditions can call for high voltages (pressures) in the region of 15 to 20,000 volts. The role of the coil, therefore, is to boost the nominal battery voltage (12 volts) to that required at the sparking plug.

To understand how the coil does this, it is necessary to have some idea of the relationship between electricity and magnetism which was covered in *Chapter 2, Doing the Knowledge* but basically, what it amounts to is that, when an electrical current is passed through a conductor (cable or wire), a magnetic field is set up around it.

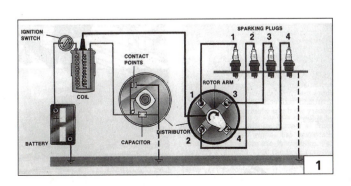

SAFETY FIRST!

Very high voltages are used in the High Tension side of the ignition circuit, which at the very best can cause an unpleasant shock. While it is unlikely that this would be harmful to a healthy person, any reaction to the shock could well be, such as spontaneously pulling your hand away and into a moving part.

It's therefore wise to take precautions - avoid touching any part of the HT system with your bare hands unless the ignition is switched off. Where it is necessary, such as when checking for a spark, then use insulated pliers, rubber gloves, a dry rag or anything of that nature - do not, for instance, rely on the cable insulation.

These precautions become even more important when working on an electronic ignition system, for a shock from some systems could prove harmful or even fatal - a shock from any system could have serious consequences for anyone with a heart problem.

It is possible to get a shock from a low tension side of a contact breaker system, where the back emf (electro motive force) of around 300 volts is produced in the primary windings when the magnetic field collapses.

Do not attempt to turn the engine over by hand with the ignition switched on, it's best to remove the key from the ignition in any case.

Some coils and ballast resistors can reach high temperatures in use so avoid touching them both when and for some time after, running the engine.

The electric fans used to cool the radiators in many modern cars, may start up some time after the engine has been switched off, so take care if working in that area. This obviously also applies when the engine is running.

Remember, sparks can start fires and a spark can occur when connecting or disconnecting any lead, or if any live terminal is shorted to earth. Unless it is required for testing purposes always disconnect the battery before working on any electrical component. Incidentally always disconnect the battery negative lead before the positive and connect it up after. Beware of any items of loose clothing - a tie or loose sleeves when leaning over an engine that is running.

Not only does a current, passing through a conductor, produce a magnetic field but, conversely, if a conductor (wire) is made to pass through a magnetic field, cutting its lines of force, then a voltage is induced into the wire. If these lines of force were cut by a number of turns of wire, then the total voltage induced would, among other things, be related to the number of turns.

Furthermore, if a coil of wire is wound around a soft iron core and a current is passed through the wire, the soft iron core is magnetised, increasing the strength of the magnetic field.

7/2 Back then to our automotive coil, which consists of two insulated windings and a laminated iron core, all encased in a metal can. Of the two windings, the outer (primary) is made up of relatively few, thicker coils of wire. Inside this is the secondary coil, made up of a far greater number of coils of thinner wire.

In operation, battery voltage is applied to one side of the primary windings and the other side is earthed (through the contact breaker). This results in a current flowing through the primary windings, building up a magnetic field around the iron core. This magnetic field encompasses the secondary windings.

When the current flow is interrupted, the magnetic field collapses and, in so doing, is cut by the thousands of turns of wire in the secondary windings, inducing a very high voltage into the secondary circuit, which eventually ends up at the appropriate plug.

Each build up and collapse sequence produces one spark and a four-cylinder engine running at 3,500 rpm needs 7,000 sparks every minute. This means there has to be some device capable of switching the primary current at this rate, and even faster. In this traditional type of ignition system, that device is the contact breaker.

Contact Breaker

Located within the distributor, the contact breaker (sometimes referred to as the 'points') is nothing more than a mechanically operated switch.

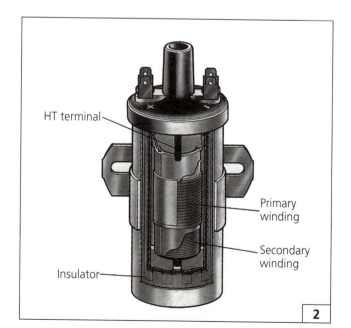

HT terminal

Primary winding

Secondary winding

Insulator

2

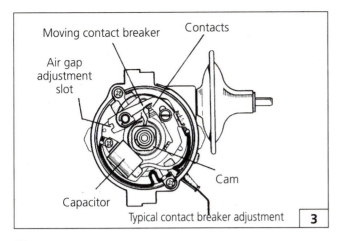

Moving contact breaker

Contacts

Air gap adjustment slot

Cam

Capacitor

Typical contact breaker adjustment   **3**

7/3 Basically, the assembly consists of two contacts, one of which is securely attached to the baseplate of the distributor - the fixed contact. The other, known as the moving contact, is mounted on a spring strip, together with fibre compound rubbing block. This block rides on a cam incorporated into the distributor centre shaft. In most cases, the number of lobes on this cam will equal the number of cylinders. As the cam turns, each lobe will force the contacts apart, after which they are closed by spring pressure.

The distributor shaft, and cam, are driven from the crankshaft at half engine speed so that, in a four-cylinder engine for example, the points open and close four times every two engine revolutions - corresponding with the compression and power strokes of the engine.

Electrically, the fixed contact is earthed and the moving contact connected to the CB terminal of the coil. As the points open and close, the current flow in the primary circuit is interrupted.

Capacitor

We have already seen that, as the contact points open, the magnetic field collapses and its lines of force are cut by the secondary winding.

However, they are also cut by the primary winding, inducing a current into the primary circuit. In comparison with the secondary winding the voltage is quite small - somewhere in the region of 350 volts - but still sufficient to arc across the opening contact points. In a very short time, this arcing would burn the points to such an extent that they wouldn't pass a current when closed.

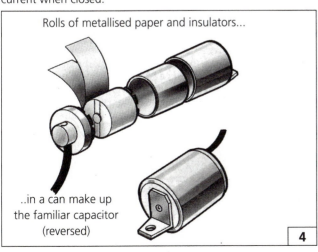

Rolls of metallised paper and insulators...

..in a can make up the familiar capacitor (reversed)   **4**

7/4 The capacitor, or condenser as it is often called, is wired electrically across the contact breaker and acts as a sort of sponge, soaking up the surge of current. Having 'soaked' up this current surge, the capacitor, once again acting like a sponge, re-asserts itself and discharges. As the contact points are now fully open, the discharged current can only flow back through the primary winding.

Besides preventing arcing of the points, the action of the capacitor also speeds up the collapse of the magnetic field, increasing the voltage induced into the secondary circuit.

Distributor

As its name suggests, the primary role of the distributor is to distribute the HT current from the coil to the appropriate sparking plug. However, this isn't its only function for, as we've already seen, it also houses the contact breaker and capacitor. Further to this, it also includes a means of automatically advancing or retarding the spark timing.

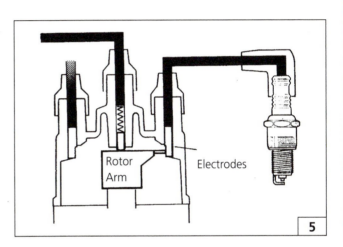

Rotor Arm

Electrodes

5

7/5 The high tension section of the distributor consists basically of the cap and a rotor arm which is fitted over (and turns with) the distributor shaft. HT current from the coil is fed through the centre terminal in the cap to a brush type connector and on to the rotor arm electrode.

Evenly spaced around the inside of the cap are a number of electrodes (segments) - one for each cylinder. These segments are connected to terminals on the outside of the cap which, in turn, are connected (by cables) to the sparking plugs, in firing order sequence - in a typical four-cylinder engine this sequence would be 1 - 3 - 4 - 2.

The whole layout is such that, as the rotor arm electrode passes each segment, the distributor shaft cam opens the contact breaker. The resulting high tension current produced in the coil flows to the rotor arm, jumping the small gap to the segment and on to the appropriate sparking plug.

Automatic Advance Mechanism

If you set fire to a certain amount of petrol it will take a specific time to burn. The same could be said for the fuel/air mixture drawn into the cylinder.

The problem is that, although this burn time may be constant, as the engine speed increases, the time allowed for it

IGNITION SYSTEMS

decreases. This means that, as the engine goes faster, it is necessary to start burning the mixture earlier or, in other words, the ignition has to be advanced.

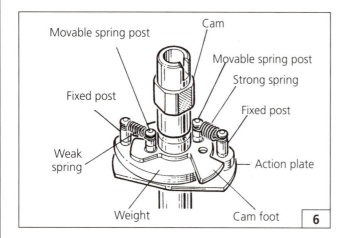

Movable spring post — Cam — Movable spring post — Strong spring — Fixed post — Fixed post — Weak spring — Action plate — Weight — Cam foot

6

☐ **7/6** To achieve this, the distributor shaft is made up of two parts; the lower section is driven from the engine camshaft, while the upper part incorporates the cam and drives the rotor arm. The two are joined by an arrangement of pivoted weights and springs. In use, as the engine speed increases, the weights move out against spring pressure, moving the upper part in relation to the lower. This has the effect of moving the spark forward in relation to the crankshaft/piston position - advancing the spark.

Vacuum Advance

Although we said that the burn time of the fuel/air mixture is constant, that only applies where the volume is also constant. However, in an engine the amount of air (and fuel) going into the cylinders changes, according to the position of the throttle.

For instance, when the throttle is only partly open, less air enters the cylinder than when it is wide open. This means that the pressure rise on compression stroke is also reduced.

☐ **7/7** The fuel/air mixture burns more slowly at lower pressures so, in these conditions, the ignition needs to be advanced even further. This is achieved by the use of a vacuum control unit, mounted on the side of the distributor and operated by the depression in the inlet

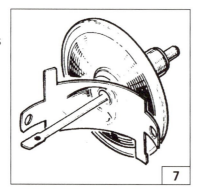

7

manifold. This arrangement is such that, as the diaphragm within the unit flexes, it physically moves the baseplate on which the contact breaker points are mounted. By moving the contact breaker in relation to the cam, the points are made to open earlier, so advancing the spark.

Electronic Ignition

The contact breaker points are regarded generally as the weak link in the ignition system. Electronic systems are used either to eliminate the points altogether or to increase their lifespan. The different types of electronic system are covered in *Chapter 8, Electronic Ignition.*

Ignition Timing

The timing of the spark is vital for efficient engine operation but, as wear takes place on the contact breaker and its rubbing block, the points gap will alter, affecting the timing. The operation known as Ignition Timing involves re-setting the distributor so that, once again, the spark occurs at exactly the right moment. It's obviously important to ensure that the points gap is correct before checking or adjusting the timing.

Sparking Plugs

Although all sparking plugs may look similar, there are a number of different types and it is vitally important to use only the correct one for your car. This will be stated in the car's handbook.

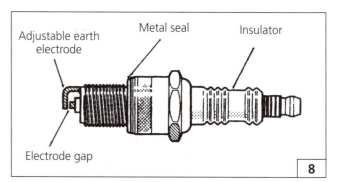

Adjustable earth electrode — Metal seal — Insulator — Electrode gap

8

☐ **7/8** In its basic form, a sparking plug consists of an outer body containing a ceramic insulator, through the centre of which is an electrode. The HT current passes down this centre electrode and then jumps an air gap at its base to an earth electrode attached to the plug body, sparking as it does so.

Ballast Resistor

When the starter is operated, it makes a big drain on the battery, in effect reducing its voltage. In turn, this reduces the coil output and weakens the spark.

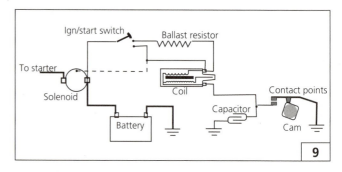

Ign/start switch — Ballast resistor — To starter — Solenoid — Coil — Contact points — Capacitor — Cam — Battery

9

☐ **7/9** To overcome this, a coil designed to operate at around 8 volts is used and a (ballast) resistor inserted in the circuit between the ignition switch and coil to reduce the voltage at the coil to that figure.

This resistor is by-passed when the starter is operated so that the reduction in battery output (when the starter is in use) has no effect on the quality of the spark.

Ignition System Maintenance

Every year around 1 million UK motorists suffer from an ignition related breakdown or refusal to start. And the situation is at its worst when the overall weather pattern tends towards the damp side.

Some of these breakdowns will be unavoidable, such as a component failure that nobody could have foreseen or a fault somewhere else that affected the ignition. But, nevertheless, many of these breakdowns result from poor (or a complete lack of) maintenance.

Practically all cars from 1985-on, and some considerably older, are equipped with electronic ignition systems of one sort or another, which although more reliable than the primitive contact breaker systems, have the disadvantage of being more difficult to sort out if they do go wrong. But these electronic systems have another hidden disadvantage in that, as one of the reasons for fitting them was to reduce maintenance costs, or rather manufacturers' publicised maintenance costs, it often results in complete neglect of the ignition system.

For example, in the old contact breaker days, when any garage or DIY motorists cleaned, adjusted or replaced the points, they also took the trouble to lubricate the advance weights and clean both the rotor arm and distributor cap. With no contact breaker service needed, these other requirements are often ignored and neither are they listed in service manuals as being required. Yet with the higher HT voltages generated in some electronic systems, it's even more important that both the cap and rotor are clean and dry.

Admittedly, some electronic systems have neither a distributor cap or a rotor arm, but most still do and neglecting both these and other components can result in a failure. In other words, regardless of whether the system is electronic or conventional, it still requires looking after and the service checks shown here are a guide to what still may need doing, although of course not all will apply to some of the electronic systems.

CLEAN AND CHECK SPARK PLUGS

With standard type sparking plugs it's advisable to check and, if necessary, clean and re-gap them at 6,000 mile intervals. Normal replacement intervals are at around 12,000 miles, but often, in a clean running engine, this can be extended if regular checks are made and, when necessary the electrodes squared up with a small file - rounded off electrodes increase the gap breakdown voltage. In some (dirtier) engines more frequent plug changes may be necessary.

Follow the car/plug manufacturers' recommendations with long-life platinum and Double Copper type plugs and only fit the recommended grade of plug - most outlets selling sparking plugs have application lists. For further information see *Understanding Spark Plugs* from page 73-on.

☐ **7/10** Numbered spark plug leads (traditionally called 'HT' or 'High Tension' leads) are fitted from new on many cars, the numbers being printed into the leads themselves. Note that the numbering starts from the drive-belt end of the engine, or the left-hand side as you look to the rear of the car.

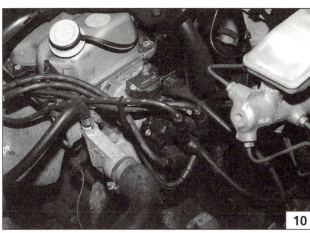

INSIDE INFORMATION: If the lead numbers are illegible or non-original leads fitted, mark them with a spot of paint - typists' correction fluid is used by many mechanics as it is easy to apply and dries very quickly. Mark them from the radiator end of the engine in the sequence one, two, three and four 'dots'. (Correct identification of the plug leads is important because if incorrectly replaced, the engine will not run!).

☐ **7/11** When this is done the plug caps can be pulled off. Be careful not to tug on the lead itself as you may pull it from the cap, which will remain on the plug!

☐ **7/12** Using a suitably long spark plug spanner or socket extension, unscrew the spark plugs. They may be 'tight' to begin with so take care to keep the plug spanner or socket in line with the plug body, otherwise the porcelain insulator of the plug can break.

INSIDE INFORMATION: If you are trying to remove a plug which gets ever tighter as you turn it, there's every possibility that it is cross threaded. Once out, it probably won't go back in again. Tighten it up again and take the car to a Main Dealer or specialist who may be able to clean up the threads with a

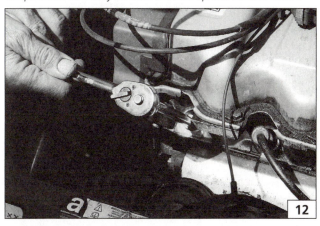

purpose-made tool. If this can't be done, he will have to add a thread insert to your cylinder head. It pays to take great care when removing and fitting spark plugs, especially when dealing with aluminium cylinder heads!

7/13 Clean the plug electrodes by vigorous use of a wire brush to remove any carbon deposits. If the electrodes of the plug look 'rounded' and worn (compare them to a new plug) they should be replaced.

making it easy! Leave the spark plug in the socket spanner while using the wire brush - this is kinder on the fingers and lessens the risk of dropping the plug and breaking it.

7/14 If using a flat feeler gauge select the 'blade' of the correct thickness and slide it between the electrodes as shown. The gap between the two electrodes should provide a sliding fit, with no 'slack'. If necessary, adjust the gap using a pair of snipe-nosed (thin, pointed jaws) pliers, carefully bending the curved side-

electrode towards or away from the tip of the centre electrode, until the feeler gauge fits the gap as described. Special gapping tools are available from accessory shops which make this easy and their use carries little risk of damaging the plug, which can occur if the electrode is clumsily moved by use of a screwdriver or pliers.

Replace the plugs when the gaps are correct, adding just a slight smear of grease to the threads to make future removal easier. There is no need to screw the plugs down with great force - just tighten them firmly.

Before replacing the plug leads, clean them by use of a maintenance spray and a piece of rag or tissue. Also clean the exterior of the distributor cap (into which the plug leads fit) using the same method.

making it easy! If you have forgotten, until it is too late, to mark the HT leads and you have lost their order, don't despair! There's an easy way of finding it again. First put the rotor arm back on the distributor, but not the cap. Then get a helper to turn the engine over, clockwise looking at the pulley end, with a spanner on the pulley bolt while you put your thumb over the plug hole of No. 1 cylinder - the one nearest the pulley end of the engine. When you feel air pressure under your thumb indicating that the cylinder is on compression, stop and then ease the pulley nut round until the timing notch on the pulley is opposite the 0 (zero) mark on the timing cover. This is Top Dead Centre, very close to the firing point for No. 1 cylinder, and the rotor arm will be pointing to the stud in the distributor cap which takes the HT lead for No. 1 plug. Notice while the engine was being turned over that the rotor arm was going round anticlockwise. So, having found No. 1 HT lead you can find the others by going round the cap anticlockwise looking at the top, marking the leads in their firing order. REMEMBER that the firing order is NOT the same for all engines - check your handbook or Porter Manual.

CLEAN AND CHECK IGNITION COMPONENTS

7/15 On some engines, the distributor may be hidden away at the back of the engine (A) and the cap lifts off after undoing the two spring

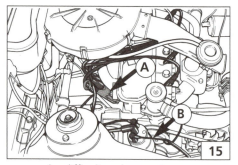

clips. However, access can be difficult and prevent sufficient leverage to spring the clips off with your fingers, so carefully use a broad-bladed screwdriver.

INSIDE INFORMATION: Distributors by Bosch and Lucas are among the most commonly used. Usually, the Bosch unit is distinguished by having a brown cap secured by spring clips, while the Lucas unit has a black cap secured by screws or clips.

7/16 On other engines the distributor is much more accessible, sometimes at the end of the camshaft housing. Before you can take the cap off you have to lift off this sprung-on metal cover on this type.

7/17 Then undo two cross-head screws or spring clips and lift the distributor cap away. Clean the HT leads and check for signs of surface cracking, and loose connections where the lead fits on to the plug connector and into the distributor cap.

7/18 Clean the distributor cap inside and out and check for any signs of 'tracking' - burnt lines where carbon has lodged in a faint crack to provide a short circuit for the HT current. Any signs of tracking means that the cap could let you down with poor starting and bad running at any time as well as increasing your fuel consumption. Check also that the centre carbon brush (see pointer) still has plenty of length and that it is springy enough to bear on the centre of the rotor arm. Check the studs in the distributor cap for burning. Light burning can be cleaned up with fine glasspaper - better than emery paper because it does not leave any conducting dust.

7/19 Check the vacuum advance by pulling the pipe off the inlet manifold end - engine NOT running - and sucking quite hard on the pipe. As you let go, you should hear the base plate inside the distributor return back to its original position with a click. (It's spring loaded.) If you can suck freely with no

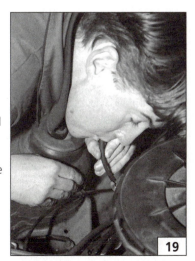

resistance, or you don't hear a click from the base plate, then either the diaphragm has failed completely or the mechanism inside the distributor has seized solid. A second-hand replacement can be a cheaper solution, but check the replacement carefully before buying it.

INSIDE INFORMATION: Be warned that you can end up with a mouth full of petrol carrying out this check! Use a bicycle pump with the valve inside turned round so that it 'sucks' - but be careful not to pull too hard and cause damage.

7/20 Clean the top of the coil tower and check for any signs of HT current tracking. Check that the HT lead, and the two low tension leads, are firm and secure.

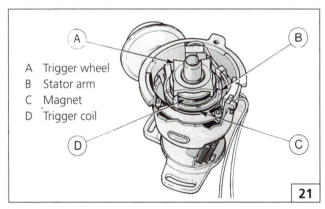

A   Trigger wheel
B   Stator arm
C   Magnet
D   Trigger coil

7/21 The inside of an electronic ignition distributor requires no attention, except a careful wipe over. Here, for reference, is the early Lucas electronic distributor. Lubricate as shown later but keep oil off all electronic components!

IMPORTANT NOTE: With some modern cars, the distributor and coil are combined and no servicing is possible.

Check/set CB Points/Dwell Angle

ENGINES WITH CONTACT BREAKERS ONLY

Check that the rotor arm (**7/22**, inset) fits firmly and not loosely on the centre cam of the distributor and check the end of it for burning. Again, light burning can be cleaned up but severe burning of either the distributor cap studs or the rotor arm means renewal - not too expensive at all.

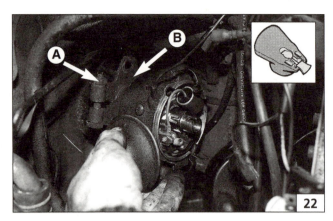

22

Distributor Removal

7/22 The distributor is not always sited in the most accessible of positions, which makes points adjustment awkward in some cases and in others downright impossible. Sometimes, you are better off taking the distributor out, and of course, unless this is done using the proper procedure, all the ignition timing will be lost. Start by turning the engine over until No. 1 piston is on its compression stroke and the rotor arm (inset) is pointing to the segment of the No. 1 HT lead with the contact breaker points just opening. Mark the way it points on the distributor body and mark also the distributor flange and the engine, as reference points for replacement.

Do not undo the clamp bolt (A), but instead take out the two bolts through the mounting flange (B). If the unit has a skew gear drive, it will rotate as you lift it up. Record the final position, as a further help to replacement, by marking the direction in which the rotor arm finally points. When you come to refit it, line the rotor arm at this second mark and then as it

---

FACT FILE: DWELL ANGLE

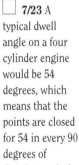

Checking the points setting dynamically involves measuring the period when the contact points are closed in relation to the distributor shaft rotation. This is referred to as the dwell and can be checked using an instrument known as a dwell meter.

7/23 A typical dwell angle on a four cylinder engine would be 54 degrees, which means that the points are closed for 54 in every 90 degrees of

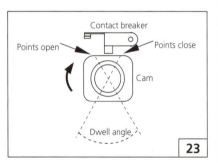

Contact breaker
Points open
Points close
Cam
Dwell angle

23

distributor shaft rotation. In percentage terms this would be:

$$\frac{54}{90 \times 100} = 60\%$$

Checking the dwell angle is a simple operation and involved connecting up the dwell meter according to the instructions supplied with the instrument, which normally amounts to a couple of connections to the car's battery and one to the distributor or coil, after which you start the engine and check the meter reading.

---

goes home it should rotate back to the first mark. Check that the two marks on the distributor flange and engine are lined up and refit the two bolts. Provided that the engine has not been turned over in the interim, the timing should now be exactly as it was before the distributor was removed.

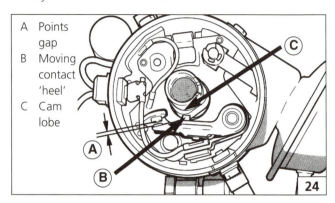

A Points gap
B Moving contact 'heel'
C Cam lobe

24

7/24 To check the points gap (A), turn the engine (via the road-wheel) until the heel of the moving point (B) is on one of the lobes of the centre cam (C). Insert a feeler gauge of the appropriate thickness between the points (see your handbook or appropriate Porter Manual).

If you find it difficult to slide the feeler gauge between the points, because they appear burnt or pitted, the points require replacement as it will be difficult to obtain a satisfactory gap if their condition is poor: see later for points renewal.

7/25 If the points are clean but need adjusting, first slacken the screw (C) holding the fixed point to the baseplate. A notch (B) is provided in the baseplate against which a screwdriver blade

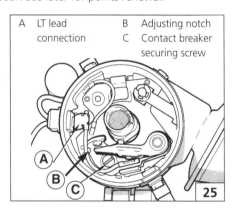

A LT lead connection
B Adjusting notch
C Contact breaker securing screw

25

can be inserted and turned to increase or decrease the points gap. Adjust the fixed point and tighten the screw when the appropriate feeler gauge is a sliding fit between the points.

7/26 The method as described will give you a points gap which is accurate enough for starting the engine but, to get the gap absolutely accurate, you need to use a dwell meter. This is a job that your dealer will do for

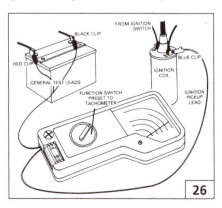

26

you, or you can buy a dwell meter - DIY versions are not expensive - and learn to use it by following the instructions. They are quite simple to use. (Illustration, courtesy Gunsons)

☐ **7/27** Before you replace the distributor cap, dribble a few drops of oil down the side of the baseplate to lubricate the mechanical advance and control mechanism. On engines which have been neglected, it does no harm to give a brief squirt of releasing fluid behind the baseplate first in case the advance and retard weights have become partially seized.

☐ **7/28** Finally, put just the smallest smear of high melting point grease (A) on the faces of the cam (B). Take care not get any oil or grease on the points faces but, if you do, clean it off with methylated spirit.

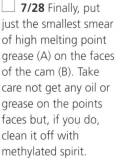

Make sure all the spirit has evaporated before you replace the distributor cap. Even points in good condition spark slightly and any spirit vapour left in an enclosed space is a potential fire bomb.

☐ **7/29** The procedure for checking and adjusting the Lucas distributor follows that given for the Bosch unit; similarities in the internal arrangement can be seen from this illustration. Note the position of the fixed-point securing screw (B) and the position of the moving contact heel (C).

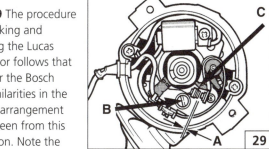

In both types, check the condition of the contact faces (A), looking for signs of burning, pitting and a build-up of metal on one or other of the contacts. If you find any pitting, it is wise to renew the contact breaker (points) assembly, as described below, as the small cost is far outweighed by the potential benefits in performance, economy and reliability.

☐ **7/30** These are the pivot post lubrication points, A is a Bosch distributor and B is one of the Lucas units.

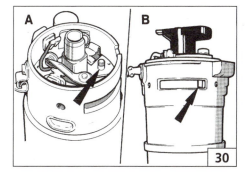

Contact Breaker Points Renewal

NON-ELECTRONIC IGNITION ONLY

BOSCH DISTRIBUTORS (TYPICAL)

☐ **7/31** With the distributor cap and rotor arm removed pull the LT lead connector (A) from its terminal, then undo and remove the points securing screw (B) and lift out the old points. Position the new set

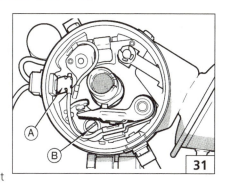

of points on the baseplate and replace the screw but do not tighten it fully; push the LT wire connector onto its terminal. Now refer to **7/23-on** for details on setting the correct points gap.

INSIDE INFORMATION: Be extra careful not allow the screw to fall down into the distributor body, otherwise the distributor will have to be removed to retrieve it.

LUCAS DISTRIBUTORS (TYPICAL)

☐ **7/32** With cap and rotor arm removed, remove screw (B) and disconnect the LT lead from the clip on the points sprung arm at (C). When fitting new points, make sure to locate the forked cam (A) on the pin

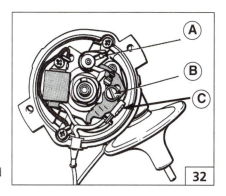

projecting from the baseplate; replace the screw (B) and connect the LT wire to the sprung arm. Carry out the points-gap setting procedure described in **7/23-on**.

With both types of distributor, position a slip of paper moistened with methylated spirits between the closed points and work it to-and-fro a couple of times to remove any oil or other anti-corrosion substance placed there by the manufacturer.

Check Ignition Timing

SAFETY FIRST!
THE ELECTRONIC IGNITION SYSTEM INVOLVES VERY HIGH VOLTAGES! All manufacturers recommend that only trained personnel should go near the high-tension circuit (coil, distributor and HT wiring) and it is ESSENTIAL that anyone wearing a medical pacemaker device does not go near the ignition system. Also, stroboscopic timing requires the engine to be running - take great care that parts of the timing lights or parts of your body or clothing don't get caught up in the moving parts! Don't wear loose clothing or hair.

7/33 INSIDE INFORMATION: To check or adjust the ignition timing with the required degree of accuracy calls for the use of a strobo-scopic timing light similar to the Gunson's model shown here. Although a 'static' timing figure may be given in some workshop manuals, this is only a guide, mostly used to get an engine started after the distributor has been disturbed and the previous settings lost.

making it easy! After removing the spark plugs - ignition turned off - turn the engine by hand so that the timing mark or 'notch' ('A' in illustration **7/34**) on the rim of the crankshaft pulley can be seen. Highlight it, and the timing marks (B) on the timing cover, with a dab of white paint or typists' correction fluid. This ensures that the marks will be clearly visible when illuminated by the timing light.

INSIDE INFORMATION: Timing checks and adjustments are usually made with the vacuum pipe (the one that connects between the inlet manifold and distributor) disconnected at the distributor end and plugged with a suitable instrument, such as a small Phillips-type screwdriver, or wooden 'bung'.

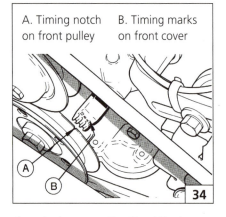

7/34 These are the timing marks as found on a typical OHV engine. Note that on this engine, the notches on the fixed pointer are numbered 12, 8, 4, 0; these numbers relate to degrees of 'advance', that is, the point at which the spark occurs

A. Timing notch on front pulley   B. Timing marks on front cover

before the '0' mark - otherwise known as Top Dead Centre or TDC. Therefore, if the timing for a particular model were specified as 10 degrees before TDC (BTDC) then the pulley notch should appear between the 12 and 8 marks when illuminated by the brief flashes of the timing light.

7/35 On other engines there are no numbers to distinguish the timing marks, but the '0' or TDC mark is made larger than the others, which in turn are arranged in 4 degree steps. (Illustration, courtesy Ford Motor Company Ltd)

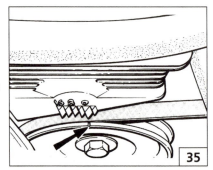

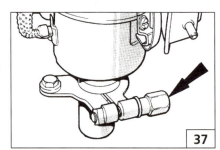

7/36 Connect the timing light according to the maker's instructions, start the engine and let it tick-over at the correct idle speed and point the flashing beam of the light at the timing marks. The strobe effect of the flashing beam 'freezes' the moving mark on the pulley and should appear stationary, adjacent to the static mark on the engine if the timing is set correctly. If the mark appears at the wrong place, the distributor will have to be slackened and turned to bring the marks into alignment, as follows:

making it easy! (Or at least, a little easier!) Switch off the engine and slacken the distributor clamp bolt as shown in **7/37** and **7/38**, just enough to enable the distributor to move under firm pressure. Turn the distributor clockwise to 'retard' the timing, or anticlockwise to 'advance' it. For example, if the specified timing for your model is given as 10 degrees B.T.D.C but the timing light shows the 4 degree mark next to the pointer, the distributor will need to be rotated anticlockwise, to advance the timing by 6 degrees and bring the 10 deg. mark to align with the pointer.

DO NOT try to adjust the distributor with the engine running; make an adjustment, start the engine and check with the timing light if further movement is necessary. If so, stop the engine, adjust, and start it again. When the timing is correct, stop the engine and tighten the distributor clamp bolt, taking care not to alter the position of the distributor while doing so. Make a final check on the timing before disconnecting the 'light.

7/37 The distributor clamp bolt on some units such as some of Ford's OHV engines can be difficult to see, being located on the bottom of the distributor at the back of the engine - locate it by touch if necessary. Slacken the bolt just sufficiently to allow the distributor body to be turned by hand, but not loose enough as to be disturbed when the bolt is tightened. Turn the distributor clockwise to increase the amount of 'advance', or anticlockwise to reduce it. Tighten the clamp bolt when the desired setting is reached.

☐ **7/38** On most other types, the distributor is retained by three bolts arranged at the base of the body - arrowed in the illustration. Slacken all three

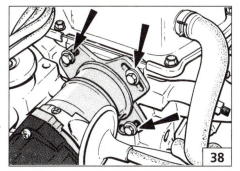

bolts but leave one with enough 'grip' to hold the distributor in position but enable it to move under firm pressure. Turning the distributor clockwise increases the amount of 'advance', while anticlockwise decreases it. Tighten the clamp bolts when the correct setting is achieved.

In all cases, double-check the setting is correct after the clamp bolts have been tightened. If correct, disconnect the timing light, unplug and reconnect the vacuum tube to the distributor.

Distributor Rebuild

Old distributors rarely die, but they most certainly fade away! He we explain what is involved in having one rebuilt.

The distributor is a vital part of any car's 'central nervous system' and yet most will continue to function when they are well past their best. Unfortunately, older cars - such as classic cars - may show signs of having gone through several engine rebuilds - they'll have 40 or more thou. oversize pistons, and thrice- ground cranks, for instance - but both the distributor and the carburettor are usually left alone until they break. This is a Big Mistake!

We took a trip to Holden Vintage & Classic, leading specialists in all things British and electrical to discuss with Jeremy Holden what is involved in overhauling a 'dizzy'. First of all, as Jeremy pointed out, identify your problems! Symptoms include a general lack of 'go' because of a defunct advance mechanism, through to a spindle that can be waggled about and 'fully floating' distributor bodies.

It's worth saying now that to attempt to rebuild your own distributor can hardly be worth considering. First, you would need a well equipped workshop, for reasons which will soon become obvious and second, you would need access to - in this case - fairly obscure information on distributor types and their advance curves, as well as information on how to set them up. Holdens seemed more than happy to tell us what goes on behind the scenes; they can be content that 99.9% of us could never consider even trying to rebuild our own distributors in any case!

But here is what you *can* do yourself, since before rushing off to have your distributor overhauled, you will want to establish whether the expense will be necessary or not. The most 'external' of the external checks will be to see if the vacuum advance is working. Disconnect the pipe from the manifold end and suck hard (but see the advice earlier against illustration **7/19**). There should be almost immediate resistance, as if you have sucked a very small amount of air out of a sealed

chamber - which you have. Then, as you let go, you should hear a small sound, a muffled 'click', as the spring inside the vacuum advance pushes the diaphragm back home. All suck and no stop means that the diaphragm has disintegrated; no return click, and the unit has seized. Holden's repairers actually cut the unit apart with a special tool, insert new diaphragm and spring into a new housing and refit to the distributor body. They say that it is very rare for an elderly vacuum advance to work perfectly and so they are renewed as a matter of course.

Other checks are best carried out with the distributor removed from the car. Take off the cap and rotor arm and try moving the spindle from side to side.

INSIDE INFORMATION: If you try this in the car, as some manuals suggest, the drive gears at the lower end of the unit can easily mask play in the spindle bushes.

If your distributor is more than a few years old, you can bet the spindle bushes are worn! A waving spindle equals variable points gap, equals variable spark timing, equals lowering efficiency. And the same is true of a worn distributor drive slot at the bottom end of the unit. Your repairers should put in a new spindle when wear is found; it will be up to you to replace the drive shaft in the block. Luckily, distributor drive shafts usually screw or pull up and out of the block once the distributor is out, depending on type, but consult your manual. Jeremy Holden assures us that wear is virtually unknown with the geared type of distributor drive.

> *making it easy!* Incidentally, if you want to fit a distributor from a later model of car, such as from a second-hand source, do consult your specialist first, as advance curves can be very different. Earlier engines might 'pink' while later engines fitted with an earlier distributor might be down on power.

Vacuum advance mechanisms work directly on to the cam pillar and the plate at its base. When the vacuum inside the manifold reaches a certain point, the plate is pulled against the pressure of a pair of springs. Also working on the same plate is the centrifugal advance mechanism. This consists of a pair of weights which push gradually outwards as the speed rises. Consequently, higher speeds and more acceleration will together cause the largest pull on the plate, advancing it furthest and fastest. To prevent things getting out of hand, the two coil springs can be 'tuned' to let the advance occur faster or slower, as required (the advance curve) and there is a stop to give the distributor its maximum advance. Holdens restorers fit new springs and ensure that the stop is the right length for the model of car in question - which is why you will have to tell year, engine size, and state of tune.

Holdens don't actually start here, of course! They strip the old unit down and send various bits, including the cam pillar away for plating. The shaft itself is checked for true running and reground 0.15 mm (5 thou.) undersize. Old bushes are pressed out of the cleaned body and new sintered (self-lubricating) bushes are pressed in. Sintered material is especially prone to distortion or even disintegration and simple but special press tools are required. Weights wear out and are always renewed while pivot posts, which almost never wear, are checked and only replaced if necessary. Finally, the rebuilt distributor is placed on the test rig and checked to ensure that the advance characteristics are exactly as required.

The newly rebuilt distributor will ensure that the engine's vital sparks are fed in at precisely the right time. In a nutshell, the bushes keep the spark exactly at the position you put it in; the correctly positioned stop ensures the optimum maximum amount of advance while the new springs control its rate. At the same time, the new weights and vacuum device ensure that the advance 'pull' happens according to plan.

A distributor's innards are a brilliantly evolved piece of precision engineering. The most amazing thing of all is that the whole thing works so precisely at such unimaginable speeds, which are mind-bogglingly high even in the typical classic car's engine. Small wonder that a badly worn unit carves into an engine's performance and makes the engine both more expensive to run and an unnecessary contributor to the frightening pool of pollution that we are all creating. And it's worth remembering that, if a good number of our classic cars are going to be able to pass the MoT test, complete with emission checks, getting the sparks and the mixture spot on is going to require engines that run as the makers originally intended.

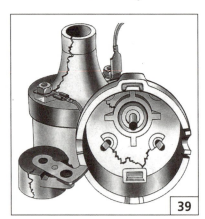

39

making it easy! **7/39** Here's some areas you can - and should! - replace yourself. Cracks in distributor cap or rotor arm, or the coil insulator (shown exaggerated here) all call for replacement! Try running the engine in the dark, at night (out of doors) with the bonnet open. If you see any blue 'lightning' going on, replace the poorly-insulated parts (including HT leads) before your car fails to start on one damp morning.

7/40 With the distributor out of the car, test for spindle and bush wear by rocking the top of the spindle.

41
7/41 Check the drive slot in the base of the spindle. Wear is quite common here.

7/42 New bushes are of sintered construction - particles of metal and carbon compressed to form a perfect, self-lubricating bearing material.

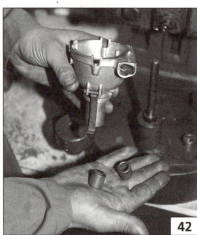

42

7/43 The old are pressed out; the new pressed in, using a special tool to prevent the sintered bushes from deforming or collapsing.

43

7/44 Some compression will invariably take place and the new bushes are reamered to size.

44

7/45 The newly reground spindle and base plate with new advance weights.

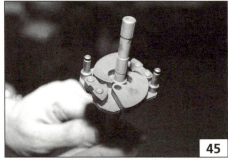

45

☐ **7/46** The replated rotor shaft pushes onto the spindle and pegs in the base locate into the weights. As the weights swing out at speed, they advance the rotor shaft.

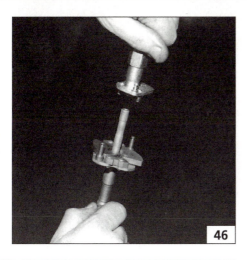
46

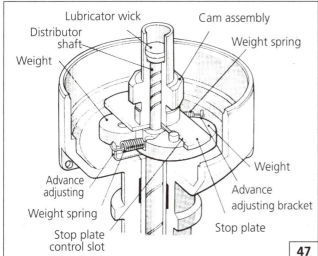

Lubricator wick Cam assembly
Distributor shaft
Weight Spring
Weight
Advance adjusting
Advance adjusting bracket
Weight spring
Weight
Stop plate control slot
Stop plate
47

☐ **7/47** The rotor shaft is normally held back at first base by a pair of springs which pull on posts mounted on the base plate. There is also a post which is also the stop for the advance limiter built into, or mounted onto, the distributor shaft. This stop can be added to by welding a bit on, in order to limit the advance, or ground off to increase it. The correct amount is stamped onto it.

☐ **7/48** Final step is for your specialist to bench test the complete distributor to ensure that the lightning is striking where and when it is wanted.

48

Ignition Fault Finding

(Both electronic and non-electronic types)

IMPORTANT NOTE: See chart on page 72.

With the wide variety of different type ignition systems fitted, it would be impossible to produce a fault finding guide applicable to all, without also making it difficult to follow and open to misunderstanding.

The problems and probable faults listed here are, therefore, of a general nature only and while they apply in most applications, they will not apply to absolutely all. For example, some cars are more prone to failure in damp conditions than others and some may be fitted with replacement parts that don't match those fitted originally. The fault sequence shown is in order of probability, but this also should only be treated as a guide, especially as regards poor and non-starters.

Some systems are also more complex than others and incorporate more (or alternative) components, so you may find that items such as a knock sensor may not apply in your case. If so, just ignore it.

On a similar theme, there are systems like the twin-coil, distributor-less variety as used by Ford (and others) which are different again. But, although they may not have a distributor, they do have a pick-up (at the flywheel) and amplifier which can be checked along with many of the HT trouble areas.

Finally, always bear in mind that this chart applies purely to the ignition, even though many of the problems listed are much more likely to arise from trouble elsewhere. For example, a flat battery, would prevent the engine from being started, either because it wouldn't power the starter motor or wouldn't supply enough power for the ignition when the starter is being used. A mechanical or fuel fault could also cause result in a non- starting engine, but neither has been included in this fault chart. For a wider view of problem solving, see *Chapter 14, Fault Finding*.

1. **Sparking plugs.**
It's extremely unlikely that all the sparking plugs would fail at the same time and, if only one does, it will result in a (regular) misfire, easily isolated by disconnecting (or shorting out) the plug lead with the engine running - note that some electronic ignition systems may be damaged by disconnecting a plug lead - check your handbook and note the *Safety First!* sections of this Chapter.

2. **HT cables.**

☐ **7/49** Again it's unlikely that all would fail at the same time and one failure would also result in a misfire. That is, unless it was the main HT lead from the coil

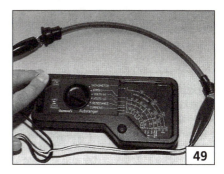
49

at fault, producing a no-start (or no-run) situation. Modern HT cables also deteriorate in use and should be checked with an ohm-meter (or a multi-meter in the ohms mode). Any with a reading of over about 25,000 ohms should be replaced, as should any that are cracked or otherwise damaged. We recommend renewing them about every four years to be on the safe side.

3. **Distributor cap.**
The most common fault with distributor caps is tracking, the tendency for the HT current to 'track' over the cap surface, either from one terminal to another, or to earth. This can sometimes be seen (especially in the dark) as streaks of

IGNITION SYSTEMS

'lightning' if it is on the external surface of the cap, and, in time, may form a greyish path over the surface. It's more likely to occur in damp or dirty conditions, and may be prevented (or rectified) by a simple cleaning operation.

4. Rotor arm.

☐ **7/50** Again, it's tracking which is the main cause of failure, although in this case it is to earth through the distributor shaft. If there are no obvious signs (or cracks) check by first removing the distributor cap, then holding the main HT lead about 6mm (1/4in) away from the rotor terminal blade with *very* well insulated pliers while an

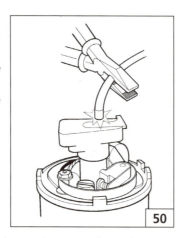

assistant cranks over the engine on the starter. If a spark jumps from the lead to the rotor, it's defective. (DO NOT attempt to carry out this check with electronic ignition's different type of set-up.)

If, in this test, the rotor doesn't turn, it's either floating on the distributor shaft (broken drive lug) or there's something wrong with the camshaft - possibly the drive-belt.

5. Ignition coil.

As with the distributor cap, tracking at the coil tower is a possibility, resulting in a no-start situation. Again, it can sometimes be seen, and sorted out by cleaning. The coil internal windings can also break down, sometimes only when they get hot and causing an engine failure after about 10 minutes (or more) running. You can check for continuity on the LT side with a testlight or voltmeter, but ideally both windings should be checked with an ohm meter against the manufacturer's specifications. Although most coils may look much the same, they do differ, and fitting any substitute may damage other ignition components, even though it may seem to work.

6. Ignition timing and firing order.

It is, of course, possible that both incorrect timing and the wrong firing order could prevent an engine from starting, but neither would be likely in the normal course of events. Indeed, the firing order won't change unless physically disturbed and, with electronic ignition, neither will the timing. Nevertheless, both should be considered in those situations shown on the chart.

7. Pick-up.

☐ **7/51** Perhaps 'trigger-device' would be a better description of this component which, in effect, is the bit that replaces the contact

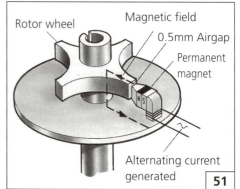

breakers. It's generally a form of magnetic switch, although in some cases an optical unit may be used and, unlike the contact breakers, neither should deteriorate in use although dirt can affect their efficiency as can the (air-gap) setting in some pulse-generator magnetic layouts. In many cases the operation of the pick-up can be checked in much the same way as the dwell setting in contact breaker systems - but don't expect the same kind of readings. It is not recommended that you try to adjust the air gap yourself.

8. Amplifier.

The voltages/currents employed in the triggering device (pick-up) circuits are far too low to be used as the switching medium for the coil. As such, they need to be amplified in order to power the electronic devices (transistors) which fulfil this role. The system therefore incorporates an amplifier, control module or igniter (depending upon terminology), but with some this may be incorporated into an ECU (Electronic Control Module) forming part of an engine management system.

The method of checking varies according to type and location and may involve special test equipment, but a typical unit would have three connections, one from the battery (through the ignition switch and coil LT) and possibly two to the pick-up unit, one at battery voltage and the other (return) at a very low fluctuating voltage, all of which can be checked. There may also be an earth connection, although in some cases this may be through a mounting bolt and a high resistance earth is not an uncommon problem. In most cases it is inadvisable to disconnect the amplifier with the ignition switched on.

9. Ballast resistor.

In ballast resistor systems, a coil designed to operate at seven to eight volts is used and a resistor wired into the circuit to

PROBLEM	PROBABLE FAULT(S)							
Engine will not start	13	3	5	15	8	7	2	4
Engine difficult to start (cold)	**9**	13	6	5	8	7		
Engine difficult to start (damp)	2	3	5	8	13	6	7	
Engine difficult to start (hot)	5	8	7	**13**	**10**			
Engine starts and then stops	**9**	5	7	8	**13**			
Engine misfires	2	1	3	5	6	4		
Engine cuts out when hot	5	8	9	7	**13**	**10**		
Engine lacks power	6	11	12	8	5	**14**	**10**	
Engine 'pinks' when accelerating	11	6	**14**	**12**	1			
Engine runs-on	6	1						
Engine uses excessive fuel	6	**11**	**12**	1	**10**			
Engine idles erratically	6	5	8	**11**	**14**	15		
Engine backfires	6	2	3					
Engine overheats	6	2	12	3				

IMPORTANT NOTE: Items shown in Bold type may not be used in some applications

reduce battery voltage to that level. When the starter is used, the resistor is by-passed and full battery voltage (less any drop due to starter operation) is applied to the coil. In a sense this can be considered as 'supercharging' the coil, producing a better spark for starting.

The resistor can be either in the form of a small (white) block, often attached to the coil, or a resistive lead in the wiring circuit from the ignition switch to coil.

Because the resistor is by-passed when the starter is operated, testing for an HT supply at the plug or from the coil when cranking the engine over, will not show up a failed resistor - in fact, the test would indicate that nothing was wrong. However, it would show up in the coil HT test when flicking the points, for there will be no spark. In any case, if there is an open circuit in the ballast resistor, the engine would only fire when the starter is operated.

To check a suspect resistor, connect up a testlight (or voltmeter) from each end in turn to earth. Then, with the ignition switched on, there should be battery voltage at the supply end (from the ignition switch) and around eight volts at the output end (to the coil). A reading at the supply end, but none at the output side, would indicate an open circuit resistor.

10. Crank angle sensor.
In some more advanced systems the ignition advance and retard is controlled electronically through a pre-determined programme (map), but the basic timing is regulated by a sensor (usually at the flywheel) which is referred to as the Crank angle sensor. In most such systems, when a failure occurs, the programme reverts to a limp-home or stand-by mode, which will affect performance. The sensor is, more or less, a form of pick-up and is usually linked to the amplifier in much the same way.

11. Vacuum advance unit.
Most electronic systems still use a basically mechanically operated vacuum unit, although, instead of being mounted on the distributor, it will be at the ECU. As such it can, and does, suffer from the same kind of problems such as a leaking diaphragm and a displaced or broken hose connection, all of which can affect the ignition timing.

12. Centrifugal advance.
Like a clock which isn't working, the old fashioned centrifugal weight system of advancing the ignition according to engine speed, gave the correct time only once, or possibly twice, throughout its (limited) range. With the advent of programmed (mapped) ignition it is now set to be confined to the dustbin of motoring history and quite rightly so too. However, it has proved pretty reliable in operation with sticking weights and sloppy springs as its chief failure points, both of which will affect the ignition timing.

13. Wiring and multi-plugs.
The main advantages of electronic systems over the old contact points ignition layouts are their reliability and performance - they don't go wrong very often and they stay in tune indefinitely. But, they do have more connections and every connection is a potential failure point.

 *making it easy!* Most failures are due to poor connections and many are sorted out only when a new (unneeded) component is fitted. Simply breaking and making the connection would be just as effective, and far less expensive.

14. Knock sensor.
These are used to ascertain the onset of detonation (pinking) and then signal to the ECU that the ignition should be retarded. The simple, but somewhat unscientific method of checking them is to connect up a stroboscopic light in the normal way and tap the engine block, near the sensor, with a screwdriver, when the strobe should show that the timing retards slightly.

15. Distributor.
This is another component that is scheduled to disappear from the scene and even in those systems that now retain it, use it for just what its name implies - to distribute the HT current to the sparking plugs. With these, it is a fixed component and cannot be moved for ignition timing purposes. It's problems depend upon its various roles. The fewer of them (no contact points, advance weights, etc.) the fewer the problems.

Understanding Spark Plugs

The humble spark plug has to be the true unsung hero of the engine department. Little else can make such an obvious improvement to an otherwise unaltered engine, in terms of performance and mpg. Consider these facts: Working at a pressure of up to 50 bar and in temperatures of up to 3,000 degrees Celsius, the spark plug is expected to deliver in excess of 30,000 volts no less than 100 times every second when the car is at speed!

Put in such perspective, it becomes clear just how important it is to use a well manufactured plug and the right one for your engine. Some spark plugs have a flat seating surface and make use of a sealing gasket; others have a conical surface and are self sealing. Clearly the correct type of plug seating designed for your particular engine has to be used; they are not inter-changeable and it's up to you to ensure that you're using the right plug for your car. If you have any doubts, consult your specialist or main dealer.

Where radio interference from spark plugs is a problem (unusual nowadays given the complexity of most radio suppression circuits, although with interference, anything can happen!), it is possible to buy plugs with interference suppression built-in. These are denoted by the letter 'R' in the type number. It is even possible to buy fully shielded plugs.

Other special plug types include those with multiple electrodes to satisfy some manufac-turers extremely long service intervals and also those with precious metal electrodes.

making it easy! ☐ **7/52** *A long reach socket is ideal for removing recessed spark plugs. Take care when removing and replacing your plugs; it's so easy to damage the cylinder head and land yourself with a massive repair bill!*

☐ **7/53** Always ensure that the plug threads are clear. The soft metal of an aluminium cylinder head is all too easy to ruin by inadvertently cross-threading a

53

plug. When refitting a plug, screw it in by hand until it is seated. New plugs with flat seats should be turned a further 90 degrees with a spark plug wrench. Used flat and conical seat plugs should be turned a further 15 degrees with the wrench. DO NOT overtighten plugs in the cylinder head.

FACT FILE: SPARK PLUG FAILURE

In the main, plugs tend to break down for one of several reasons. One is that the plug's internal insulation fails, which leads to internal shorting out. A plug working outside its optimum temperature range will be prone to failing in this way.

Therefore, it is important that you use the plug with the correct heat range to suit your car. If the engine is standard, then check against the manufacturers catalogue and follow its recommendation.

However, if your engine had been tuned, refer to the tuner and follow his advice.

Leaving the plug in place for too long could also lead to breakdown. Again, it could be failure of the insulation or the centre electrode could have become contaminated, leading to reduced efficiency. Alternatively, the electrode could have become eroded.

☐ **7/54** Using a spark plug gap/measuring gauge.

A. Measuring the electrode gap. The measuring wire should pass through with only the slightest resistance.

B. Checking platinum plugs for wear. Bend the side electrode back; push measuring wire into the hole in insulator nose;

when wire goes in as far as plastic stop, wear limit has been reached.

C. Opening the electrode gap with a 'bottle opener' type bending device on the measuring tool.

D. Close the gap by tapping lightly and carefully on a smooth, hard surface.

☐ **7/55** The construction of a typical spark plug.

1. Terminal nut
2. Thread
3. Current leak barrier.
4. Insulator
5. Conductive seal
6. Terminal stud
7. Fitting; swaged and heat shrunk
8. Gasket (flat seal)
9. Insulator top
10. Centre electrode
11. Ground electrode

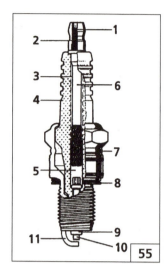

55

☐ **7/56** Those plugs with either silver or platinum electrodes (denoted as 'S' and 'P' respectively by Bosch, for instance) are inherently more efficient than ordinary plugs and the extra efficiency is especially welcome in high performance engines, all the way up to racing standards.

The advantages of platinum plugs are: Ignition conditions remain practically constant throughout the recommended service life of the plugs; plugs warm up quicker and so self-clean earlier, and heat transfer properties are improved.

A. Very long insulator nose ensures extension of the thermal operating range.

B. 0.3 mm diameter platinum centre electrode.

C. Platinum centre electrode sintered gas tight in insulator nose.

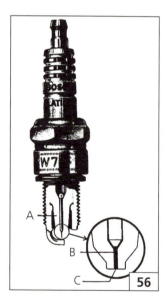

56

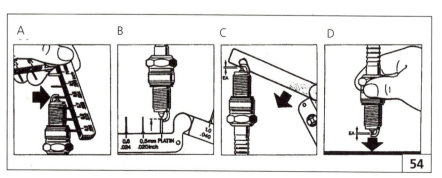

54

CHAPTER 8
ELECTRONIC IGNITION

It was back in 1908 when Charles F. Kettering, an engineer working for the Dayton Engineering Laboratories Company (Delco), took out a patent on an ignition system in which the flow of current from the battery to an induction coil (transformer) was interrupted by a set of mechanically operated contact breakers. It was, in effect, the type of ignition system described in the previous chapter and which is now often referred to as 'conventional'.

Other than the fact that it was much cheaper to produce, Kettering's form of ignition had one major advantage over the magneto versions then in widespread use. It produced its best spark at low engine speeds, whereas the magneto was at its best with the engine turning over at pretty high revs. Consequently those cars fitted with Kettering's ignition were infinitely better starters than those with magnetos, a good selling point when most engines were still being cranked by hand. Incidentally, CFK was also the inventor of the electric starter.

It's now somewhat ironic that this one major advantage of Kettering's coil ignition system is, in a sense, the reason why it is now being superseded by an electronic switching arrangement. Because it gives its best spark at low speeds, then by definition it must give its worst at high speeds.

Way back in 1908 this didn't matter, for very few engines exceeded 1,000rpm anyway and the modern versions of Kettering's ignition system are quite capable of producing satisfactory sparks for a four-cylinder engine running at speeds of up to 10,000rpm.

It is true that other than those used in racing cars, very few modern engines exceed 10,000rpm. Indeed, most car engines shouldn't go faster than around 6,500rpm. On face value then, it would seem that this form of ignition should be more than adequate for the cars of today, so why, you might ask, is it that you won't find a new car in any showroom, fitted with the Kettering (contact breaker) system.

The operative word here is 'capable' for while the system can produce satisfactory sparks at the required rate for these higher engine speeds, it can only do so when in perfect condition, and it's only in perfect condition for a very short time.

The weak link or Achilles Heel of a conventional system, is the contact breaker which, from new, reaches its peak of efficiency once it has bedded in, after about 200 miles or so. From then on, it's a downhill slope. Very gradual perhaps, but downhill nevertheless.

This decline in contact breaker performance may not be noticed, at least, not to begin with, but even so, it will affect spark quality, especially at the top end and possibly result in a high speed misfire. This, in turn, results in loss of power, heavier fuel consumption and increased emission levels. But that's only at the beginning, for in addition to decreasing spark quality, wear on the contact breaker fibre heel causes the spark to be produced later than it should, again with an adverse effect on power and emission levels.

A further disadvantage of the Kettering system is that although it may be capable of producing satisfactory sparks, it will only do so for engines for which emissions control was not considered important. It's doubtful if the spark quality would be good enough for any 'lean-burn' engines or those with sophisticated emission controls.

The limiting factors here are current flow through the coil and the time allowed for the coil to 'charge-up' - the dwell period. The contact breakers are physically incapable of switching anything more than about 4 amps (at least not for very long) and their mechanical (cam) operation restricts the time they can remain closed and 'charge' the coil.

It is true that most of these limitations could be overcome, but at some expense and additional complexity with consequent reliability problems. Far better to get rid of the contact breakers completely and use some other means of switching the primary current, which is basically what electronic systems do - at least most of them.

ELECTRONIC IGNITION

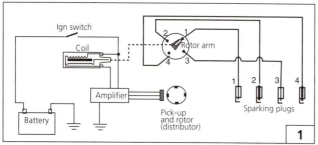

1

8/1 Although there are different forms of electronic ignition and different applications, the layout of a typical system is as shown in the illustration. However, there are some (aftermarket) systems which retain the contact points and therefore have no pick-up as such. There are also electronic ignition systems which are linked up with fuel injection as part of an overall engine management system controlled by one (or more) central computers (CPUs or ECUs - electronic control units). These may appear quite complex but, other than in the actual switching arrangement, don't differ much from the conversion kits shown here.

While any electronic system is more efficient than the contact breaker set-up (and generally much more reliable) it's just as well to check the HT side of the system, when changing over from the old contact breaker system. The reason for this is that with some layouts (and especially if a performance coil is used), the higher secondary voltages are more likely to show up any defects in that part of the circuit.

8/2 Typical HT checks would include a test of both the main HT cable and the plug leads, replacing any that are obviously damaged or record a resistance of over 25,000 ohms or so.

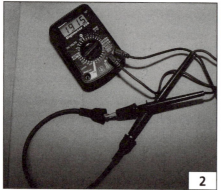

2

8/3 It would also be wise to inspect the coil tower and the distributor cap, checking for signs of tracking (thin greyish lines) either between electrodes or from an electrode to an earthing point.

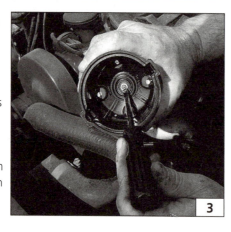

3

Transistor Assisted Contact (TAC) Systems

8/4 These (first generation) electronic ignition systems, retain the contact breaker points, using them as a trigger device for the electronic process, whereby a transistor actually

switches the coil primary current. Although no longer fitted as original equipment, conversion kits, such as those shown in **Fig 8/4** are still

4

available and are an excellent way of improving the efficiency of classic car engines.

Instead of switching the coil current of around three to five amps, the contact breakers in these systems have to contend with less than around one third of an amp and therefore electrical erosion of the contact faces is virtually eliminated. With this form of ignition, a contact set should last at least twice as long as with a normal system.

But, that's not the only thing in their favour. In a contact breakers system, the dwell period (when the points are closed) gets shorter as the engine speed increases, with a consequent drop in spark quality. This problem can be made less acute in TAC systems, with the contact points just initiating the process and the duration of the dwell period being controlled electronically, giving the coil a longer 'charge time', particularly at higher engine speeds. In this sense these TAC systems can give an improved spark even when compared with a conventional system in good order.

Advantages of these systems over the contact-less versions include:
1. Much cheaper to buy.
2. Relatively easy to fit.
3. Easy to change from one vehicle to another.
4. Easy to change back to the conventional system in the event of electronic failure (many have a change-over switch).
5. If the distributor and its drive gears are worn, removing the contact breakers points (contact-less systems) also removes the pressure and drag they put on the shaft. This may then result in the shaft oscillating with consequent timing errors at individual cylinders.

Disadvantages include:
1. Although points erosion may be eliminated, wear (particularly on the fibre heel) is not, so the points will still need periodic adjustment and renewal. Any wear will also affect the timing.
2. The problems of 'points bounce' in high-speed applications can still arise.

Contact-less Systems

As their name implies, these systems eliminate the contact points completely. However, with most, the coil primary current is still switched by a transistor (as in the TAC systems) but it is the method of triggering the electronic process that differs. There are, in fact, three different methods in use - optical, magnetic and what is termed the Hall Effect.

OPTICAL SYSTEMS

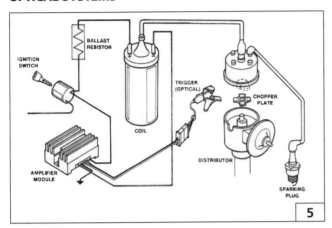

5

8/5 Optical systems are the favourite aftermarket kits and generally come in two packs. One made up of the module (amplifier) and the other, generally referred to as the distributor kit, containing the chopper plate and diode/photo-transistor components.

8/6 In these systems, a horseshoe-shaped bracket containing a light emitting diode in the end of one leg and a phototransistor directly opposite in the other, is fitted in place of the contact points. When the ignition is switched on, a beam of light is projected from the diode onto the photo-transistor.

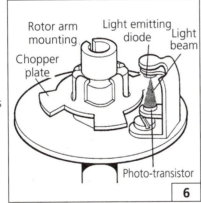

6

8/7 A segmented disc (chopper plate) is mounted on the distributor shaft so that, as the disc rotates (with the shaft), its blades interrupt the beam of light, producing a signal which is then used within the control module to switch the primary current. As the number of blades on the chopper disc corresponds with the number of

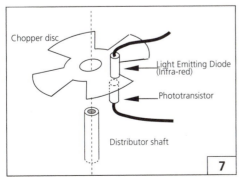

7

cylinders, it acts in much the same way as the cam in a conventional system.

MAGNETIC SYSTEMS

8/8 Magnetic systems vary, but a typical arrangement consists of a spoked iron rotor (reluctor) mounted on the distributor shaft, a pick-up unit fitted in place of the contact breaker points and a control module.

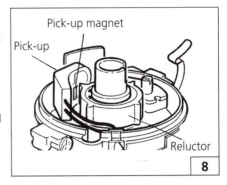

8

The pick-up unit consists of a permanent magnet and a small inductive winding (coil), making what is, in effect, a pulse generator.

As the iron rotor turns (with the distributor shaft), each spoke in turn passes close to the pick-up unit. This produces a change in the permanent magnetic field, inducing a small electrical current into the winding which again is used as a signal by the control module for switching the coil current - the number of spokes on the rotor corresponding to the number of cylinders.

Another form of magnetic triggering uses ferrite rods (small rods of high-permeability magnetic material) set in the rotor, but the general operating principle is much the same as with the iron rotor.

As with any of these contact-less systems, eliminating the contact points also removes the need for a capacitor.

HALL EFFECT

8/9 Named after its discoverer, the American E.H. Hall, this works on the principle that if a chip of semi-conductor material (silicon chip) is located in a magnetic field and has a current passed through it, a small voltage is generated in the chip at right angles (physically) to the current.

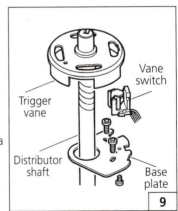

9

In practice, the chip and a permanent magnet (vane switch) are mounted on the distributor base plate in place of the contact points, with a gap between the two of them. A segmented disc or vane (attached to, and rotating with, the distributor shaft) interrupts the magnetic field and generates a voltage in the chip which is used, by the control module, to switch the primary current.

Unlike some other systems where the dwell period is determined by the control module, the vanes in the Hall Effect segmented disc switch the primary both on and off. The dwell is therefore related to the width of the vanes and is constant throughout the engine speed range.

DISTRIBUTOR-LESS SYSTEMS

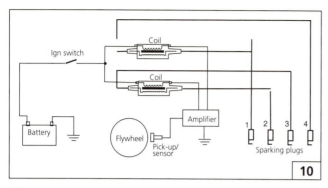

10

☐ **8/10** Eliminating the contact points and centrifugal weights turned the distributor into just that - a device for distributing the HT current. However, it was still the only component in the ignition system with moving parts and, as such, potentially the most unreliable component.

Some manufacturers have therefore introduced ignition systems with no distributor whatsoever. Some, such as Saab, use a separate coil located directly over each sparking plug whereas others, notably Ford, use two coils, each 'feeding' two sparking plugs - this, of course, on a four-cylinder engine. A typical layout is the one shown here.

The ignition process is triggered by sensors at the flywheel and, in the Ford case, produces two sparks per cycle or, in other words, a spark every time the piston approaches TDC. One of these will be on the exhaust stroke and is, in effect, a 'wasted' spark in that it doesn't do anything.

Although flywheel sensors initiate the ignition process, the actual spark timing is regulated by the ECU (Electronic Control Unit) using data stored in its memory to advance or retard the spark as necessary - this is now, more or less, standard practice in all engine management systems.

Capacitor DIscharge (CD) Ignition

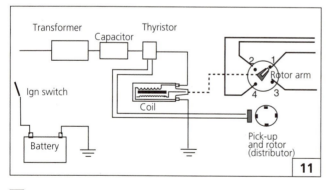

11

☐ **8/11** All the electronic ignition systems mentioned so far work on the inductive discharge principle, in that the collapse of the magnetic field induces a voltage into the secondary windings of the coil. This means that the coil has to be 'charged up' over the dwell period and that the energy for the spark is 'stored' in the coil until released by whatever triggering system is used.

The CD ignition system works on an entirely different principle in that battery voltage which would normally power the coil is used through a special type of transformer to charge a capacitor at around 300 to 400 volts. When a spark is required, an electronic switch (thyristor) discharges this voltage through the coil primary winding.

This results in the secondary winding producing a very high (but brief) voltage pulse which translates (at the sparking plug) into an extremely high energy, short duration, spark.

The main advantage of the CD system is its speed. With no coil 'charge-up' time, CD systems are capable of producing many more sparks per minute. Hence the reason for them being mainly used on high speed multi-cylinder engines. A further factor in its favour is that the very high secondary voltages tend to 'blast' through any resistive areas (such as fouled plugs) that could possibly result in a failure in an inductive system.

But there's also a down side to this potential high speed capability - the duration of the spark. In practice the air fuel mixture is neither static, nor evenly mixed and it is possible that the ignitable part of the mixture may not have reached the plug when the spark occurred. This is even more probable on those engines designed to run on a 'lean burn' or weak mixture.

A number of these systems use extra electronic circuitry to extend spark duration or produce a series of sparks. However, the problem with many of these is that the 'follow up' sparks can be much weaker than the original. So weak, in fact, that they may fail to ignite the mixture.

Adaptive Ignition

☐ **8/12** With the highly advanced adaptive system developed by Lucas, the ignition point is always suited to the conditions prevailing at any instant, whatever the conditions. Although the

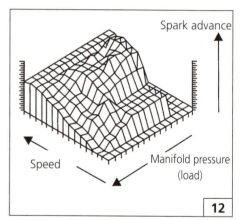

12

system's ECU is initially programmed with the usual basic timing data in the form of the three dimensional map shown here, it also has the ability to either slightly advance or retard the timing from the mapped point and see what effect it has on the engine torque. Engine speed is monitored by a crankshaft sensor so if it detects an increase in speed then torque must have increased as a result of better combustion. The map is then updated for that particular engine load and speed.

By altering spark timing to give maximum torque an adaptive ignition system can compensate, to some extent, for normal engine wear and for defects such as fouled injectors, slight differences in compression and oil burning due to defective valve seals.

CHAPTER 9
LIGHTING

It goes without saying that lights are vital! You couldn't drive safely at night without them, the police are likely to stop you if there's anything wrong with them and the MoT Test broadly requires that all lights fitted to your car must be working properly. It pays, in more ways than one to make sure they all give of their best!

Wiring

☐ **9/1** The basic outline of a lighting circuit is shown here and is broadly common to many modern cars, despite being illustrated differently in various technical publications. Some follow more or less the pattern shown here with the various components linked by lines representing the cables, whereas in others more emphasis is made on where the components are actually located in the car and less on how they are connected. In other cases no interlinking cables are shown, but each terminal is given a number along with that of its opposite connection at the other end of the line.

If this all seems a little confusing, just think of the whole layout being made up of a number of individual circuits, each of which is fairly easy to trace on its own. In ours, for example, the wiring is common from the battery to the main lighting switch. From there, individual circuits reach out to the side and rear lights, and also the headlights via the dip switch. Not shown is a take-off from the sidelight circuit for the instrument panel lights and another from the rear lights for number plate illumination.

Cables are given a two letter code to denote the colour, with the primary colour being given first. For example, GR would mean a green cable with a red trace. For those cables with no trace the main colour may be repeated, in which case a blue cable may be listed as UU or it might be given just one descriptive letter.

The circuit shown is both basic and typical but there are variations. In some cars, for instance, the side/tail lights circuit passes through a single fuse, instead of the two shown. The headlights may also have just one fuse or one each for dip and main beam and, in each case the location of the fuse within the circuit would be different to that shown here.

Obviously, the more fuses the better, in that should there be a problem in one circuit, it would be less likely to affect anything in another. But there are still many older cars around with just two fuses, one for the ignition controlled circuits and one for everything else. Indeed, in older times, there were cars with no fuses whatsoever, but with those, what should have been minor electrical problems tended to be major disasters. In fact you could say that there are fewer of

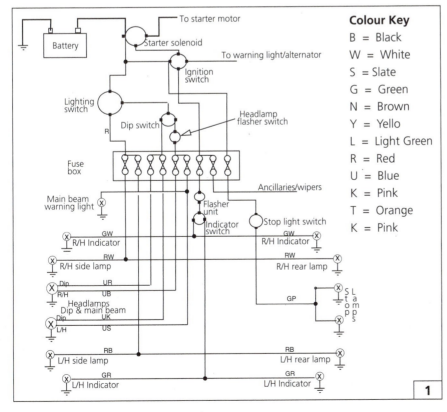

Colour Key

B = Black
W = White
S = Slate
G = Green
N = Brown
Y = Yello
L = Light Green
R = Red
U = Blue
K = Pink
T = Orange
K = Pink

1

these cars around than would have been the case if only they had been fitted with fuses!

Flashing indicators are generally wired through the ignition switch and may be fused (as shown in our diagram) or not, in which case they would take their power straight from the ignition switch, just as the stop lights are in the illustration. These wiring colours are in accordance with the standard British/Lucas system in which specific areas are all given a primary colour, with sub-areas shown as a trace on that colour. For example, the insulation on the main feed cable for the side/tail lights is coloured plain red (R), but from where it splits at the fuse box it acquires a white trace (RW) to the right hand lights and a black trace (RB) to the lights on the left hand side of the car. Similarly, the main feed to the dip switch is plain blue (U), which then acquires a red trace (UR) from the fuse to the right hand headlight dipped beam or a black one (UB) for the main beam wire. Note that these colours are for circuits with individual fuses; for those sharing a fuse, the trace colours may be different. The principle is the same for most other systems.

Although this may all seem a little complex on paper, in practice it all works out fairly easy. This is especially true when checking for wiring faults, in that it becomes relatively easy to identify both ends of any particular circuit.

Headlights

9/2 Headlights may be either a combined lens/reflector unit with a separate bulb or, less commonly nowadays, a sealed beam unit which incorporates the bulb in the unit. Obviously in the former case, it is possible to change the bulb only, in the latter, the whole unit has to be renewed.

Methods of access for both are very similar in the traditional 7in. round light, but where the trapezoidal (rectangular) or specially - shaped types are concerned, there are many different ways in which they may be fitted.

making it easy! If you want to check that a bulb is working, the simplest way is to use the car's battery and a couple of test leads. Connect one to the earth terminal of the bulb and the earth terminal on the battery. Connect the other to the 'live' battery terminal and touch it onto the other two bulb terminals, one at a time of course, to see if both main beam and dipped beam filaments light up. You can use exactly the same procedure to check a sealed beam unit - after all the whole thing is virtually one big bulb, and it's got the same three terminals.

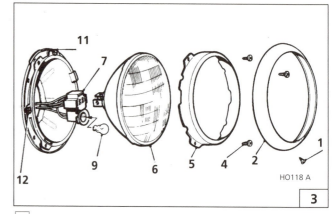

HO118 A

9/3 The components for a sealed beam set up are simplest to deal with. The beam is set by turning in and out screws shown at numbers 11 and 12 on this example.

9/4 Tackle the traditional round type by locating and undoing the single bezel fixing screw (self tapper) at the bottom under the light.

9/5 Then pull the bezel forward and push upwards to 'unhook' the lugs at the top. Perseverance may be necessary! Sometimes, no screw is fitted - you push the bezel down and pull out at the bottom.

9/6 Next there's an inner retaining rim held by three screws. Once this is removed (be careful not to undo the adjustment screws by mistake)...

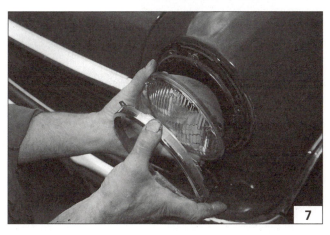

9/7 ...the light unit or sealed beam unit can be pulled forward for disconnecting. On an alternative type, the retaining ring is not held by screws. Here you push it forward against spring pressure, turn it slightly anticlockwise until the round holes in the rim line up with the heads of the adjuster screws, and lift off.

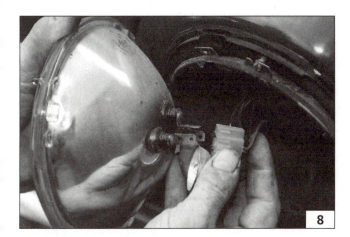

9/8 On a sealed beam unit, the three terminals are moulded into the back of the reflector and the three pin connector is simply pulled off to free it. With a bulb unit, after pulling off the connector, it is necessary to remove a wire clip to free the bulb.

9/9 There may also be a sidelight incorporated, which means there is a small bulb fitted into the side of the reflector. This may simply pull out, or it may be necessary to turn it to free it.

9/10 With modern cars, all this procedure is unnecessary - the bulb can be reached from under the bonnet behind the light.

9/11 There will be a plastic or rubber cover (2), a retaining plate on the bulb itself (4) and a wire retainer (3), or some such system. This method of access may apply only to some normal round headlights, but will almost certainly be the one used with trapezoidal types.

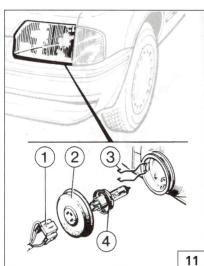

When replacing normal bulbs, there is no problem other than ensuring that a slight projections on the bulb flange engages the matching depression in the reflector. Remember when replacing a quartz halogen bulb, however, not to touch it with the fingers. Handle only the metal flange part.

ADJUSTING HEADLIGHTS

☐ **9/12** It is a legal requirement that headlights on dipped beam should not dazzle oncoming drivers, and that means keeping them properly aligned by means of the adjusters that all headlights have.

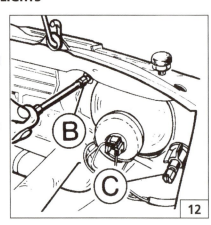

☐ **9/13** The best idea is to have them set up by a properly equipped garage, using a beamsetter, but it is possible to do a reasonably accurate job yourself if you have them checked later.

☐ **9/14** You will need a bit of open space (flat ground) in front of a wall, or the drive in front of the garage doors will do. Drive the car square on about a foot away and mark the centres of the lights on the wall as two crosses. Chalk is the easiest thing to use and the cross should be in the form of a 'plus' sign, not an 'ex'. Double check the centres by measuring both vertically and the distance between the lights.

Drive the car straight back for about 3.8m (10ft). Switch the lights onto main beam and cover the one not being adjusted. Use the adjustment screws to bring the bright centre of the light centrally onto the vertical line of the chalk cross, but just below the horizontal one. Cover up the light that you've already done and repeat the procedure on the other one.

This method works quite well with round headlights, but is not always so easy with the trapezoidal sort. The bright centre spot is likely to be less well defined, so here proper equipment is much more a desirable option.

On older 7in. round headlights adjustment is usually a matter of two screws located behind the front decorative bezel (**see 9/3**). Once this is removed, the screws are directly accessible. With many more modern cars, the adjustment points are behind the light units and are reached from under the bonnet (**see 9/12**).

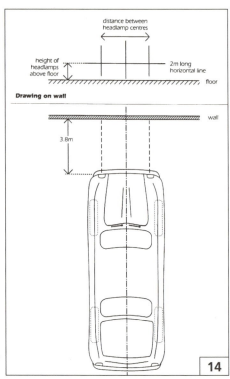

Side and Tail Lights

The circuit for these is generally quite straightforward, from the lighting switch through one, or two, fuses to the lights themselves. Invariably, where the two fuse layout is used, the lights on one side of the vehicle share one fuse, with those on the opposite side sharing the other.

☐ **9/15** In most modern cars the tail lights form part of a rear light cluster incorporating the stop, turn-signal and reversing lights and with the bulbs mounted on some kind of printed panel board. Many rear light problems are associated with this board or the multi-pin connector linking it to the vehicle wiring loom and earth. These faults can include the tail lights working (sometimes dimly) when the brake pedal is pressed or when the indicators are switched on, or alternatively, the indicators lights coming on with the stop lights or, indeed none of them working. Should any faults of this nature occur, they can often be cured by running a separate cable from the earthing point on the printed board to the car body.

In nearly all cases, both side and tail lights are incorporated into the general vehicle styling and the procedure for changing bulbs will vary accordingly - usually from inside the engine bay or boot. See your Porter Manual or maker's handbook for details.

Stop Lights

The feed for this very simple circuit is invariably taken from one of the accessory fuses (which may, or may not be ignition controlled) through to the stop light switch and from there to the stop lights themselves. Testing for faults follows very much the sequence already described, starting with checking the fuse, testing the bulbs and then tracing through the circuit and testing the switch using a testlight or multimeter. Note that in some installations where the brake light switch is mounted adjacent to the brake pedal arm, it may be adjustable for position, so if the switch appears to be not working a simple adjustment could solve the problem.

Direction Indicators

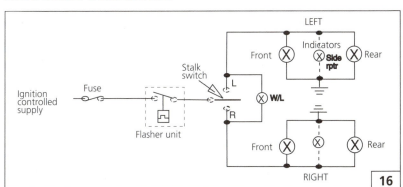

16

To test check the circuit using a test light or multimeter (volts scale), clip one lead to a good earth, touch the other to the B terminal on the flasher and turn on the ignition. A reading or the bulb lighting up indicates that you have current as far as the flasher. Test next from the L terminal to earth, and if that works, it means the fault is in the wiring or in the switch. If it doesn't, the flasher is faulty. Carry on testing from there as described for all the earlier circuits to find out if the switch is faulty or to locate a wiring problem.

9/16 Slight variations in the circuit layout are possible, depending on the type of flasher unit fitted, but most follow more or less the pattern shown here. Although, in the diagram, we have shown the flasher unit between the fusebox and the indicator switch, its physical location varies from car to car. It might simply hang from its wiring, it may be held in a spring clip, supported by a bracket or it may plug into the fusebox. It may be hidden away under the dash or it can be fixed onto the steering column. Finding it is usually a matter of operating the indicator switch and tracking it down by the clicking sound it makes. Obviously then it's best to know where it is before anything goes wrong and it becomes silent!

9/17 It may also be useful to know what it looks like for flasher units now come in all shapes and sizes, making them even more difficult to find on the car - especially when they are not working!

Troubleshooting the direction indicator circuit is a mixture of the logical step-by-step sequence suggested in *Chapter 14, Fault Finding*, along with the more specialised information given below.

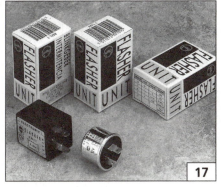

17

Hazard Warning Lights

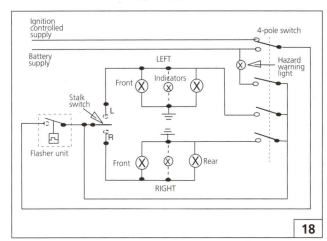

18

9/18 This is basically the direction indicator circuit with the hazard warning switch added between the fused supply and the flasher unit. Operating the switch cuts out the normal direction indicator switch and the normal source of supply. Power now comes directly from an unswitched source (virtually at the battery) and all four indicator lights are energised. Fault finding procedures are much the same as those described for the direction indicators.

Reversing Lights

The basic reversing light circuit is another very simple one, with wiring running from the accessory fuse to the switch and then on to the light(s).

On almost every modern car, the switch will be an automatic one in the gearbox housing, although in some cases it may be mounted on the body or transmission and linked to the gear change mechanism by a spring.

INSIDE INFORMATION: Some systems differ in that the switch is positioned on the earth side of the lights instead of the live side. That means that the switch is earthed instead of the lights, and the bulbs in the lights are different in that they have double-pole contacts instead of the side of the bulb being earthed.

Another variation on some cars is that the feed for the reversing lights come through the main lighting switch, the reasoning being that you only need their light after dark. Most are only ignition controlled, however, which means the provide a warning during daylight hours that the car is about to reverse.

Bulbs

There is a wide variety of bulbs used throughout the car, and although in most cases it is not possible to fit the wrong one, care must still be taken. We have listed many of the more common types here, but details of those fitted to any particular car should be given in that car's handbook and can be found in the appropriate Porter Manual for your car. If you don't have a handbook, take the old bulb with you when you buy a replacement.

BULB CLASSIFICATION

Light bulbs are broadly classified according to the end cap, wattage and voltage and in most cases it would be difficult to use the wrong bulb in any particular application, because of either the difference in end cap fitting or physical appearance of the bulb itself. However, this doesn't preclude the possibility of fitting different wattage bulbs.

Always carry a bulb replacement kit with the spares kit in your car. It could save you being stopped by the police on a long trip. A bulb kit is a legal requirement, incidentally, when touring some European countries.

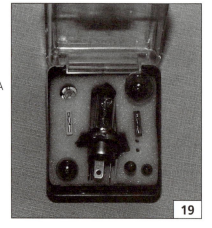

19

It's not possible to go into detail about how you gain access to all these different bulbs, there are far too many variations. Often the front lens is taken off by removing screws. In other cases, access is from the rear of the light. Once access is achieved, the actual job of replacing the bulb is usually straightforward,

but be aware of the offset lugs in those dual-wattage bulbs used in stop/tail applications. They are designed so as to only fit one way.

CHANGING A BULB

20

☐ **9/20** Changing a faulty bulb is theoretically simple, but in the real world, there are often problems such as the light unit being found to be corroded and in need of replacement, or the bulb being rusted into the light unit itself. If you find a seized bulb, start by squirting in releasing fluid and leaving it to soak for a day, if possible.

21

making it easy! ☐ **9/21** Take a clean rag, place it over the bulb to give yourself extra grip and to protect your fingers in case the glass breaks, and try working the bulb clockwise and anticlockwise. If the glass starts to come loose, don't give up straight away although your chances of getting the bulb out will of course be a little diminished.

☐ **9/22** If the glass breaks, clear as much of it out of the way as you can with a screwdriver and try pressing and turning on the shank of the bulb still left in place with a cork out of a bottle.

22

☐ **9/23** If all else fails, push the shank inwards with a screwdriver and grasp it with a pair of pliers, twisting, turning and encouraging it to come loose until it does so. If the inside of the bulb holder is equally badly corroded, you may have to cut your losses and buy a replacement light unit either new or from a breaker's yard. If you use the latter source, go to the trouble of stripping the bulb out of the light unit and inspecting its insides before bothering to remove it from the car. Place a smear of Vaseline or copper-based lubricant around the bulb shank before pushing it back into the bulb holder.

23

If you can, always take the opportunity to inspect the interior of the light unit for rust. There shouldn't be any, but there may be if the glass lens has been cracked at some time in the past. Rust on the reflector is an MoT failure point (and could seriously reduce light output) and rust elsewhere can cause all sorts of earthing and poor contact problems. Any of these faults could seriously reduce light output. A rusty reflector will absorb, rather than reflect light and a poor contact in the circuit will reduce the voltage at the bulb and, in turn, its light output.

To put this in perspective, tests on auxiliary lights have shown that line resistance (poor wiring and bad contacts) can cause a two volt reduction in the power available at the bulb and almost a 50% loss in efficiency as the following table shows:

Voltage at light

Voltage at light	Light output
13.5V (100% voltage)	100% luminous output
12.8V (95% voltage)	83% luminous output
12.2V (90% voltage)	67% luminous output
11.5V (85% voltage)	53% luminous output

Note that the normal voltage on a 12V system should be around 13.5V

What this means is that it's often far more effective to get the right voltage than simply plugging in 'bigger' bulbs. Indeed, fitting larger wattage bulbs without taking into account the available voltage can actually lead to a reduction in light output and, in the case of headlights it could be illegal.

COMMON BULB APPLICATION LIST

Application	Category	Base type	Nominal power
Headlights (Main beam/dip)	R2	P45 t	45/40
Headlights (Main beam/dip	H4	P43 t	60/55
Side & tail lights	R5W	BA15 S	5
Stop and flashing indicator lights	P21 W	BA15 s	21
Stop/tail lights (combined)	P21/5	BAY 15 s	21/5
Fog lights	H3	PK 22 s	55
Number plate lights	C5W	SV 8.5	5
Interior lights	W3W	W2.1 x 9.5 d	3

BULB USAGE

By far the majority of bulbs used in motor vehicles are of the incandescent variety in which a filament is heated until it is white hot. They are, in effect, small scale furnaces and, as such, are terribly inefficient as light sources with over 90% of the energy consumed being given off as heat. However, given the current state of technology, they are, at the moment, the most practical form of lighting for this purpose.

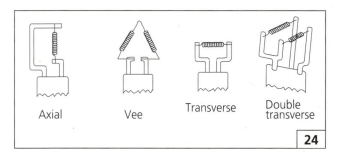

Axial   Vee   Transverse   Double transverse

24

☐ **9/24** The filament (the most common types are shown in 9/12) in an average car bulb is very thin (0.1 - 2mm or 0.004 - 0.008in) tungsten wire coil which, if fully drawn out would measure about 80cm (32in). It's the size of this wire which determines the wattage, a thicker wire making for the higher wattage bulb and, of course, an increased power consumption.

In use, the (white hot) tungsten wire virtually evaporates, very slowly perhaps, but it gradually gets thinner (and therefore hotter at its thinnest point) until it either breaks or melts. This is what is generally referred to as a 'blown' bulb. However, during this evaporation process, minute particles of the wire are given off and deposited on the inside of the glass, slowly turning it black and making the bulb even less efficient as a light source.

In what are termed halogen bulbs, the glass envelope is pressure filled with a gas belonging to the halogen group, usually iodine or bromine. This not only allows higher temperatures to be achieved (and therefore more light) but also reduces the extent of filament evaporation. However, due to these pressures and temperatures, the physical size of the bulb is limited and a special type of glass or high-strength quartz used for the envelope.

Touching this envelope with bare fingers leaves traces of perspiration on its surface which, due to the high temperatures involved, can have a detrimental affect on bulb life, so either use a tissue, rag or gloves when handling the bulbs or, only touch the metal base. Although more expensive than the conventional variety, nearly all car manufacturers now specify halogen (H4) bulbs for use in the headlights.

Lighting Fault Finding

Methodical fault finding procedures follow very much along the lines of those outlined in *Chapter 14, Fault Finding*, but before starting out, it would be as well to have some idea of the sort of the faults you might be looking for.

Poor connections are among the most common causes of lighting circuit failures. Examples include a loose connector on a terminal, acting like an intermittent On/Off switch. It can be corrosion inside snap connectors, or it can be corrosion in the light itself or, indeed, at the bulb. It can be a bad connection on the earth side - between side of the bulb and its holder, between holder and light, or between the light body and earth. It can be a fault at any of the connections between the power take-off point at the fuse or junction box and the light, or even at the fuse itself.

9/25 The procedure you adopt to find the problem depends very much on what the indications of the trouble are and, of course how the various circuits are fused. If, for instance (and discounting the fuses), you have lost both the main beams, but not dipped beams, the fault probably lies in the dipswitch, or the wiring between it and the snap connector where the main beam cable divide. If there is power

at the bulb socket (**9/25**) then obviously the trouble must with the bulb or the earth connection.

In another example, if only one tail light has failed, and a check indicates that the bulb is sound, the fault lies somewhere in the circuit after the snap connector where the cable divides to go out to the second light. Because the first light is working, you know the switch and the feed cable to the rear of the car are sound. It's a case of checking only the part of the wiring that can be responsible for the fault.

Take a case where the rear lights and number plate lights aren't working and the fuse blows every time you renew it. What you do is disconnect all the lights, switch on again with a new fuse. If it blows again, you know you're looking for a wiring fault (the lights are OK). If the fuse doesn't blow with the lights disconnected, you simply reconnect them one at a time until it does blow. Then check out the last one connected.

If the rear lights aren't working in a car where there's no fuse and the wiring hasn't melted, you've probably got a break in the circuit. Connect your testlight or multimeter to a good clean earth point and touch the probe to a known 'live' point to check the light or meter is working. Touch the probe to the first snap connector you can find after the lighting switch. If there's no current there, the fault is between there and the switch. If there is current, work backwards towards the lights themselves, until you find the point where it fails.

Not a lot happens to the lighting circuits without some outside cause, like some work being done on the car - someone not replacing cables correctly after a repair or actually trapping cables during a repair. At other times, the fault is more likely to be due to corrosion of the more exposed components, like the lights themselves.

Finding lighting faults can sometimes be a lengthy process, especially when the fault is an intermittent one with no obvious pattern. However, even then it's more often tedious rather than difficult and can, eventually be sorted out.

CHAPTER 10
INSTRUMENTS

Some gauges, such as that for the fuel contents are relatively easy to understand in that they provide a definitive reading. Others, such as an ammeter or the oil pressure and vacuum gauges are also diagnostic instruments requiring a degree of interpretation if their full value is to be recognised. Of course, not all gauges are electrical, the majority of speedometers, for instance, are mechanical, as are all vacuum gauges but even so, they are included here.

Fuel Contents

There are two basic types of fuel gauge in current use - the electro-mechanical versions generally found on older cars and the far more common bi-metal strip devices.

In operation an electro-mechanical gauge will show an instant reading when the ignition is switched on and will immediately fall back when

switched off, whereas the bi-metal strip versions will take a little time, both to reach the indicated level/temperature and to drop back to zero. To understand why this should be so, it's necessary to have some idea of how the different types work.

Gauges working on the electro-mechanical principle incorporate two fine coils wound on soft iron cores with a pivoted needle between the two. This is attracted or deflected by the relative magnetic strengths of the two coils, which, in turn, are dependent upon the current flow through them. Needle movement is almost instantaneous, which has the disadvantage, when used as a fuel gauge, of constantly changing readings as fuel sloshes around in the tank.

Bi-metallic gauges, as their name implies, use a two-metal combined strip which bends when subject to heat (the two strips of metal expand at different rates, hence the bending action). As the gauge needle is attached to the strip, it moves across the scale as the strip bends. In most cases the heat is produced by current flowing through a coil, more current means more heat and greater needle deflection.

In both cases, current flow, other than through one (control) coil of mechanical gauges, is dependent upon the resistance felt at the sender unit. With fuel gauges this is made up of a float attached to an earthed wiper arm, which moves across a resistor coil as the float rises or falls with the level of fuel in the tank.

☐ **10/1** This shows a typical electro-mechanical fuel gauge circuit. When the ignition is switched on, current passes through both coils, but whereas that flowing through the control coil can be considered as being constant, the current

flow through the series coil is determined by the resistance of the sender unit at the tank.

As the tank is being filled, the float rises and the wiper arm moves over the resistor windings, in effect increasing its resistance and reducing current flow through the series coil in the gauge. This weakens the magnetic effect around the series coil and the needle is attracted to the (stronger) control coil, moving over to the 'Full' position on the dial. Obviously, as the fuel is used up, the float falls, decreasing the resistance at the sender unit. This results in a greater current flow through the series coil, strengthening its magnetic field and attracting the needle towards the 'Empty' mark, depending upon how much fuel is left in the tank.

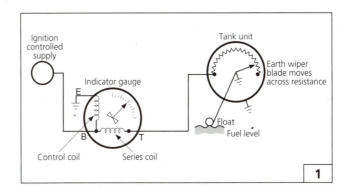

With this type of gauge, variations in battery/generator voltage won't really make any difference, for it will affect both coils equally.

☐ **10/2** This is not the case with the bi-metal gauges, a typical layout of which is shown here. Once again the current flow through the coil (and therefore its temperature) is determined by the (variable) resistance of the tank sender unit, but in this case differences in the applied voltage would also affect current flow. To overcome this a voltage regulator or stabiliser is used in the circuit to provide a constant supply of around 8 to 10 volts.

INSTRUMENTS

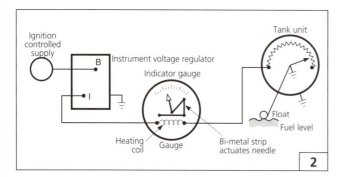

2

Water Temperature

There are two basic types of water temperature gauge, electrical and mechanical, easily identified by the dials. If it has a full scale dial, it's mechanical, whereas those with a quadrant (part) scale are electrical. Most of the standard original equipment gauges are electrical, but generally are no more than indicators, with the scale marked as Cold, Normal and Hot or just coloured segments - they don't give an actual temperature reading.

Both types require a sender unit, the difference being that the electrical versions have a separate unit linked to the gauge by a length of cable, whereas with the mechanical versions the sender is permanently attached to the gauge by a length of capillary (fine-bore) tubing.

In either case, the sender has to be inserted into the coolant, preferably in an existing threaded hole in the cylinder head or thermostat housing. Should this be impossible, it can be fitted into a hole drilled in the radiator header tank (well below the water line) or, by using a special adaptor, into the top radiator hose.

☐ **10/3** The capillary tube on the older mechanical versions cannot be separated from either the gauge or the sender unit. This means that the

3

sender, which can be about 3/8in diameter, has to be fed through a hole in the bulkhead into the engine compartment. In addition, the tube from the sender unit to any fixing clamp or grommet on the body or bulkhead, needs to be wound into about four to six coils of around three inch diameter, so as to help absorb vibration and engine movement.

☐ **10/4** Electrical gauges can be either electro-mechanical or bi-metal strip, more or less the same as the fuel gauge, but obviously the sender units differ and, in this case, it takes the form of a temperature sensitive bulb screwed into the engine's cylinder head water jacket. This bulb incorporates an electrical conductive spring attached at its upper end to the unit's electrical terminal and at its lower end to a temperature-

sensitive disc of semi-conductive material with what is termed a high negative coefficient of resistance. In simple terms this means that (unlike most metals) as it gets hotter, its electrical resistance decreases. As with the tank sender units, a lower resistance means a greater flow of current.

4

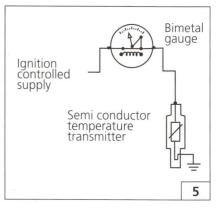

5

☐ **10/5** Once fitted, the gauge should show the temperature of the coolant. Depending on the engine and where the sender is located, the reading should be somewhere in the region of 90 degrees C, give or take 10 degrees C, once the engine has reached its normal working temperature.

Thrash the engine by accelerating hard or, labouring it before it has reached its working temperature, and it won't last as long as it otherwise would. So there's the first possible benefit of fitting such a gauge.

With the sender unit fitted in the cylinder head, the gauge should start reading within a few minutes of starting up from cold. If it doesn't, then the thermostat may be stuck in the open position (or maybe there isn't one fitted). With the sender unit in the top hose or radiator, the gauge will show a low reading at first, then go up quickly once the thermostat opens.

Conversely, a thermostat stuck in the closed position (which is more likely than sticking open) would probably result in a high reading on the gauge. However, this could also be due to a number of other causes, such as: lack of coolant; a frozen, scaled up or fin-encrusted radiator; a broken fan belt or inoperative electric fan; an excessively weak carburettor mixture; incorrect ignition timing or binding brakes.

If the gauge reads normal, but then drops suddenly, it probably means that the coolant level has dropped below the sender unit.

If, in the winter, the gauge quickly moves into the 'Hot' zone, but the heater output is virtually zero, you've probably got a frozen-up radiator/block. Another indication of a frozen block could come about before the gauge has even moved - it's a screeching sound from the fan-belt as it slips on the pulley of the (frozen) water pump. Of course, on some engines the water pump is driven by the cam-belt and, if yours is one of these, and the water pump freezes, you could be in big trouble.

Oil Pressure

As with the coolant temperature gauges, those recording oil pressure can be either electrical or mechanical, the difference being that the latter has a capillary tube which is not permanently attached either the sender or gauge in its unfitted state. Again, as with that used in the coolant temperature application, the tubing should be coiled up to cater for engine movement/vibration.

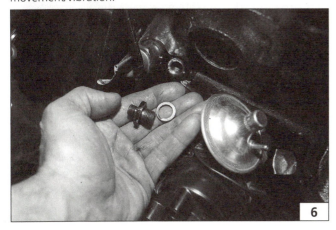

6

☐ **10/6** Practically all engines have a tapping somewhere (usually in the region of the main oil gallery or filter housing) for oil pressure measurement. On most, this will accommodate the oil pressure warning light sensor. The sender unit for an oil pressure gauge can be fitted in place of the warning light sensor (in which case the warning light will not work) or a T-piece adaptor can be fitted to take both the sensor and sender units. Some instrument manufacturers produce sender units with a connection for the warning light - with these there is obviously no need for any adaptor.

Gauge readings will vary considerably from car to car, but with a good engine, expect somewhere in the region of 15psi (1.0 bars) at idling and about 60psi (4.1 bars) when running at about 3,000rpm, both with the engine (and oil) warm.

Low pressure could be due to a worn oil pump, a defective or sticking (open) pressure relief valve or worn main bearings. Incidentally, in a situation where one main bearing is defective and shows signs of seizing up, don't just change the one bearing. The real problem could be with its (worn) neighbour allowing the oil to escape.

Oil diluted with petrol, possibly due to a leaking fuel pump diaphragm, can also result in a low reading, as can using a thin (10W/40) oil in an older, partially worn engine. Much the same will apply if the engine oil temperature becomes excessive, possibly because the level in the sump is low.

A spasmodically low reading, noticed when braking, accelerating hard or cornering, will also probably mean that the sump level is low and the pump pick-up is being left high and dry.

An excessively high reading would be unlikely, but could be due to a blocked filter or that the pressure relief pump is sticking closed.

Battery Condition Indicator

☐ **10/7** As its name implies, the function of this instrument is to give an approximate idea of the state of charge of the battery. It is, in reality, nothing more than a voltmeter connected across the two terminals of the battery.

7

In practice, as the unit does make a small (minute) drain on the battery, it is wired from an ignition controlled (fused) supply, so that it is not in use when the engine is switched off.

The (quadrant type) scale is usually divided into three, different coloured sectors. If the battery is healthy, the needle should stay in the middle sector at around 11.5 - 12.5 volts when the ignition is switched on, rising up to a maximum of around 15 volts when the engine is started. The reading may drop when there is a heavy load on the battery, such as when the headlights are switched on and/or the heated rear window is in use.

An excessive movement of the needle when any heavy load is switched on may also mean that the battery is nearing the end of its useful life or just that the electrolyte level is low.

If the instrument always reads low, even with no load (other than the ignition) on the battery, it's probably due to a problem in the charging circuit - maybe just a slipping fan belt. A high reading would also indicate trouble with the charging circuit, most likely a defective regulator, although it could also be due to a defective battery. In either case, a high gauge reading could be accompanied by excessive gassing of the battery.

Ammeter

☐ **10/8** In the old days, when dynamos were the norm, it wasn't uncommon for cars - especially the more expensive ones - to be fitted with an ammeter. However, since the alternator arrived, the reverse

8

is true, with hardly a car leaving the production lines sporting such an instrument. Some may be equipped with a Battery Condition Indicator despite the fact that an ammeter can give a far better indication of how the charging circuit is performing.

Disregarding costs, one of the major reasons for this is that, should any fault occur in the ammeter circuit, it would almost certainly ruin the alternator.

10/3 This also shows earthing the feed to the sender unit and other circuit checks which can be carried

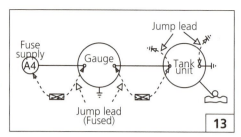

out on electro- magnetic layouts with nothing more than a jumper cable, although the terminal numbering may be different to that shown here. The tests showing the used of a fused jumper lead are checks of cable continuity between the various components

10/14 Similar checks on bi-metal gauges are shown in here, but take care not to put a direct battery supply to the

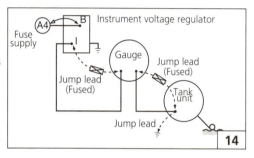

output (I) terminal of the voltage stabiliser. Incidentally, a faulty stabiliser unit can cause low, high or no readings, but would do so on both the temperature and fuel gauges, so if both are reading incorrectly, this should be your first check, although no readings on either could be a fault in the supply to the stabiliser unit - check with a voltmeter of jump lead.

10/15 Problems with temperature gauges generally be sorted out using checks similar to those for the fuel

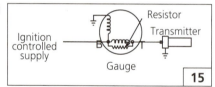

gauge and typical circuit layouts are shown in this drawing of a electro-mechanical temperature gauge circuit and...

10/16 ...this, a Bi-metal temperature gauge circuit with voltage stabiliser.

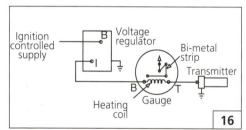

Disconnecting the lead at the temperature sender unit should make the gauge move into the 'Cold' position and earthing it should make the gauge go to 'Hot'. If these readings are obtained, then suspect the sender unit. That is, of course, again assuming that there is nothing wrong with the engine or cooling system.

SPEEDOMETER

Sorting out a problem with the speedometer is really a job best left to the experts. In any case, they seldom go wrong and many faults, such as a rhythmic clicking noise, fluctuating needle or no needle movement whatsoever, are more likely to be due to a defective drive cable than trouble with the

instrument itself, and this is something the average DIY motorist can check out.

Probably the easiest check is to disconnect the cable at its lower (gearbox) end and turning the inner to see if it registers on the clock. If you're careful, you can do this with an electric drill, set on a slow speed. No response at the speedo head could mean a broken cable or a defective head and the only sure way of determining which is to disconnect the cable at the top end as well and see if the inner is turning there.

If the cable does now turn, connect up the bottom end again, then raise the driving wheels off the ground and either turn them or start up the engine, engage a forward gear and drive them, while at the same time observing the top end of the cable. You could take the car for a short drive instead, but with no speedo, you would be breaking the law. If the cable turns, it undoubtedly means trouble with the speedo head, whereas if it doesn't you probably have a problem with the drive gear in the gearbox.

However, as stated earlier, many of the problems are associated with the cable itself, so check that the squared ends aren't rounded off and that it is fitted correctly.

Fitting Extra Instruments

MOUNTING THE DIALS

This can be a problem, particularly with more recently produced models where there is little space or opportunity to install additional gauges. Sometimes there are alternative instrument panels available with more instruments incorporated - usually from a more up market version of the same car - but this would mean using the manufacturer's own instruments and layout, and could be expensive. In any case, you may find that the wiring looms and connecting blocks are incompatible.

10/17 The simplest expedient is to use a supplementary panel which can be purchased ready drilled with one, two or three 52mm holes for standard instruments, per perhaps a larger

hole for a tachometer. Such a panel is normally fitted under the dash panel, but the necessary horizontal clear surface is not always available. The best ones come complete with all the components needed.

An alternative is to use a pod mounting, which is a shroud for the instruments, leaving only the actual dials showing. It is usually mounted on top of the dash and can look quite neat. The snags are that the position is too prominent, the instruments look like an afterthought and they can suffer from vibration.

One of the better possibilities is that of buying a console designed as an accessory to fit around the gear lever area. It can often look very attractive and in some cases will already be equipped with 'pop out' panels to take instruments.

CHAPTER 11
ELECTRICAL ANCILLARIES

There are certain electrical components and circuits on a car which are essential to its very operation - these include the ignition, lighting, charging and starter systems. However, there are also many other electrical items, some of which may be legally necessary, some as an aid to safety or comfort and others which may be just desirable - the following are a few examples.

Horns

It is a legal requirement that the car has a means of producing an audible warning and, in most cases, this is achieved with either one, or a pair, of electrically operated horns.

Most manufacturer fitted horns are one of two types - HF (high frequency) or Windtone, both of which operate on the same principle. Operating the horn button energises, what basically amounts to a relay with a diaphragm attached (within the horn). However, as the relay is energised it opens a set of contacts, breaking the circuit and allowing the relay to resume its normal rest position. As it does so the contacts close again and the process is repeated - many times every second.

☐ **11/1** In the HF horn, a resonator plate attached to the diaphragm amplifies the sound it makes. In the Windtone, there's a trumpet containing a column of air, and diaphragm actions sets this in motion to provide the sound. Windtones are often installed in pairs, giving two different notes (marked L for low and H for high). They require considerably more power than the HF type, so if fitting them as an aftermarket accessory as shown here, it's important to check on cable sizes and advisable to use a relay in the feed circuit.

A third type of horn, known as an air horn (see **Heading Picture**), is available as an accessory. In this, a compressor feeds air into a trumpet or series of trumpets to provide a harmonic sound - usually much louder than other types of horns.

☐ **11/2** The horn circuit, particularly if it is an older car, might well be one with the switch (horn push) in the earth side of the circuit. Later cars, on the other hand, may have them wired in the same way as lights - with the switch in the live side as shown in the circuit diagram. On very old cars, the circuit can be fed from a point before the ignition switch, so they are continually live. On later cars, they are likely to be fed through a relay, powered from an ignition controlled point.

Troubleshooting methods depend on which way the horn is wired - something your wiring circuit should be able to tell you. With the earth-switched type, if the horn has stopped working, use the testlight or multimeter, connecting one lead to earth and the other to the fuse from where the feed is taken. The result should indicate the supply is sound. From the fuse, transfer the probe to the horn live terminal. If the supply is there, the light should light.

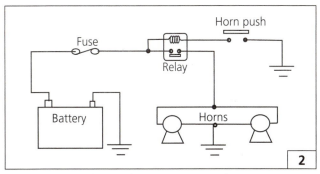

To check the earth side of the circuit, use a plain test lead, connecting one end to earth and touching the other to the second horn terminal. If the horn does not sound, it is faulty; if it does sound, the problem is in the wiring or the switch. Check closer to the switch at the point near the steering column where the horn push wiring joins the main wiring (either snap connector or plug and socket). At this point, if it is the horn push that's faulty, it's not always easy to put things right, particularly if the horn push is on the end of the stalk. A new switch might well be the answer.

With the steering wheel boss type, it's sometimes possible to clean dirt off the slip ring connector or bend the contact finger to restore continuity. Another possibility is a broken cable which can possibly be repaired or by-passed.

> *making it easy!* The horns themselves are often situated in a very hostile environment, right at the front of the car in the path of all weather. Corroded contacts may well be a possibility here and cleaning them up could do the trick. Again there is the possibility of a broken cable. With the type of horn that is bolted together and can be dismantled, it is sometimes possible to bring it back to working order by cleaning up the contacts inside.

If your car has only one horn and you feel it would benefit from the addition of a second, just in case you might be overloading the switch, fit a standard-type relay in the circuit - that is, if it doesn't have one already.

Windscreen Wipers

If your windscreen wipers have ever failed on a dark, wet night, you'll know just how difficult it is to drive without them. It is also totally illegal, of course, and very, very dangerous.

By far the majority of windscreen wipers are electrically powered, although both vacuum units operated from the engine induction manifold and engine (camshaft) driven versions have been used many years ago. Both are fairly straightforward mechanical devices, both are rare and neither is covered in this section.

There are two basic types of motor used in electrical windscreen wipers. The older shunt wound unit similar in nature to the dynamo and starter motor (but much smaller) and the more modern, and even smaller, permanent magnet type. As a general rule it's fairly easy to distinguish one from the other because the later permanent magnet type is round, the older one is a more square shape.

☐ **11/3** On some cars, the rotary motion of the motor is converted into a push-pull actions by means of a connecting rod, attached to the wipers by means of a rack moving in a tube and meshing with gears fixed on the wiper arm spindles. While this arrangement does provide some latitude as to the location of the wiper motor (and therefore better access)...

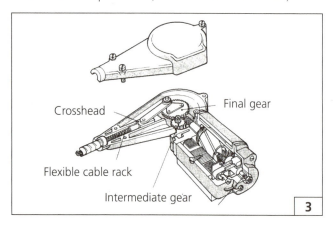

Crosshead

Final gear

Flexible cable rack

Intermediate gear

3

4

☐ **11/4** ...the modern trend is to use the more efficient crank and linkage layout with the motor hidden away behind the engine bay bulkhead.

Although the basic wiring circuit is not complicated, the wiper motor itself and its switching arrangement are a bit more involved, especially as regards the multi-speed control and blade parking arrangement.

Various forms of multi-speed control have been used, but all involve either some method of incorporating one or more resistances in the circuit or, on permanent magnet motors, adding a third brush to the commutator arrangement. Modern windscreen wiper layouts also include an intermittent wipe arrangement, most of which now use some form of electronic control.

Blade parking may be achieved in a number of different ways, but the essential element is that the blades go on moving after the wipers are switched off, but only as far as the parking position. Then the parking switch operates, so that they remain in that position.

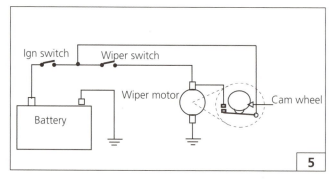

Ign switch   Wiper switch

Wiper motor

Cam wheel

Battery

5

☐ **11/5** In this simple self-parking layout, a cam attached to the motor armature, opens a set of points every time the wiper blades reach the 'park' position. When the wipers are switched on this will make no difference as there is a direct feed to the motor. However when the wiper switch is in the Off (open) position, there will be a current path through the points until they open.

Almost universally, the wiper switch is a stalk type mounted on the side of the steering column. Unfortunately, the motor is not always so accessible. It could be mounted on the bulkhead or elsewhere in the engine bay, but might just as likely be hidden under the dash.

ELECTRICAL ANCILLARIES

Troubleshooting

If the wipers stop working, the first item to investigate is the fuse. If changing it sorts the problem out, it may just have been a defective fuse; but if changing it makes no difference, or the fuse blows again, you'll have to look further.

Checking through the wiring is simply the same technique as with any other accessory. Using either a testlight or multimeter and testing as far as the switch, then closing it to check that it's not the switch at fault. The final reading will establish whether or not it is the motor itself that's faulty. In going through the wiring, you'll be looking for all the usual faults - dirty, corroded or loose connections are the major possibilities. That is, of course, if switch and motor prove satisfactory. If it's a motor fault, the most likely possibility is worn brushes and, in most cases, to gain access to these, the motor has to be dismantled. This primarily involves removing two long screws which secure the body to the magnet assembly, but before doing this, mark the body so it can be placed the same way round. If you don't do this, the motor may well run backwards!

☐ **11/6** Checking the condition of the commutator and brushes usually involves dismantling the motor, or at least, part of it. If the brushes have worn down to 2 or 3 mm, they should be changed - on most a matter of fitting a new complete brush carrier assembly. Make sure you get the right one for your car. Fixing is a matter of screws only, but the brushes will have to be tied back in their holders while the commutator is reinserted. Alternatively, in some motors, the individual brushes are soldered in position.

☐ **11/7** However, before even partly stripping the motor, check on the availability of spare parts. Quite frequently there will be none!

Most of the other possibilities of wiper failure are mechanical. If the motor runs, for instance, but the wiper blades don't move, there are several possibilities.

☐ **11/8** First, the main gearwheel in the gearbox may have stripped and will have to be replaced. The mechanism is held to the gearwheel by a circlip.

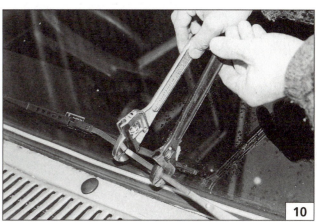

☐ **11/9** Simply ensure that the new one you buy has the right sweep angle - it should be marked on the wheel.

If, on a rack drive system, the movement of the wipers becomes excessive so that the blades contact the bottom or the sides of the screen, probably the easiest remedy is to disconnect and pull out the rack drive, rotate the two gears in the wheel boxes through 180 degrees and refit. This brings a new set of teeth into engagement and hopefully eliminates the slack.

☐ **11/10** Although not an electrical fault, wiper blade judder can be a problem and is frequently caused by the blade wiping the screen at the wrong angle - it tries to 'dig in' to the glass. First determine whether the judder is on the up, or down, sweep, then using two adjustable spanners as shown, bend the blade arm accordingly. The blade should 'flip' over on each change of direction and lean back the way it has just come.

Thermo-Controlled Cooling Fan

In the past most engines were fitted with a cooling fan which was belt driven from the engine crankshaft and in operation whenever the engine was running - even during its warming-up phase. This not only tended to overcool the engine, but also wasted power - and consequently fuel.

Now, nearly all engines have a thermostatically controlled electric cooling fan. This does not cut in until the engine reaches a pre-set temperature, operates until it cools down, and then switches off again.

11/11 Electric fans are available as an aftermarket fitting and are attached to the radiator by thin straps or by support brackets to the surrounding area. When fitting, ensure the blades do not strike the radiator fins - and make *certain* that the fan runs the correct way round! *It must* draw air *into* the engine bay on all front-mounted radiators.

These fans (original or aftermarket) are normally trouble free, but if they do go wrong there are only three major components to investigate - the fan motor, thermo-switch and the relay (if fitted), plus of course the wiring and connections.

Checking that the fan is working is simple. Just run the engine up to operating temperature with the car at a standstill and watch to see if it cuts in. If it doesn't, use the testlight or meter to check if power is reaching the input terminal at the motor. If it isn't, the problem will be further back in the circuit.

An alternative would be to make a temporary connection (using a fused lead) directly between the motor input and the battery. If the motor runs, the fault must lie elsewhere - the thermostatic switch perhaps. The simplest way of checking this is to 'short' the two switch terminals together, either using a screwdriver blade of a length of wire. If the fan motor then works, obviously the switch is the component to change.

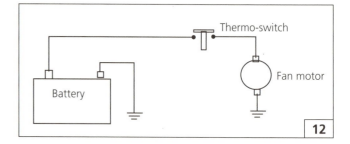

11/12 If the motor doesn't work, use the test light or meter to see if current is reaching the switch (the illustration shows a typical circuit layout). If it isn't look for a fault in the wiring from the feed point, like loose, corroded or dirty terminals. If there is power at the switch, that really only leaves the relay to check. The way to do this is to short out the thermo-switch with a screwdriver, turn on the ignition (don't pull the leads off in this case) and listen to see if you can hear the relay contacts close. If you can't, use the tester to see if there is current at the 'live' feed terminal of the relay. If there is, but you get no reading at the terminal which connects to the fan motor, the relay in faulty and must be replaced.

You should be able to find instructions for changing the fan motor in your workshop manual. Usually it comes off together with the fan blades and the job may also mean draining and removing the radiator. Make sure you connect the replacement up the right way round - polarity will be marked with the usual plus and minus.

The thermo switch may be housed in the radiator's bottom tank or in the cylinder head. You'll have to drain the coolant below its level before unscrewing and replacing it.

Rear Screen Heater

This is another simple circuit with the power feed picked up from one of the accessory fuses. There's a switch of course, usually with a built-in 'tell tale' light, and invariably a relay, while the heater itself is simply a thin heating wire built into the rear screen.

11/13 If it stops working totally, check the fuse first and then go through the circuit. It's often easiest to work backwards, checking from the heater terminal at the rear screen back to the switch, although if you know the location of the relay it might be best to check that first if there is no power reaching the rear screen.

14

16

making it easy! ☐ **11/14** The most 'popular' place for a break in the cable on cars with tailgates is inside the trunking connecting tailgate to body - or the contacts can become in need of sanding clean where contacts replace cables.

If there's power at the screen heater but it doesn't work, the probability is that the element has been damaged. This is even more obvious if only part of the screen works, as does sometimes happen. A further possibility, if the screen heater doesn't work, is that there is a problem with the earth circuit - a not uncommon fault on hatchback cars.

15

☐ **11/15** If the element is faulty, the obvious cure is to fit a new screen, but that's expensive. However, there is sometimes an alternative if the break in the element can be found, and that is to use a special conductive paint available from most accessory shops.

Electric Screen Washer

Another basic circuit here, wired from the ignition switch through a fuse to the switch and from switch to the pump - this being connected to earth. The motor is usually a permanent magnet type with a small centrifugal pump built onto it. The simplest way to test it (after checking the fuse) is to run a (fused) lead from the battery live terminal to the pump motor input. If the motor doesn't run, check further that the earth connection is sound. If it does run, you'll know that the fault lies either with the switch, the wiring or the connections.

☐ **11/16** If the motor is faulty, you can sometimes change it on its own, but in other cases the whole reservoir will have to be replaced. If so, investigate the possibility of a separate pump and motor unit, and adapting both the plumbing and wiring.

Heater Blower Motor

In circuit terms, this is very similar to the previous item, and checking follows along similar lines. The major difference lies in the switch which may be a multiple position type, possibly incorporating a resistance, and that gives a couple of extra check points - at either end of the resistance, although a problem here would probably mean the heater not working on one speed only. In some cases it may be possible to overcome this by replacing just one resistance.

Generally, it is not possible to repair the blower motor, which is usually a sealed unit, and it will have to be replaced as a unit. It is not unusual to find that the motor has burn out because 'foreign' objects have fallen down the demister ducts into the impeller, jamming the motor.

Cigarette Lighter

This is normally wired direct to the auxiliary terminal on the ignition switch - that's the same terminal as the radio, which means the lighter can be used when the ignition switch is switched to 'auxiliary' as well as when the car is running. It works by pushing the lighter element in, where a sort of push switch brings power to the element. It is held in contact by spring clips, until the heat of the element expands them, allowing the element to pop out.

Check for power (using test light or meter) at the centre contact and also the earth. If both are sound, the lighter is faulty (probably the element has burn out) and it will need replacing.

CHAPTER 12
IN-CAR ENTERTAINMENT

A car radio or radio-cassette player is viewed by many as a basic necessity, but quite often, when you buy a second-hand car it will either have had the radio removed or the one that is fitted will be unsatisfactory. However, to many, the thought of wiring up a replacement radio/cassette deck is unbearable - all those wires; all those complications! While it is true that some care has to be taken, it should not be beyond the reach of the average owner

The type of equipment you choose is a purely personal matter and, when buying a set, much will depend on individual choice. If you spend most of the time listening to the radio, there's not much point in paying for a super CD/cassette combination when something with an elaborate tuning system would be preferable.

INSIDE INFORMATION: The only problems you are likely to encounter will be either because some clot has butchered the aperture in the dash. (See your local in-car audio specialist for a special repair plate if this has happened.) Or, it will be because the car manufacturer has not applied a standard DIN-sized aperture (almost always older cars) in which case you're going to have to get the file out!

With the main decisions made about what sort of equipment you want, there are a few practical points to look at. Check, for instance, whether the price includes mounting bracket, fascia panel and speakers - and if so, that they are suitable for your car. Think about the aerial and, if electric, the switching arrangement on the set. Most cars these days have a prepared

radio position in the dash, probably with a blanking plate, so that the question of mounting brackets might be irrelevant, but just the same it is well to check there is a slot before you buy and if there is, that the set you're contemplating is standard size and will fit - most will.

Normally the front of the unit is supported on the adjustment knob spindles and if brackets are not used for the back end, it may be a case of fitting a piece of slotted steel strip which does double-duty as a support and as an earth.

If there is no pre-prepared place and brackets have to be used, you're going to need a good firm horizontal surface, such as under the fascia or under the parcel shelf, made of metal and strong enough and wide enough to take the self tapping screws needed to secure the brackets. Again, a slotted metal strip can support the rear end. If none of these is possible or convenient, investigate the viability of a small central console. They are available to suit a great many different models and normally have a knock-out panel to take a radio.

PART I: CHOOSING AND INSTALLATION

Fitting a Radio/Cassette Unit

☐ **12/1** First things first. This car, a Ford Capri was never equipped with a DIN E size aperture as standard. This is more than a little inconvenient, as that is the size that the ICE manufacturers work to! But all is not lost, for although the hole in the plastic dash panel is too small, there is plenty of room behind it to house the bigger sets. Cut the new size. It is very important to cut to the left of the panel, as this will suit the hole in the metalwork. The previous owner of this car had cut to the right and then compounded his error by cutting and hammering the metalwork to suit. Think twice; measure twice; cut once!

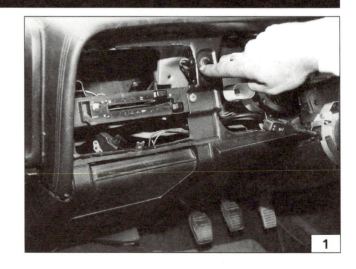

1

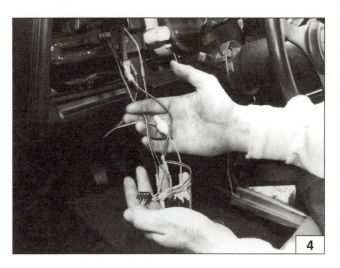

12/2 Many sets can be wired for either two or four speakers. There will be, of course, two diagrams showing the relevant wiring instructions. Should you want to add a separate power amp (or two!), make sure you buy a set with all the wiring in place and which simply requires connecting up to the item in question.

In this case, being a removable radio/cassette deck (though with the option to be mounted 'normally'), it is not actually the set which is wired into the car - rather the 'mother case'. The wiring goes to the plugs on the back of the case which align with the sockets on the rear of the set. When the set is inserted into the case, the connections are made and you're in business.

INSIDE INFORMATION: Make sure the speaker polarity is correct - see later!

12/3 When the set is in situ, it is held there securely by two pins at each side which lock into the mother case as the handle on the deck is closed.

12/4 Having removed your old set, you should draw together all the wiring for identification. An older car is likely to have seen several attempts at ICE fitment and so you can't expect to see the nice, neat factory wiring job. You're likely to meet a whole load of electrical spaghetti, as we did here. Though the original factory plug was present, there were a number of 'interesting' connections, the nature of which had to be determined before we could carry on.

FITTING THE SET

Disconnect the battery, then connect the set's power feed. Usually there's a 'flying lead' permanently fixed to the set and with half a plastic line fuse on the other end. Wiring is simply a matter of running a cable from the accessory terminal on the ignition switch, and equipping the other end with the line fuse holder and fuse. This is normally 3 amps or 5 amps, but follow the set manufacturer's recommendation about this. If the ignition switch does not have an accessory terminal (a position which allows the set to be turned off with the ignition, but which also allows it to be played when parked by turning the key to 'Accessory'), you have a choice of wiring either to an ignition controlled point, which means you must switch on in order to listen to the radio, or to a non-ignition controlled point where the penalty is that you must remember to turn the set off when you park and leave the car.

INSIDE INFORMATION: Before you remove the battery earth terminal, it is important to ascertain which are power carrying leads, and, in particular, which are ignition fed or permanently live. This is the right time to find yourself a good earth, the lack of which is the cause of more ICE problems than anything else. In this case, we used the original earthing strap. Having sorted out which is which, use masking tape as a reminder. Wrap a piece on each wire and write on it.

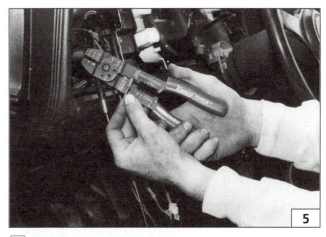

12/5 We decided that the wiring had already been messed about with too much for us to try and alter still further. So, we simply cut off the offending bits and pieces and fitted some nice new wiring and connectors. While retaining the original plugs, etc, is desirable from some points of view, you can soon end up with a real hotchpotch of wiring which could lead to problems with the set and, in really bad cases, damage to the vehicle wiring system itself.

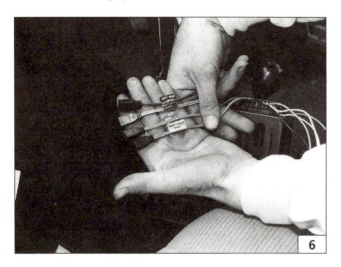

☐ **12/6** New speaker leads usually have DIN speaker sockets fitted as standard. If your car speakers have corresponding plugs fitted, then it's easy. If you are not so lucky, then you will have to fit DIN socket ends to your speaker leads.

☐ **12/7** Each speaker has two connections on the back of it. It is essential that they are all wired up the same way with no cross-overs between negative and positive terminals. In other words, all the 'positives' must be wired up to the same source, and all the 'negatives'. Otherwise the cones in the speakers will reverberate in a pattern that exactly opposes each other and cancels out much of the sound.

☐ **12/8** As the speaker wires pass through the A-posts and door frames they should be protected with grommets. The two holes should not be on a level with each other, otherwise they will tend to push the grommet out as you close the door. Make their

heights an inch or two different (see arrows) and the speaker wire will loop gracefully out of the way as the door is closed.

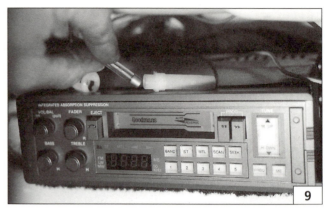

☐ **12/9** Fuses are vital to the well being of your car and to your in-car entertainment. Make sure that you get it right! The thin in-line fuse for the live feed is there to protect your set. Don't replace fuses of a given amperage with one of a different amperage.

FACT FILE: WIRE CONNECTION

A word about electrician's tape. You should, of course, have some - its insulating properties are ideal for in-car entertainment fitting and it's useful for 'looming' similar wires together (ie, speaker or power leads, but not mixed!). What you must never do, however, is twist wires together, secure it with tape and call it an electrical joint - it isn't! At best, you may get away with it, for a while at least. At worst, you'll end up with a poor sound system, possible damage to your equipment and even end up causing a fire. It's not hard (or expensive) to make good electrical connections - see *Chapter 3, Electrical Circuits.*

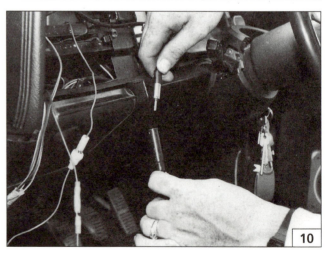

☐ **12/10** Having wired the set, as per the diagram supplied, it's almost time to reconnect the power - but don't forget the aerial; there's little more annoying than wasting time looking for complex reasons as to why the radio won't work, when it just isn't connected.

☐ **12/11** Take some care when you ease the mother case into the standard DIN aperture. You will have to 'tease' the wiring back into the depths of the dash to ensure that it doesn't foul anywhere and that it is not kinked or damaged in process. Make sure that speaker leads and power carrying leads are kept as far apart as possible, so as to reduce the risk of power-bourne interference.

☐ **12/12** Once in place (and having been tested once more, to ensure that none of the leads have come adrift), the metal tags in the case are bent down to prevent it coming out whenever you remove the set.

making it easy ! ☐ **12/13** *Always try the set before you get carried away fitting it in place. It's far easier to sort out any problems - swapped over speaker leads are a favourite - while it's still like this. Temporarily reconnect the battery, then check that all the functions - tape, radio, speaker fader/balance, etc - work as they should before removing the battery earth lead once more.*

Choosing and Fitting Speakers

When choosing speakers you should always make sure that they are capable of handling the amount of power your set will put through them. First of all, make sure that when you compare the power outputs of set and speakers, you are comparing like with like. Power can be given in a variety of ways, although most manufacturers state and MAX power output - that is, the maximum amount of power that a speaker/amplifier can handle for a short period of time. Allow an overlap, in favour of the speaker, of at least 50 per cent. So, if your amplifier produces 20W per channel MAX, your speaker should be rated at around 30W MAX. Ideally, of course, you will choose a speaker which can handle considerably more power than that, which will allow for a power increase later on without the expensive need to uprate your speakers again. When buying speakers, as well as the power rating, you should also look for the Frequency Response. This is a technical term which refers quite simply to the highest and lowest notes a speaker (or head unit) is capable of reproducing. The measurements are taken in Hertz (or Hz) or thousands of Hertz (KHz), where the lower the number, the lower the note. Again, this is something you need to match with your set.

☐ **12/14** Buried, as they are, beneath your car's trim, it's very easy to ignore your speakers when considering an ICE uprate; all too often lots of cash has been

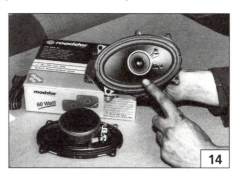

poured into the front-end equipment, amplifiers, graphics, etc, but the speakers have been left untouched. What's the point? Would you expect your 200bhp Turbo, to perform correctly on 5 inch wheels with 70 series tyres? Of course not. In fact, you should always look to replace your speakers *before* you touch the rest of your system, using the simple formula shown above. Standard speakers (where fitted) are usually wide range, ie, all the frequencies are handled by a single unit. However, the more you can split-up the frequencies, the better the quality of sound you will have.

☐ **12/15** Moving up somewhat, these are triaxial speakers which have three speakers within the same enclosure. With a power handling capacity of 150W max, you'd need some system before you overload these speakers! More importantly, with a reasonable power output, you will not be working the speakers anywhere near their capabilities and thus get a much better performance from them. You should note that, like all really high

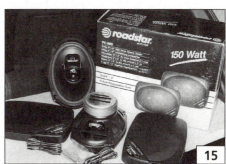

IN-CAR ENTERTAINMENT

performance speakers, they are heavy and not suitable for fitting, say, on the standard hatchback rear shelf.

12/16 The larger, outer speaker handles the lower frequencies, the centre speaker the mid range and the lower speaker is, once again, a tweeter. By separating the sound frequencies like this, the clarity will be still further improved. A variation on a theme is...

12/17 ...a triaxial unit. It differs in that the speakers are totally separate, although still inside a single enclosure. Their 100W max capability would be more than enough for most!

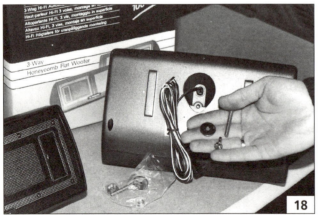

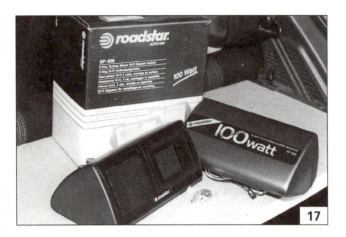

12/18 Although there are three speakers, there is only one speaker lead to wire-up. They are mounted by using the stud provided. Again, the standard rear shelf is not up to taking the weight. Another point is that you should cut the studs to length, rather than leave a dangerous piece sticking out into the interior of the hatch.

12/19 We used the 8mm socket on a screwdriver attachment to remove the four speaker securing nuts. The grille, already removed at this stage, simply unclips.

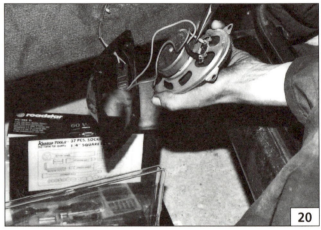

12/20 You may find that the speaker leads are reluctant to come off - use long nose pliers and tug so as not to bend or break the speaker terminals.

12/21 With the speakers removed, you have a choice with regard to some car's standard backing plate. You can replace it with the new speaker or leave it off - you'll see why later.

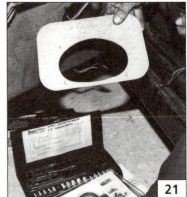

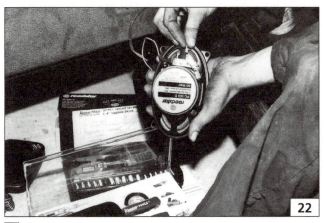

12/22 Many modern speakers are fitted with three different sizes of terminal, so there should be problem fitting the speaker leads to them. Make sure that you keep the polarity right in order to avoid 'phasing'.

12/23 And here's the backing plate problem. The screws stick out too far to allow the new grille to fit. Your choice is to use the standard grille or take out the backing plate completely and fix the speaker with the self-tappers supplied with the new kit or, as we did, saw off a little from the end of the screw to suit. The result is that...

12/24 ...there's a good, solid mounting for the speaker and you're able to use your stylish new grilles.

12/25 At the rear of most cars, the obvious mounting place for speakers is in the rear shelf - if you have one, of course! Shelves only appear as standard on certain models, so if you're fitting this MDF shelf you'll need to sort out some shelf supports. Using the standard item is OK for relatively small speakers designed to handle small amounts of power, but as the power output in 'our' car had been increased substantially (to 64W), the owner was looking to introduce more amplification and possibly more speakers at a later date, we took another route and fitted a custom rear shelf. It is designed to fit exactly in place and comes complete with acoustic speaker cloth covering, available in a range of colours.

FACT FILE: SPEAKER POSITIONING

When mounting speakers, remember that the higher the frequency capability, the more sensitive they are to positioning. So, the tweeters and mid-range speakers need to be as far apart as possible in order to get good stereo imaging. The lower frequencies, particularly sub-bass, are felt rather than heard and thus can be placed much nearer together.

12/26 Cutting out the holes for the speakers calls for great accuracy when marking out. Take your time and always remember the old adage; 'Measure twice, cut once' - you can't undo a hole once it's cut!

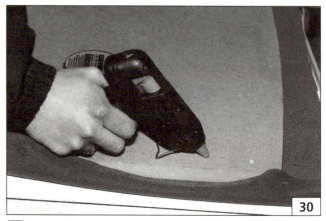

12/27 Templates for the speaker holes are provided as part of the box lid. We used a craft knife (watch those fingers!) to cut out the centre portion from the template and then...

12/28 ...carefully placed the template in the previously marked position. In order to make sure that it didn't move while we marked out the hole in pencil, we used masking tape around the edges of the template.

12/29 We placed the speakers toward the outer edges of the shelf, for the best possible stereo separation and toward the front of the shelf to prevent them from fouling when it was raised to carry luggage. It also allows for larger bass speakers (woofers/sub-woofers) to be positioned in the centre of the shelf at a later date.

12/30 The speaker cloth has to be stretched tight over the shelf before it is inverted. Then, it has to be cut so that there is only a two inch overlap around the whole shelf and pulled tight once more. It has to be fixed securely in place. You could use a staple gun for this, although we found a mains power glue gun to be ideal. It takes some time and you'd be well advised to have a second, or even third pair of hands to help keep the cloth absolutely taut.

12/31 If you think you will need to remove your shelf fairly frequently, it's a good idea to fit a plug/socket to the speakers. This will enable you to unplug them and remove the shelf unit in a matter of seconds. You must take great care to ensure that you maintain the polarity of the speaker wiring otherwise you'll end up with phasing. These plugs cost only pence and are available from most in-car entertainment specialists.

Compact Disc Players

In essence, fitting a purpose made CD player (CD/tuner or CD only) is as easy as fitting a DIN size radio/cassette deck. However, because of the very nature of the compact disc player, it is much more important that the unit should be very firmly held in place, to enable the complex suspension systems to work correctly and prevent the lasers from 'skipping' over parts of the disc. This is the single biggest problem with DIY fitted CD players.

12/32 Should you opt for a multi-disc autochanger, then the same principle applies, but it is also important to ensure that the 'changer' is kept away from sources of extreme heat and moisture and where it will not get damaged by care-lessness (if mounted in the hatch, for example).

Amplifiers

Any decision to uprate the amplification of your ICE system should not be taken lightly. Neither should it start with the amplifiers themselves, curiously enough. It should start with the speakers. There are plenty of folk willing to pump hundreds of watts through poor old standard speakers which were not meant to handle that sort of power. So, sort out the speakers first. Then take a good look at your deck. If it's a CD player, then you should be OK in terms of sound quality. But radio/cassette decks come good, bad and rather ugly, and if you've good a poor sound source, there's not much point in amplifying it; it will sound just as bad - but louder! You should always match your amplifier to the equipment already in your car, preferably by make.

12/33 Once you've got a good system, the only way is up and it's a natural extension to want to boost the power. This 'amp' produces 50W + 50W max.

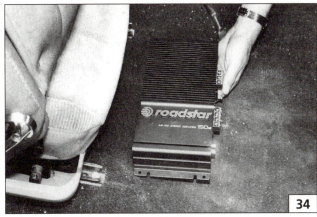

12/34 This amp pushes out 50 per cent more power. Note that the terminals are all positioned on one side of the amp which should be mounted so that these cannot be damaged. For example, if you mount it under the front passenger seat, the terminals should face forward to avoid being accidentally kicked.

12/35 A favourite mounting place in some cars is under a false floor in the hatch. Mounting here, to the side of the spare wheel, is a good position, not least because it's well away from the fuel tank! If you decide to mount your amp(s) vertically (say, on the back of the rear seats or rear bulkhead), then you must make sure that the fins run end-on to the amp, otherwise the air cannot circulate properly and the amp will overheat.

Graphic Equalisers

The graphic equaliser is best described as a more versatile tone control switch. Effectively, your car is its own tone control and because it modifies the sounds at random (due to the effects of engine, tyre and wind noise, etc), the chances of getting the sounds you would really like are minimal. You can choose to have a separate graphic equaliser, although the crowded confines of many cars may lead you to consider an amplifier unit with a built-in graphic.

☐ **12/36** There's rarely room to fit a graphic in the dash. The bracket supplied can be adjusted to suit the angle of the dash in question. As you can see, it fits quite nicely under the centre dash area. The wiring is not for the faint hearted, although it's not quite as bad as it looks.

Fitting an Aerial

The car aerial suffers from problems that don't beset the domestic aerial, most of which revolve around the fact that it is attached to a moving vehicle and the radio tuner is constantly changing its position in relation to the radio signals. This can lead to poor reception, not only if the transmitter is too far away, but also if it is too close. If the set is close to a strong signal, but it is tuned into a more distant one, it may mix up the two. The resultant audio melange is called 'cross modulation'. If the set is already tuned into a strong signal, there is a danger of overloading. If the signal is too far away, there is an opposite problem. (This is noticeable with FM, where the signal travels in 'sight' lines and is easily interrupted by the horizon or tall buildings). The volume will fall, but interference will increase. These difficulties can be overcome by fitting a quality aerial.

AERIAL SURVEY

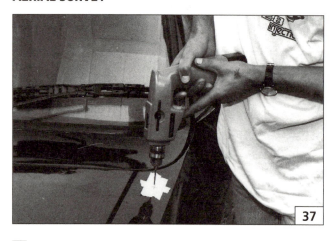

☐ **12/37** Before doing anything drastic, check and double check the spot you propose fitting the aerial to make sure first that there is enough space for the base underneath, if it telescopes down flush with the surface and that the bodywork isn't double skinned at that spot. Then make sure by bouncing the car that the suspension won't foul it.

A good aerial will come with a fitting kit and it should contain a template for marking out the hole. Care must obviously be taken here to minimise the possibility of damage and with that in mind the first step is to cover the site with masking tape. Mark out onto this the position of the centre of the hole and use a metal punch and hammer to just lightly mark the metal ready for drilling.

The hole you need will usually be 7/8in (22mm) diameter, and there are several ways it can be cut out. The crudest method is to use successively larger drills, finally opening it out to size with a rat-tailed file. An alternative is to use a hole saw in the electric drill, and this is a good method provided that you've got a good quality hole saw. The third alternative is a tank cutter - probably the best of all. All of these need a pilot hole and the masking tape will be found invaluable in preventing the drill bit from skidding and scratching the paintwork.

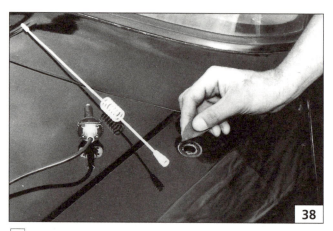

☐ **12/38** One of the most important aspects of aerial fitment is to have a good earth. Use emery paper to ensure that there is metal for the aerial to make good contact with (rather than paintwork), and then use a dab of Comma's Copperease as a means of preventing rust but still retaining the electrical conductivity.

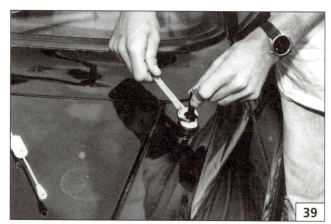

☐ **12/39** The aerial is inserted from under the wing and the securing top nut tightened with a 17mm spanner. Don't overtighten this nut or it could damage the rubber seal. At this point, the aerial can be screwed into place. The base of the aerial is flexible, allowing it to be 'bent' to whatever position is desired - a 90 degree angle is best. It also means that you can remove it when you park the car to prevent undesirables tying knots in it for you!

CONNECTING UP

Route the aerial lead through to the back of the set without taking it through the engine compartment. Any holes in metal panels that it passes through should be fitted with a rubber grommet to prevent chafing. Do not shorten the coaxial cable. Fit the aerial firmly nad permanently and do the same with the set. Somewhere on this there will be an aerial trimmer - see the instruction book with the set. Turn the set onto a weak station and turn the trimmer until the signal is at its strongest.

ELECTRIC AERIALS

☐ **12/40** The fitting procedure for an electrically operated aerial will be much the same but with additional wiring work involved. In most cases the circuit will be similar to that shown in the illustration.

side-loading and front-loading versions from most accessory stores. By inserting a long key into the end (or side, depending on the version required) of the lock, two clamps lock over the capstans of the cassette deck and make it virtually impossible to extricate without destroying the set.

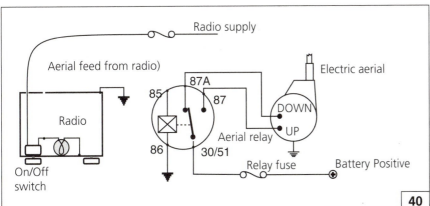

☐ **12/42** The ingenious cassette-shaped device is loaded into the deck as you would a normal cassette. This model sticks out a large yellow 'tongue' in no uncertain manner, warning potential thieves to look elsewhere.

Security

The old adage 'you can't take it with you' doesn't apply to the car thief who, given half a chance, would be more than happy to take your newly installed equipment with him!

☐ **12/41** If you haven't got a removable unit in your car, then you could use a Security Lock, available, as seen here, in

PART II: ELIMINATING INTERFERENCE

You should not be too surprised if you get some form of interference, especially if your set or car (or both) are fairly old.

Before attempting any form of interference suppression, it is important that you have a good quality aerial, correctly fitted and earthed properly. If you can get improved radio reception by touching the aerial when tuned into an AM station, then it is not earthed properly.

A further aerial check to carry out is to tune the set to a station and then tap the aerial. If interference, in the form of a crackling noise is present, then this points to the contact between the various sections being intermittent or non-existent. The only answer here is to buy another aerial.

Most forms of radio interference come from various electrical items already fitted to the car. In some cases (plug leads, for example) they could be faulty. In others, they may be working perfectly, but just need suppressing.

Metal Bodied Cars

To carry out the following checks, it is important that the car is parked in a reasonably open space otherwise confusing signals could get in the way. Also the doors, hatch/bootlid and bonnet should be shut.

With any car, the metal bonnet provides an excellent screen for unwanted noise. However, to be totally effective, it must be well earthed. If your bonnet does not have an earthing strap,

FACT FILE: NOISE SOURCES

Listed here are some of the most common sources of interference and the types of noise they are likely to make.

ITEM	NOISE
Clock (analogue)	Regular ticking, even with ignition and engine switched off.
Windscreen wipers	Crackling sound when in use.
Heater fan motor	Crackling, as above, or a whine.
Windscreen/rear screen washer motor	Whine
Fuel pump	A fast irregular ticking, fast and then slow.
Coil/plug leads/plugs	A crackling sound which rises and falls with engine revs.
Alternator (or dynamo)	A whine in unison with the engine revs.

then you should fit one - most accessory shops will be able to supply a universal item to suit. If it does have one, then you can lose nothing by removing it, cleaning up the contact areas with emery paper and smearing a little copper grease on both contact surfaces before replacement. In successfully suppressing any source of interference, the first task is to isolate the culprit. Essentially, it is a task which requires patience and a logical mind to work steadily through the various stages of isolation until the offending item(s) is(are) found.

Start by sitting in the car with the engine and ignition off and the radio on. Most in-car electrical items require the ignition on for operation and so interference at this point will almost certainly be the clock. Switch on the ignition and, one by one, switch on all the electrical items (wiper motor, heater fan) you can think of and listen for interference. If interference occurs simply by switching on the ignition, it points to a fuel pump problem. If you cannot locate the problem, switch on the engine and listen for the sounds given in the table listed earlier. All modern cars are fitted with spark plug caps with internal suppressors. Over a period of time, these fail and cause interference. Another common cause of complaint is the distributor, which often develops hairline cracks in the cap or a loose or worn rotor arm. Straight replacement is the answer. Similarly, fitting a metal shield around it can sometimes help; indeed, some vehicle manufacturers now fit these as standard equipment.

It could also be some non-standard electrical item that you have fitted as an 'extra' to your car. Listen for this in the same manner as above.

If you are getting interference from only one speaker or pair of speakers, it could be that the wiring loom is causing it via the speaker cables. Re-routing the speaker leads usually eradicates the problem. Ensure that the speaker cables do not run close to any power carrying leads or electric motors. It is also possible for the radio's power lead to induce interference. This is usually solved by selecting a different power source.

Often, an interference problem because evident after fitting an uprated system. However, it does not mean that the problem is new - it could have been present for years, but has only become noticeable given the extra capability of the new system.

☐ **12/43** You should note that FM (VHF) signals are much more prone to interference than AM signals. Take extra care when earthing the set and a roof aerial will help to get a better signal. Because of the nature of FM signals, they tend to bounce off hard objects and in certain causes, you could find that your tuner is receiving the same signal twice. A reflected signal could take much longer

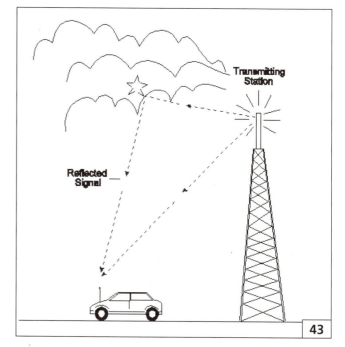

Transmitting Station

Reflected Signal

43

than the original to reach your set and, as such, there could be distortion and fading. There is not a lot you can do about this, although, because the car is constantly moving, there is more than a probability that the car will soon move away from whatever is causing the reflection.

☐ **12/44** A kit like this one allows you to update several possible areas of interference at one fell swoop. It comprises; four spark plug caps, one for the distributor cap, one for the coil, a braided earth lead. This is not a job to do when the engine is warm!

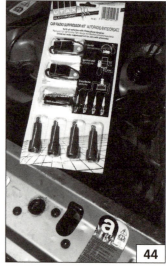

44

45

12/45 Fitting the spark plug suppressors is easy. Pull off the spark plug cap, push-fit the suppressor into it...

12/46 ...and replace the whole lot onto the plug. Don't mix the plug leads up otherwise your car will be reluctant to run. Always replace one lead at a time. The caps have a tendency to be a tight fit on the leads and so a healthy tug may be necessary to get them off. Don't forget to give a similarly healthy push when you replace them. Remember that the leads themselves are also subject to wear and tear and that after a few years, it could be that their suppression

46

qualities are on the wane. Replacing a set of plug leads with a new set of silicon replacements may well be a good idea if your car is any age.

If you have fitted the suppressors and replaced the leads but are still getting interference which sounds as if it is coming from the HT circuit, it could be the plugs themselves. Some plugs have in-built suppressors and can be identified as they have the letter 'R' as a prefix or suffix. Again, replacement of plugs is a simple task and it could well solve your problems.

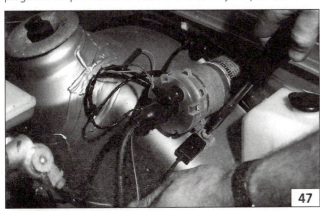

47

12/47 Fitting a suppressor to the coil is equally simple. The suppressor has to be securely earthed by its mounting bracket. The best way is to place it under the coil mounting brackets.

The size of capacitor depends on whether your radio has FM waveband (almost all do, nowadays). For FM sets, the capacitor rating needs to be 2.5 microfarad but for AM sets it need only be 1 microfarad.

48

12/48 The suppressor lead then has to be connected to the ignition side of the coil.

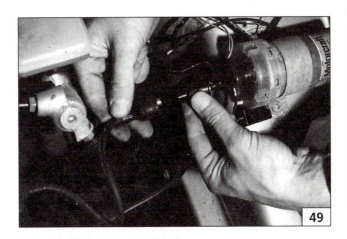

49

12/49 The high tension lead to the coil can also be covered by using the in-line suppressor, which is fitted in the same way as the spark plugs.

50

12/50 The vehicle bonnet makes and excellent screen (as long as it's a metal car) but it must be earthed to the car body. This kit includes a strong metal braid for this purpose. In this case it was not required, as the vehicle was so fitted as standard. However, many cars are not equipped with one and it could make a big difference to your radio reception, especially on FM.

Whether you are fitting a new one or checking on the old one, make sure that there is a good contact at both ends by cleaning the metal surfaces with emery cloth and adding a dab copper grease to prevent the build-up of corrosion.

Generator Suppression

Later model cars tend to have alternators while earlier models were equipped with dynamos. Both are a common cause of radio interference.

ALTERNATORS

Some alternators will have capacitors already fitted, which should be visible and situated close to the other electrical connections. All you can check is that it is securely held and that the leads are firmly attached. If all appears to be well, but you still think that it is the root of the problem, then any good motor electrical dealer should be able to test it for you quite cheaply. If it is found to be faulty, the it should be replaced. Use a 3 microfarad capacitor for an alternator.

DYNAMOS

Use a capacitor between 1 and 3 microfarad. Bolt the capacitor to a good, clean mounting point on the car's bodywork and place the lead from the capacitor under the large terminal on the dynamo.

FACT FILE: SUPPRESSION OF MOTORS

Having established which motor is causing the problem, the first task is to ensure that it is earthed correctly. Where it is earthed through its casing, remove the motor and clean up its earthing point and that on the bodywork with a fine emery cloth. If this has no effect, try running a separate earth wire from the motor to a known good earth. If the problem persists, you will have to fit a either a 1 microfarad capacitor or a 7amp, in-line choke or, in extreme cases, both.

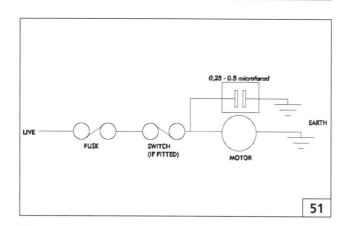

12/51 The capacitor lead needs to be connected into the power lead of the motor. In some cases, it is possible to use a 'piggy back' spade connector. In others you will have to use a Scotchlok connector. The capacitor should be tightened securely to a nearby earthing point, as shown in this diagram.

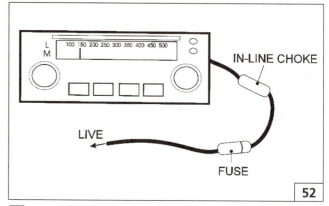

12/52 An in-line choke is basically a small coil of wire which produces a magnetic field when fitted in the supply lead of a component. This effectively cancels out interference. It should be fitted as close as possible to the item in question. It is fitted in a similar manner to a capacitor, usually by Scotchloking into the power lead and then attaching a good earth.

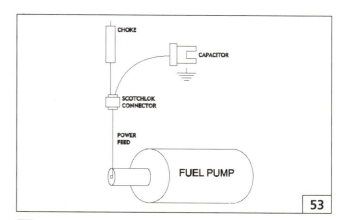

12/53 A fuel pump should be suppressed in the manner shown here, with a capacitor and/or a choke.

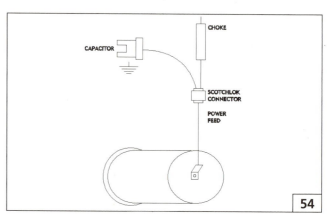

12/54 A clock can be treated in a similar way. Don't forget that while using Scotchloks is a simple way to achieve the desired result, you **must** make sure that a good connection is made. Bear in mind also that they need to be protected from the elements when fitted in the engine bay.

Fibreglass Cars

Owners of cars with fibreglass bodywork (Lotus, TVR, many kit cars etc.) will not need reminding that dealing with interference without the aid of a metal body is difficult. The fibreglass makes earthing (either aerials or audio equipment) hard work. In addition, the metal bonnet of a 'normal' car makes an excellent screen for the interference-laden engine compartment.

Thus, fitting ICE in such a vehicle demands more of the fitter than usual. You must make sure that the equipment you fit has a good earth. The best way is to take a separate braided lead directly to the chassis. Mounting the aerial away from the engine bay is much more important than in a metal bodied car. If possible, mount it at the rear of a front engined car and the front of a rear engined car, again, ensuring a really good earth. If you have to extend the aerial lead, use a proprietary extension with pre-fitted plugs/sockets. For power, take it direct from the battery, remembering, of course, to maintain the presence of an in-line fuse.

In the engine bay, some manufacturers fit a small metal shield over the coil etc. If you do not have one, it is worth contacting the makers to see if it is available as an official spare. If not, you could look to making one up yourself. However, where and how to mount it is likely to be a problem. Clearly, it must not foul on the engine or the bonnet when closed.

It is possible to regain some of the interference repelling properties of that metal bonnet by adapting a fibreglass bonnet accordingly. By fitting a special foil to the underside of the bonnet, some screening against interference will be gained.

It may be possible to glue it in place or possibly fibreglass resin could be used. You must make sure that there is absolutely no possibility of it falling off while the car is in motion, as this could be very dangerous. Many ICE specialists keep a supply of specially perforated metal for specifically for this purpose. The foil you use to cook your turkey at Christmas is not suitable - it will cook your engine in much the same manner!

Having fitted the foil, you should ensure that it has a good earth to the chassis.

Interference Fault Finding Chart

IMPORTANT NOTE: Ensure aerial is properly earthed, properly connected to set and fully extended before carrying out checks

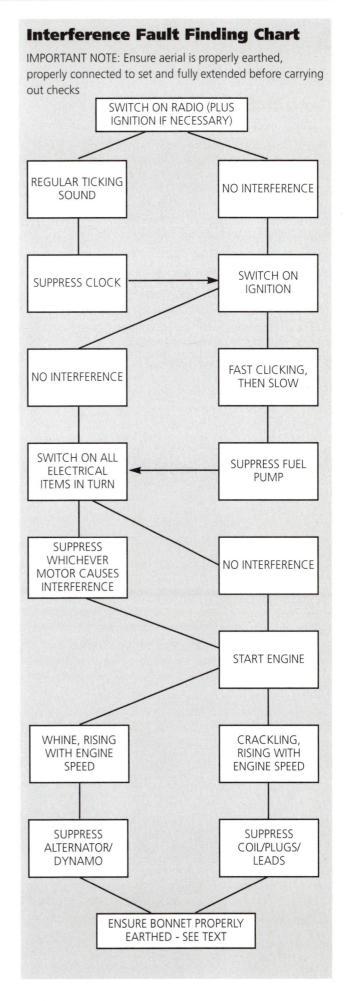

CHAPTER 13
ADDING ACCESSORIES

Compared with their equivalents built twenty or so years ago, modern cars are particularly well endowed with electrical accessories and most now come complete with some form of radio-cassette player, reversing lights, heated rear window, rear fog light(s) and much else besides. All classed as extras a few years ago, but now fitted as standard equipment.

Even so, there is still a considerable demand for even more - upgrading the ICE (In Car Entertainment) equipment for instance (see *Chapter 12, In-Car Entertainment*), or fitting extra fog/driving lights, additional 'High-level' stop lights or, for the more adventurous, items such as power windows or central locking. By far the majority of these extra accessories are readily available, many of them in kit form and with full fitting instructions.

However, there are a few factors to consider which are seldom referred to in any instruction leaflets. These include the extra load on the existing electrical system, the legal requirements and advice on planning your work. Fitting a set of driving lights, for instance, isn't just a matter of finding a suitable place to mount them, there are regulations about where they can go (and how they might be used). Wiring just one additional stop light into the existing lighting circuit may be acceptable, but two could well overload the switch and, if you intend fitting such lights, then think about the possibility of other accessories at the back end of the vehicle (reversing lights or trailer socket) and lay down the necessary wiring at the same time.

Extra Lights

☐ 13/1 Only a few years ago, fitting extra lights to your car was a fairly simple operation. In most cases it was just a matter of drilling a couple of holes in the bumper or body and bolting the things on. These days it can be far more difficult for two main reasons. The first of these is that on most modern cars the

bumpers have all but disappeared into the bodywork, and the second is that we now have regulations by the score regarding where the lights can, and cannot, be fitted.

☐ 13/2 With the majority of modern cars, some form of bracket for mounting the lights will be needed, especially for those at the front. Most of the major light manufacturers provide mounting kits as well, but with the vast range of different cars around, it would be virtually impossible to provide kits suitable for all, so it may be that you will have to make your own brackets, or be prepared to modify some 'general purpose' versions. If so, it's important that they are firm and stable, especially any for spot lights, in fact you may also need a steady bar on the light unit as well, unless you buy a kit from your local main dealer which *could* be expensive - but *would* be right for your car.

If there is a performance version, or more up-market edition in your car's particular model range, it could well have additional lighting fitted as standard. If so, you could have a look at one to see how it's been done. In most cases, you can buy identical brackets or whatever from your local dealer, indeed, as we said, many manufacturers also sell the same type of lights as well - following this line of action would also ensure they comply with the regulations. Broadly speaking these are as follows:

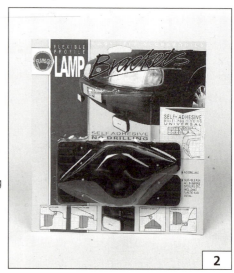

FACT FILE: FOG AND DRIVING LIGHT POSITIONS

SPOT (DRIVING) LIGHTS

These must be mounted so that the outside edge of the illuminated area is not less than 500mm from the ground or not more than 1200mm. They must be fitted in matched pairs, equi-distant from the centre of the vehicle, at the same height and each must be within 400mm from the outside of the vehicle - this last applies to cars first used after 1st January 1971, cars built before that date may differ from this standard.

☐ **13/3** Both lights must emit the same colour light and must be wired so that they both come on or can be switched on only when the headlights are on main beam. In other words they are extinguished when the headlights are switched to dip beam.

FOG LIGHTS

Basically the same rules apply, except that these can be mounted below the 500mm mark, when they then become in bureaucratic terminology 'permitted lights'. Here's where it gets a little confusing, for you are allowed two 'permitted lights', either both fog or one fog and one spot.

☐ **13/4** In conditions of fog or falling snow, these two lights can be used instead of the headlights. However to confuse things even further, the regulations state that if only one is fitted or used, it must only be illuminated with the headlights. The best advice is to only fit fogs below 500mm and only in pairs.

REAR FOG LIGHTS

All vehicles manufactured after 1st October 1979 or first used on or after 1st April 1980 must be fitted with one or two of these lights. Where only one is fitted it must be on the right hand or off-side of the vehicle, whereas if two are fitted they must be equi-distant from the centre and at the same height. They must also emit a light of the same colour and intensity. In addition

they must not be lower than 250mm from the ground or more than one meter above it.

The rear fog lights fitted to any car of whatever age must also conform to the following regulations:

a) The wattage of each light must not exceed 25 watts.

b) The illuminated surface of the light must be at least 100mm from a stop light.

c) The light must not be wired so that it is illuminated by the application of the vehicle brakes.

REVERSING LIGHTS

Either one or two of these are permitted, but neither must exceed 24 watts. Operation must be automatic or by a manually operated switch in which case a warning light must be used to show the driver when the light is in operation.

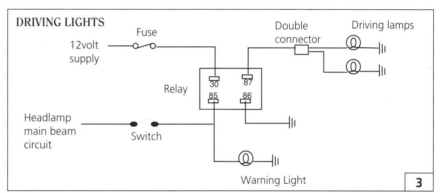

DRIVING LIGHTS — Fuse, 12volt supply, Double connector, Driving lamps, Relay (30, 87, 85, 86), Headlamp main beam circuit, Switch, Warning Light. **3**

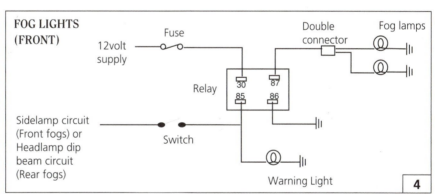

FOG LIGHTS (FRONT) — Fuse, 12volt supply, Double connector, Fog lamps, Relay (30, 87, 85, 86), Sidelamp circuit (Front fogs) or Headlamp dip beam circuit (Rear fogs), Switch, Warning Light. **4**

Connecting Up

☐ **13/5** You must never touch halogen bulbs with your fingers. Like this is safe, but only remove the bulbs from their protective boxes when you are ready to put them into the light. If you do touch the bulb by mistake, then you should clean the glass carefully with methylated spirit.

5

☐ **13/6** The 2.8i Capri we used for this fitting has a couple of fog light mounting holes pre-drilled in the valence at either side (one for the light and one for the wiring to it). Naturally, if you have a car which does not feature them, you'll have to drill some new ones. Even in this case, it was necessary to make the holes slightly larger in order to accommodate the 8mm mounting bolts.

6

7

13/7 When routing the wires, be careful to avoid areas of extreme heat and cold and keep them well away from moving parts, such as the alternator. The relay should be mounted with the same care and we found that this earthing screw was ideal, not least as it meant that we didn't have to drill an extra hole in the bodywork. Foglights can be used with or without headlights and are operated by a separate switch mounted on the dash - we would suggest one of the standard switch blanks under the steering wheel.

8

13/8 The brackets are supplied with the kit and each light simply bolts to the bracket, which in turn is bolted through the hole in the valence. Make sure that you don't forget the lockwasher, otherwise the vibration will soon relieve you of your extra lighting equipment!

WIRING

Our suggested methods of connecting these lights up are shown in the relevant wiring diagrams. In some case there are alternatives which produce the same results, and if you prefer one of these, then go ahead, but the lights must only be in use as the law demands, so make sure you have wired them correctly. IMPORTANT NOTE: The diagrams shown here are to be used only if you don't have the appropriate manufacturer's recommended instructions. Manufacturer's instructions take precedence!

Another factor to consider when wiring in any accessory is the cable size. Use too small diameter a cable and a drop in voltage along its length may occur. Not only would this mean that your accessory wouldn't be getting its full quota of power but, in extreme cases, the cable itself may get hot and even start a fire. Check on the cable size chart in *Chapter 3, Electrical Currents*.

However it isn't only cable size that causes a volt drop, the length of the cable can also affect it. Basically the longer the cable, the greater the resistance to current flow and the greater the volt drop. For this reason it is always advisable to keep all cable runs as short as possible.

As for the current, most accessories of this nature are rated in Watts, the standard unit of electrical power. This is covered in *Chapter 2, Doing The Knowledge*, but basically to determine the current flow, divide the total wattage by the voltage. For example, a headlight rated at 60 watts would consume 5 amps (60 divided by 12). Two headlights of this size would amount to 120 watts, consuming 10 amps. All this, of course, assumes we are talking about a 12 volt car. These lights would require a cable size of 28/0.30 or larger. If you are in any doubt always use a larger cable.

If you are wiring into an existing circuit, always calculate the total current consumption, that is the sum of your additional accessories and all the other (original) equipment on that circuit. You may find that the grand total exceeds the capacity of the existing cable, in which case one answer would be to wire the new equipment through an in-line fuse directly from the battery or to use a relay, so putting only a small load on the control circuit.

E MARKING

13/9 If you are in the market for any additional lights (of any sort) and regardless of when or where you intend fitting them, make sure they carry the 'E' approval mark (Europe only).

This mark is as shown in our illustration. The number in the circle E11 indicates the country carrying out the approval. The symbol above the circle shows the use for which the component has been approved (the B is for a fog light). The number below the circle is that given by the approval authority to the manufacturer of the equipment and the number before the 'R' is the approval number. The numbers are for illustrative purposes only and should not be applied to any particular component.

```
┌─────────────────────┐
│  ┌───┐              │
│  │ B │              │
│  └───┘              │
│    ╱─────╲          │
│   │ E11  │          │
│    ╲─────╱          │
│   15R2343           │
│                   9 │
└─────────────────────┘
```

Anti-Theft Devices

While it's true that hardly any burglar alarm would stop a professional crook who has designs on your particular car, even a simple anti-theft device would deter the opportunist thieves who are responsible for most car crime.

Although concealed switches and other isolator devices won't stop thieves breaking into the car, they might stop it being driven away and one of the easiest to fit is the simple cut-out switch in the ignition system - in reality, nothing more than an additional ignition switch.

ADDING ACCESSORIES

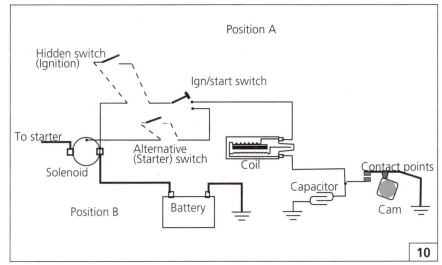

Position A

Hidden switch (Ignition)

Ign/start switch

To starter

Alternative (Starter) switch

Solenoid

Coil

Capacitor

Contact points

Cam

Position B

Battery

10

SAFETY FIRST! The fitting operation of even these most basic alarms will invariably mean breaking into the wiring of the courtesy light switches, the ignition switch, the hazard flashers and the horn. And every connection must be well made for, at the very best, a failure could result in the alarm sounding. At worst, it could again result in the engine stopping while on the move. Have any DIY installation checked over by a qualified auto-electrician before using the car.

DIY IMMOBILISERS

☐ **13/10** On the older contact-points systems this (concealed) switch could be wired either side of the ignition coil and, if connected to the distributor side, could be earthed. Unfortunately, this arrangement could result in terminal damage to most electronic systems and on these it would be better to wire the new switch in series with the ignition switch and coil - simply cut the feed cable to the coil and extend each end of the cut cable up to the 'secret' switch. The switch itself should, of course, be hidden either under the dash or, elsewhere within easy reach of the driver. Do not hide it where it might be accidentally operated once the car is on the move and make sure all the connections are sound as any problem could result in the engine cutting out.

Diesel car owners can do much the same by connecting the hidden switch into the feed wire to the fuel cut-off solenoid on the fuel injection pump. However, the same problems associated with a wiring or switch defect could arise, and result in the engine stopping.

A safer alternative, suitable for both petrol and diesel engined cars, would be to wire the hidden switch in series with the ignition/starter switch and the starter solenoid. Cut the (thin) cable to the solenoid and extend each end of the cable up to the hidden switch. This would prevent the starter motor from operating but would mean that the car could still be push or tow started. However, the consequences of any failure in the circuit (or hidden switch) wouldn't be so serious as with an ignition cut-out switch.

CAR ALARMS

Many modern cars are fitted with quite sophisticated burglar alarms, some of which are linked to the central locking system and even close any open windows and the sunroof. Most have some form of remote control operation and a few even sound a remote alarm if the car is interfered with.

Similar systems are available as an aftermarket fitting, but most are best installed by the professionals. Indeed, many

are not available as a DIY fitting. Those that do, all come with full fitting instructions, but beware, for even the more basic versions can be somewhat difficult for the inexperienced.

☐ **13/11** A quite simple alarm system can be installed on most cars using nothing more than an ordinary On/Off switch and a standard relay. This should be wired up as shown in the illustration with the switch located inside the boot. With this arrangement, the alarm would sound whenever one of the doors is opened, but would stop when it was closed again - that is of course assuming the system had been switched on.

This layout would be unsuitable for those cars with a boot light linked to the interior light system and in this case an externally operated key switch would be required. This should be fitted in so that its terminals are inaccessible from the outside - in the side of the boot is generally the most convenient place.

The standard horn(s) on many cars are low down at the very front and, as such, are relatively easy to get at. It's also relatively easy for any potential thief to pull off the wires so, if this is the case, it might be advisable to resite the horn somewhere else or to fit another.

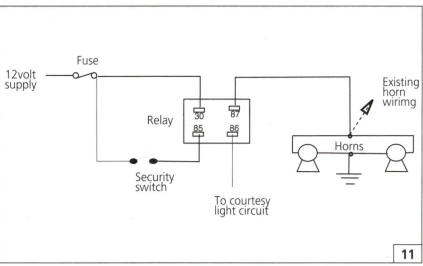

Fuse

12volt supply

Relay

30   87

85   86

Security switch

To courtesy light circuit

Existing horn wirimg

Horns

11

12

Safety First!

☐ **13/12 Before starting work on the electrical system disconnect both terminals of the battery.**

13

☐ **13/13** There are a number of low-cost, DIY alarms, such as the Sparkrite SR70. Also shown here is an optional shock sensor unit which Sparkrite's senior engineer, Neil Smith fitted as an optional extra on this particular installation. This picks up the vibrations if anyone smashes a window and sets off the alarm. The basic unit itself instantly detects any current drop caused by a door being opened (and the interior light coming on) or by anyone turning the ignition key and in both cases, the alarm sounds noisily.

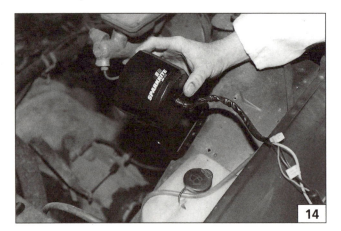

14

☐ **13/14** The alarm unit itself should be situated in the engine compartment close to the front of the vehicle and away from areas of extreme heat and at least 30 cm (12 in) away from the ignition system. After drilling the bodywork, Neil

bolts the bracket to the car using the nuts and bolts provided and then fits the alarm unit onto the bracket.

☐ **13/15** The shock sensor unit has to be placed on a hard surface - a soft-mounted surface would absorb the vibrations that it needs to pick up - and the wires are led through the bulkhead using an existing wiring grommet and fitted to the main alarm unit using the plugs and sockets fitted by the manufacturers to the respective components.

15

☐ **13/16** The SR70 only has four wire connections coming from it. One is fitted with a socket into which you can plug the optional extras available with the SR70; two more go respectively to the feed wire and the earth while the fourth, the yellow cable, is for fitting to the fan on those

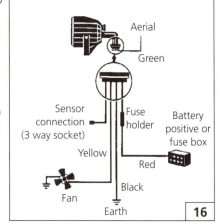

16

vehicles where the electric fan can come on after you've turned the engine off. If you didn't use this connection on those vehicles, the cooling fan turning itself on would of course trigger the alarm.

17

☐ **13/17** Neil holds the red and black terminals on to the positive and negative terminals on the battery (battery connections re-made), asks someone else to arm the alarm by pressing the remote sensor and then after allowing 30 seconds for the alarm to set itself, one of the car doors is opened. This is just to check that the alarm is working correctly. He then carries out a further test by re-arming the alarm and then banging the car doors outer panel with the flat of the hand just to check that the shock sensor is working and not too sensitive. The sensitivity can be adjusted by turning a screw mounted on the unit.

13/18 On this Ford Escort, the alarm was found to work perfectly when connected to the battery and so Neil fitted crimped-on terminals which allowed the wires to be bolted on to the battery terminals. You could easily purchase the right type of terminals from your local accessory shop and crimp them in place with a pair of pliers. If the alarm has not worked satisfactorily when connected to the battery, it

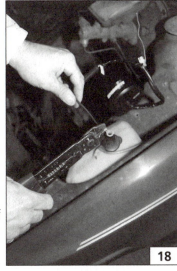

would have been necessary to connect the positive wire to the fuse box following the instructions supplied with the kit.

SCOTCHLOK CONNECTORS

13/19 The Sparkrite SR100 is a slightly more advanced unit and should only be fitted by those who feel they have a basic competence in identifying the correct wires from a wiring diagram in the workshop manual and in making effective wiring connections. Otherwise, it could be quickly and inexpensively fitted by an auto-electrician. Top right of this picture is the SR915 ultra sonic sensor unit which is a plug-in optional. The SR100 comes with two remote control transmitters and a facility for automatic arming. It can easily be set so that the alarm automatically comes into operation 30 seconds after closing the last door on the car. It also has a built-in impact sensor and it immobilises the starter motor circuit when the alarm is sounding. As the alarm sets it not only gives the "chirp" sound of the SR70 but it also flashes the indicators. It is also possible to wire the SR100 in to a central locking system so that the same remote sensor operates both the alarm and the central locking at the same time.

13/20 Sparkrite supply sufficient Scotchlok connectors to enable you to wire in to your existing wiring circuit without the need for any wire stripping. It is essential that you ensure that all such wiring connections are carried out inside the passenger compartment of the car and away from any damp which could cause corrosion to be set up in the connections.

13/21 The alarm unit itself is fitted inside the engine compartment following the same guide lines as for the SR70. The sensitivity control for the shock sensor is built in to the alarm unit and is "tweeked" with a screwdriver, as shown. You are also provided with a key which enables you to turn off the unit via a connector on the back of the unit.

13/22 Neil mounted the LED flashing light near the ignition key. You could fit it anywhere that would be easily visible to the would-be thief. If you purchase one of the more simple units such as the SR70 you can also buy a separate flashing LED to operate in conjunction with the alarm supplied. It is easily connected in to the ignition circuit.

13/23 The movement detectors are clipped behind the door trim and the wire run down the back of the door trim.

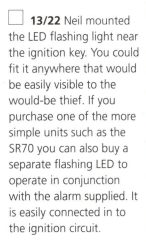

13/24 The connection is simply plugged in to the "black box" which you will later mount under the dashboard. Here, Neil adjusts the sensitivity control so that it picks up any potential movement inside the car without being triggered by air coming through vents that you may inadvertently have left open.

13/27 ...but still connected the alarm into each of the door and the tailgate interior light switch wires. That way, the belts-and-braces approach of current sensing and wire connections was followed.

13/25 The majority of the connections on the SR100 and its accessories are fed into the wiring harness through simple plugs and sockets.

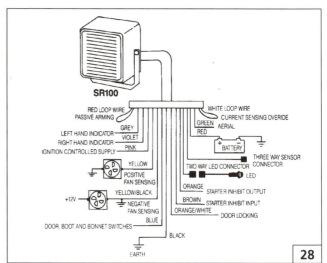

13/28 The SR100 certainly has a lot more connections than the SR70 but everything is clearly described in the instructions supplied with the kit.

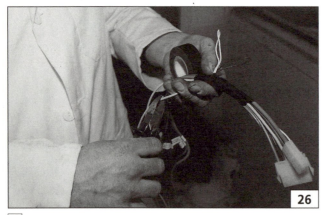

13/26 Neil is shown here snipping through the wire that connects the unit to the cooling fan in the case of those cars where the fan can run on after the ignition is switched off. If it's not wanted, it should be cut and insulated. The two loops of wire shown by Neil's left thumb are also for cutting or keeping as required. If you cut the red loop, passive alarming works i.e. 15 seconds after shutting the car's door the alarm automatically alarms itself. If you cut the white loop the current sensing facility is done away with. Neil left both loops in place...

13/29 Finally, Neil tries out the alarm unit, checking that everything works properly. You can always purchase extra switches for tailgates, rear doors or bonnet, if your car doesn't have them as standard.

Wired Up For Towing

Most modern caravans (and some trailers) have two 7-pin plugs, so two sockets must be fitted to the towing car. One socket (12N) is for the road lights - tail, pilot, stop and flashers. The other socket (12S) is for the accessories - 'split' charging of an extra battery, feeds for the refrigerator, interior lights and so on.

Assuming the tow bar and all the necessary bracketry is fitted, start off by connecting up the two lengths of 7-core cable which are provided in most kits to the two 7-pin sockets as shown in the illustration - the terminal numbers should be marked on the socket and both these and the cable colours are always standard. Then route the two cables through into the lower part of the car boot - if you have to drill holes for the cables, make sure that suitable grommets are fitted.

Connect the 12N socket cables to the appropriate cables in the boot which feed the tail, stop and flasher lights. It's often easiest to use 'Scotchlok' type connectors for this - they should be provided in the kit.

The white cable should be connected to a suitable earthing point on the car body such as a metal stud or mounting bolt.

INSIDE INFORMATION: Don't rely on an earth by simply splicing into an existing spare earth cable - it could lead to all sorts of problems.

Once the 12N socket is fully connected, check the circuits with a test light. This should light up when connected between terminals 58R and 58L and earth with the side/tail lights switched on. Similarly it should light from terminals L and R with the left and right flashers in operation and from terminal 54 when the stop lights are operated. If there are any faults, check the socket wiring - the space allowed is limited and it's relatively easy for just one strand of wire to short across an adjacent terminal or even to earth.

☐ **13/30**

12N TRAILER SOCKET WIRING

Terminal	Code	Cable colour	Function
1	L	Yellow	Left-hand flasher
2	54G	Blue	Fog light
3	31	White	Earth
4	R	Green	Right-hand flasher
5	58R	Brown	Right-hand side/rear lights
6	54	Red	Stop lights
7	58L	Black	Left-hand side/rear lights

In some cases, it will be necessary to fit either a heavy duty flasher unit to the towing car or a supplementary unit in the car boot - the owners manual for the car should give some idea of what may be required.

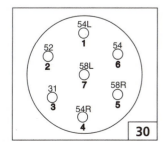

It may also be necessary to add a relay into the stop light circuit to avoid overloading the stop light switch. This would be best incorporated as near to the switch as possible with the switch connected to the relay winding.

BULB FAILURE MONITORS

Where bulb failure monitors are fitted, they will be current sensitive and therefore any trailer socket connections must be made in the relative circuits before the monitor unit - not between the unit and the lights. As, in most cases, the monitor units are located within the boot area, this shouldn't present any great difficulty.

ACCESSORY SOCKET

The basic wiring for the 12S socket can be a little more complex in that it will probably involve running extra (fused) cables the length of the car. If so, it would be best to do so for all the services regardless of whether you currently intend using them or not.

Connections for the interior light(s) and reversing lights are straightforward, but those for the 'fridge and battery 'split' charging circuits would both need a relay. Both would also need fairly heavy gauge cable for the power feed circuits - at least 44/0.30.

13/31

12S TRAILER SOCKET WIRING

1. Reversing light
2. Battery charging
3. Common return (earth)
4. Interior lights
5. Sensing device
6. Fridge
7. Spare

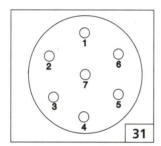

In most cases it would be best to wire the 'fridge relay so that it is energised from an ignition controlled supply. This will ensure that the unit is only working when the engine is running and so avoid the possibility of a flat battery - but full details should be supplied with the refrigerator.

The 'split' charge relay serves much the same purpose in that its purpose is to isolate the car battery from that in the caravan whenever the engine is not running, again preventing the car battery from becoming fully discharged when the caravan electrics are in use. Some manufacturers supply a single unit incorporating both types of relay which helps simplify the wiring details. Full fitting and wiring instructions should be supplied with each unit.

CHAPTER 14
FAULT FINDING

The causes of so many car electrical faults often appear to be blindingly obvious - after they have been located! One of the tricks of accurate diagnosis is to always keep an open mind. This will avoid falling into those traps which are so often set by mysterious electrical happenings. The obvious can so easily be overlooked. A blown fuse can of course be due simply to a shorted cable or accessory - but it can also be caused by a crossed connection.

When checking a car's electrical system it is essential to approach the job in a logical way, starting off with the most obvious. For example, the first check on an inoperative light should be to see if the bulb is serviceable - if you can't see any obvious fault such as a broken element, try swapping the bulb with another that's known to be good. (Illustration, courtesy Autodiagnos UK Ltd.)

defective switches, cables chafing on bodywork or other components and, possibly most important of all, check for poor earths. Where appropriate also inspect other 'linked' components - such as the alternator drive-belt if there's a charging problem or earthing straps if the starter doesn't work following an engine repair.

☐ **14/1** If the bulb appears to be good, the next step would be the fuse, but only if there were a separate fuse to that light. If the circuit to both sidelights, for example, is through a single fuse, then if one light is working the fuse must be in order. On the other hand, if neither light was working, the fuse would be the number one suspect along with the added problem of what caused the fuse to blow. The modern trend is to site the fuse box inside the car where it is better protected. Check where it is on your car and if it contains any spare fuses.

Should both the bulb(s) and the fuse be in order, the next stage would normally be to check for a power supply at the faulty light but, in the absence of any test light or meter, the best alternative would be to carry out a visual check of the circuit as far as possible. Look for loose or broken connections,

☐ **14/2** One of the more common so called 'starter' problems is a loose connection at the main solenoid terminal. This, and the smaller terminals are, on many cars, subjected to spray and debris thrown up by the front wheels.

Terminals do need to be very carefully inspected, particularly at the point of attachment to the inner conductor of the cable - a crimped or soldered joint can look and feel perfect - yet a sharp tug may result in the terminal simply pulling away. This can happen where the joint has parted underneath apparently sound cable insulation, and it is not as unusual a fault as one might expect. Where an intermittent cable or terminal break is suspected, try wriggling the cable and tugging the terminal end connections while applying a continuity test with either a test light or meter.

Don't be disappointed if you cannot find an intermittent short at the first attempt: if necessary, disconnect each circuit from the blowing fuse individually, leaving all the others connected. Once the faulty circuit is disconnected the fuse will no longer blow - and the accessory which is now not operating through disconnection will be the only one requiring serious attention. If the problem is permanent, rather than intermittent, go through the checks as detailed under the 'Short circuit' heading - it saves on fuses.

Blowing fuses can sometimes prove to be a problem, particularly when the fault is intermittent. An intermittent short-circuit is almost always due to occasional movement, where an insulated terminal or cable momentarily touches a metal part of the car. When the insulation chafes through, allowing the inner conductor to touch metal, there is always some indication of this by close visual inspection. Look for signs of glinting bright metal wherever cables come into close proximity with the car bodywork or sharp edges of metal. A chafed cable will probably be more likely to occur in the engine compartment, but it can also occur where any movement is present, such as steering column, brake and clutch pedals, or handbrake.

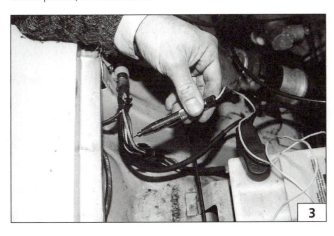

14/3 The best test lights are those with a 'prick-through' probe which can be used to penetrate a cable's insulation without damage.

Open circuits (breaks) can sometimes be just as puzzling, especially where a poor connection or defective terminal the cause. These breaks can be located eventually by progressive use of a test light, but occasionally it is necessary to test a circuit in a wiring harness which is disconnected from the car

On occasions, it may be extremely difficult to gain access to the actual fault area, even though it may be obvious where it is. If it's a cable or connection fault, the easiest answer could well be to run another cable either alongside it or along a different path and disconnecting the old cable and taping up the ends. Try it first on a temporary basis, then if it works well make it a more permanent installation.

at both ends - such as a multi-cable circuit from an electronic ignition amplifier or perhaps an electronic fuel control, to the appropriate electronic module. In such a case there may be no alternative but to test each cable separately using a continuity tester or ohmmeter connected across each individual cable, following the circuit colour coding.

Most car electrical problems are (fortunately) fairly routine - that notorious slipping fan belt which gradually drains the battery; resistive connections in the main starter and battery circuits causing odd starting problems; water on the ignition HT which can actually stop the car in its tracks; intermittent earth connections to lights which will often cause other lights in a combined light housing to glow as the current attempts to return to battery negative earth via any other available path; blowing fuses caused by short-circuits in cables or components, etc. These defects will always be with us, hopefully in small degrees. But at the same time we should always be on guard for the less obvious and more elusive faults. It's so easy to be led right up the garden path when sorting out some car electrical problems!

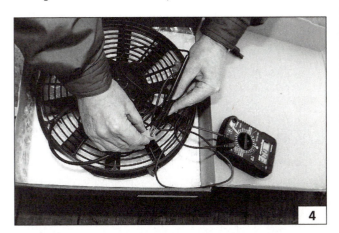

14/4 A simple check on an electric motor (in this case on a cooling fan) is to test for continuity across its input and output terminals. Switch the multimeter to ohms and connect it to each of the terminals - no reading means no go!

14/5 Lack of continuity (across a motor terminals) could mean a break in the armature windings, but is far more likely to be a problem with the commutator and brushes as on this power windows motor.

One of the major hurdles you will need to overcome is to find your way through the circuit diagrams in most workshop manuals - some are pretty good, some are not too bad, many are not far short of a disaster. But really in most cases you don't need a circuit diagram showing a mass of lines which are difficult to trace even with a magnifying glass. What you need to know is what colours the wires are and where they go to or come from. The modern trend is to show this in pictorial form, where it is much easier to follow, than in other forms of circuit diagram.

But then often you can also get away without a diagram of any sort, for although those wiring diagrams may look awfully complex, each circuit is fairly simple, with a line from the battery to the switch, sometimes with a fuse in between, then from the switch to the consumer unit (light, wiper motor or whatever), with an earth (chassis) return back the battery. Where problems can arise is that other circuits may go off from this one, for instance there could be side light, interior light, heater motor, horn circuits all taken off one fuse. So if a defect in one causes the fuse to blow, they are all affected and, as stated earlier, you will have to find which one is at fault..

SHORT CIRCUIT

Probably the most common example of this kind of fault is when for some reason or other battery current leaks directly to earth. It's like connecting one side of the battery to the other and results in a very high rate of current flow through the cable concerned. Normally this will blow the fuse, without causing any further damage, but if it is in a part of the circuit which isn't fused. or if someone has used a piece of wire in place of a fuse, it could result in the cable overheating, burning out and starting a fire.

One further problem that can occur in situations like this is that if the burnt cable is a part of a loom, it could also have burnt other cables in that loom. If so instead of cables shorting to earth, they could short to each other and produce some very strange effects.

Unless there is a fire, the immediate action in the event of a short circuit is to disconnect the battery and then to trace and rectify the defect.

If the short has caused the fuse to blow, connect the test light (or voltmeter) across the two fuse holder clips and re-connect the battery. If there is no fuse connect the test light between the vacant battery terminal and the disconnected battery cable. In both cases the light should come on, assuming any switches in the circuit to be in the 'On' position.

In most cases there will be a number of circuits leading off from the fuse connection. You should now disconnect each of these in turn until the light goes out (or burns very dimly), when it does you have found the defective circuit, which you can then check through. Leave this cable connected and move

on to the next junction or terminal and repeat the test (disconnect it). Carry on until eventually the light stays on; when this happens you have just passed the defect.

☐ 14/6

1. Connect the test light across the blown fuse. With all switches in the circuit closed, the light should glow brightly due to the short.

2. Disconnect each cable in turn; when the light goes out or dims, the faulty circuit is located.

3. Disconnect the suspect cable at the various junctions, numbered 1 to 4 in our drawing. If the light goes out when you do so the problem area has not been reached, but if the light stays on (as it would at 3a), it has been passed.

4. Where the end component is the prime suspect, check this first by disconnecting its power lead. If the test light (across the fuse) goes out, the consumer unit is at fault. (All switches in the circuit must be 'on'.) Obviously if the fuse blew when you switched on any particular consumer unit, you can generally assume the fault to be in that circuit and not bother with disconnecting any others.

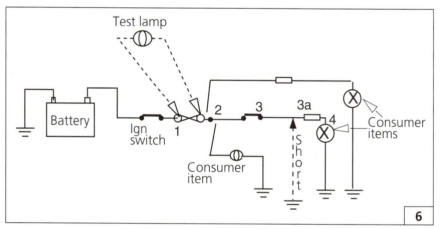

6

---

making it easy! Quite often the fault is not in the circuit as such, but in the end component be it a light, motor or whatever. If you suspect this, ignore the previous checks and go straight to the component, disconnecting its power source, when the test light (connected as before) should go out. If it doesn't it's not the component at fault, but a fault back in the circuit. Any switches in the circuit should be in the 'On' position for this test.

OPEN CIRCUIT

An open circuit is a break or gap somewhere in the line, preventing a flow of electric current and may have resulted from a short circuit. A blown fuse, for example, creates an open circuit.

Other types of open circuit could be a relay or switch not operating, a cable pulled out of its terminal or indeed, a break in the cable.

Tracing an open circuit is relatively easy. Leave the battery connected and wire one side of the test light to a good earth, then with the affected component switched on, follow the circuit back from the component itself, touching the free end of the test light on every junction or connection in turn. If the light comes on brightly you need go no further, from there on back the circuit should be in order.

7

14/7

1. With all switches in the circuit closed, connect the test light between the component power supply and a good earth. If the light comes on the circuit is in order and any fault will be in the component or its earth.

2. If the light does not come on, move back through the circuit, checking (with the test light) from various junctions or terminals to earth.

3. If at some stage, the light does light, go no further - you have passed the defect.

4. It can be assumed that if circuits A, B and C are all out of action, the fault is either at the fuse or the power supply to it. Carry out similar checks on the battery side of the fuse.

If the light comes on at the first stage of this test, that is at the consumer unit, the fault is either in the unit itself or its earth.

HIGH RESISTANCE CIRCUIT

This type of fault can be very similar to an open circuit and both are most likely to occur at a junction or terminal, rather than in the cable itself. In many cases this will be at the earth connection and will result from either dirt or rust or perhaps both.

A typical high resistance circuit would be loose battery connection, resulting in poor starter operation. This could be checked out with a voltmeter, simply by connecting the meter between the battery live terminal and the live terminal at the starter, leaving the original cable connected. When the starter is operated any reading of over would indicate a high resistance. A similar test can be carried out on the earthed part of the circuit, but in this case hook up the voltmeter between the earthed side of the battery and the body of the starter motor, when once again the reading shouldn't exceed 0.2 volts when the starter is operated.

In each of these cases make sure the connection is made to the battery post and not the cable clamp as the high resistance could be in the clamp itself.

This type of voltage drop test can be carried out on any electrical circuit, but a current must be flowing in that circuit, while the test is in progress and the test leads must be connected to each end of the circuit being tested. For example if checking the circuit through a switch, the leads should be connected to each of the its terminals and the switch should be in the 'ON' position.

To some extent a high resistance circuit can be traced in much the same way as for an open circuit, except the test light can vary in light intensity, instead of being extinguished.

MoT Electrics

A large percentage of MoT failures are attributable to problems with the electrical system, the majority of which are lighting defects. These may range from simple bulb failures to more complex wiring troubles, but nearly all could, and should, have been sorted out before the vehicle was submitted for test.

The following list gives some idea of what the examiner will be looking for and includes some related but non-electrical equipment such as windscreen and reflectors. It does not include electrical problems associated with other possible test areas such as an ignition problem causing an emissions failure or starter troubles.

Not all items apply to all vehicles. For example, flashing indicators, rear fog lights and windscreen washers (or even wipers) are not required on some older vehicles. However, if in doubt, work on the assumption that, if they are fitted, they are part of the test.

Lighting Equipment

Includes: Headlights; Side/Tail lights; Stop lights; Rear fog lights; Rear number plate lights; Hazard warning lights; Direction indicators and Reflectors.

All lights that are subject to the test must be in working order, clean and not damaged to such an extent that the light output, colour or function is impaired.

Although proprietary repairs to lenses/reflectors are not excluded, the requirements of the previous paragraph will, effectively, rule out many such repairs.

In general, additional lights (front fog, spot, etc.) are not subject to test, but this doesn't apply to extra stop lights, which are.

INSPECTION

Check that all lights work as they should and that each pair give off more or less the same light intensity. Don't forget the rear number plate and rear fog lights - many people do.

Ensure that all lights are secure and don't flicker if the car is bounced or if the surrounding bodywork is tapped slightly.

Check that operation of one set of lights doesn't affect that of another - most likely with rear lights, rear indicators and stop lights, due to earthing problems.

Ensure that the flashing indicators are operating between 60 and 120 times per minute and that the drivers 'tell-tale' warning light is working. Check also in the 'hazard warning' mode.

Although headlight aim can be checked at home (on a vertical wall) it may not be sufficiently accurate. If any doubt exists, ask the MoT examiner to align the lights if necessary.

General Items

Including windscreen, washer/wipers and horn(s).

INSPECTION

For the purpose of the test, the (wiper) swept area of the windscreen is divided into two zones. The first, a 290mm vertical band centred on the steering wheel, must be free of any damage which cannot be contained within a 10mm diameter circle or a combination of minor damage areas which seriously restricts driver vision. The same basic rules apply to the remainder of the swept area, but that 10mm diameter circle, becomes a 40mm one.

Check that the windscreen washers supply sufficient liquid (in the right direction) to clean the windscreen with the help of the wipers. Make sure the wipers also clean an area large enough to give the driver a clear view forwards and to the sides of the car.

According to the rules any two of three rear view mirrors must be in good condition, secure and, of course, provide a view to the rear. You would be advised to make sure all three do.

The horn should, of course, sound when the control (button) is operated. The sound should be continuous and uniform (but not strident) and loud enough to give adequate warning of approach.

Jump Starting

In the event of a flat battery, it may be necessary to resort to some other method of starting a car engine. This could involve either pushing or towing the car, then engaging gear and letting the clutch up, but in some cases and generally on those cars with automatic transmission and those with catalytic converters, the only answer may be connect the battery of another car up to that of the casualty - a process commonly called slave or jump starting.

To do this you will need a special set of connecting cables, again called slave or jump leads and available from most accessory shops. There are two basic types of jump lead sets available, those with aluminium cored cables and the more expensive copper cored versions. While both may do the job, the copper models are less likely to get hot in use, they will have a much lower voltage drop along their length and generally their terminal clamps are much better made as well.

FACT FILE: EMERGENCY STARTING

Pushing or Towing

NOTE: This is not possible for vehicles with automatic transmission. Diesel engines: only attempt in warm weather or with a warm engine.

Turn off all unnecessary electrical load; switch on ignition and depress the clutch pedal. Select second or third gear; release the clutch when the car reaches a person's running speed.

Starting with Jump Leads

Safety First!
This process can be dangerous and the following instructions must be followed to the letter. Also see **Chapter One,** *Safety First! and the relevant part of* **Chapter 3** *for information on safe handling of car batteries.*

Ensure that the battery providing the jump start has the same voltage (12 volt) as the battery fitted to your car.

Do not lean over the battery during jump starting.

Switch off all unnecessary electrical loads and apply the hand brake. Auto. Transmission: Place gear selector in 'P'. Manual Transmission: Place gear shift lever in neutral.

Note that on some batteries and on battery connections, '+' (positive) terminals are coloured red and '-' (negative) terminals are coloured blue or black.

Run the engine of the vehicle providing the jump start (if battery fitted to vehicle).

(The following instruction numbers refer to the numbers on the drawing.)

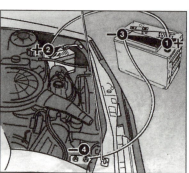

1. Connect one end of the jump lead to the positive ('+') terminal of the battery providing the jump start.

2. Connect the other end of the same lead to the positive terminal on the car being started.

3. Connect one end of the other jump lead to the negative ('-') terminal on the 'slave' battery...

4. ...and the other end to the negative battery lead on the car, or to some bare metal in the car's engine bay.

Now try to start the car as quickly as is reasonably possible.

IT IS IMPORTANT that the leads are removed in the exact reverse sequence to that shown above. Keep hands, hair and loose clothing away from moving parts in both engine bays.

IMPORTANT NOTE: Some cars with catalytic converters, electronic ignition and fuel injection systems may be damaged if jump started in this way. If so it should be stated in the car's handbook. The only alternative on many of these is to remove the battery (although check this too in the handbook) then connect up the jump leads as before (+ to +, - to -) and run the donor car for about 20 minutes at a fast idle. This should provide sufficient power for the battery to start the casualty.

APPENDIX 1
GLOSSARY OF ICE TERMS

AUTO STOP - A cassette deck feature used on sets which do not have auto-reverse and whereby the cassette will stop automatically when it reaches the end of one side.

AUTO REVERSE -A system whereby the tape direction is automatically changed at the end of the cassette.

BALANCE - The control on a head unit which 'moves' the sound from side to side.

BASS - Sounds occurring in the low frequency range, up to approximately 600 Hz.

CD-IN PLUG - To the most sophisticated and modern units a possibility of inserting a CD sound source is available. A portable CD player can be plugged in and the radio/cassette deck provides the amplification for playing through the vehicle speakers.

CHROME DIOXIDE TAPE - This is a cassette tape which has a magnetic coating of chrome dioxide (CR02) in order to give better reproduction.

DOLBY NOISE REDUCTION™ - A system developed by Ray Dolby as a means of reducing the tape hiss inherent in the cassette format. There are now two types, Dolby 'B' and Dolby 'C'.

FADER - A balance control allowing the sound to be regulated between the front and rear of the car with four speaker set-up.

FERRIC TAPE - A tape with a magnetic coating of iron oxide particles. Improves the quality of tape reproduction, though not as much as chrome dioxide.

GRAPHIC EQUALISER - Basically a sophisticated tone control, capable of altering individual frequency ranges. Highly desirable in the un-acoustic box of the motor car.

HERTZ (Hz) - A measurement of frequency in cycles per second. The lower the figure, the lower the sound. The other measurement you are likely to meet is Kilohertz (KHz) being thousands of Hertz. Thus a reference may be either 10 KHz or 10,000 Hz.

LA.C. (Electronic Interference Absorption Circuit) - The electronic systems of your own and of other cars generate radio noises. This electronic circuit eliminates them. It also acts as a noise suppressor for static generated from any other source.

LINE-OUT - The DIN 45326 plug allows the head unit to be connected to an external amplifier, taking the preamplified signal from the sound source.

LOUDNESS - At low sound pressure, the human ear loses sensitivity to low and high frequencies. The loudness circuit amplifies these two extremes, to offer a better perception of sound detail and finesse.

MID RANGE SPEAKER - A loudspeaker which is designed to handle frequencies from the middle of the range, from approximately 300 - 12,000 Hz.

MUSIC POWER - The maximum (peak) power available from an amplifier for a short period of time, whether a separate unit or as part of a radio/cassette deck. See also Rated Power.

NOMINAL POWER RATING - The maximum electric power, measured in Watts, that a loudspeaker can handle continuously.

PHASING - The odd effect caused by incorrect wiring of the speaker terminals, where one speaker cone is moving out as the other is moving in. Loss of bass response is one side effect

PLL CIRCUIT - This is a radio feature. PLL stands for phased locked loop, an electronic circuit with a quartz stabilised frequency scanning system into which frequencies are locked and held with high stability.

PRESET SCAN - By pressing this button, the tuner will 'scan' each memorised station, pausing for approximately five seconds before progressing to the next. When you reach the station you require, simply press again to retain it,

RATED POWER (RMS) - The average continuous maximum power output of an amplifier.

RDS - A system of electronic codes sent with certain FM signals. These can be decoded by sets equipped with special tuners and provide such services as traffic information and automatic same station following.

SENSITIVITY SELECTOR - This means that you may choose. during automatic search function, between receiving all stations (DX) or the stronger ones only (LOCal).

SPECTRUM ANALYSER - A graphic equaliser function showing visual display of how the sound is made up throughout the frequency range. The display is usually in the form of LED lights.

SUB-WOOFER - A loudspeaker for reproducing only the very lowest of frequencies and whose sound is visually felt, rather than heard. Will usually handle frequencies up to 200 Hz but work best below 80 Hz.

TREBLE - The sound which occurs in the high frequency range, approximately 4,000 - 20,000 Hz.

TWEETER - A loudspeaker which reproduces very high frequencies.

TWO-WAY LOUDSPEAKER - A speaker which has two speakers of different types in a single housing. For example, a mid-range and a tweeter. Also called a co-axial speaker.

WOOFER - A loudspeaker designed to handle only base frequencies, up to approximately 600 Hz.

WOW AND FLUTTER - Uneven sounds caused by speed variations in the cassette deck tape transport mechanism.

APPENDIX 2
GLOSSARY OF GENERAL TERMS

Ampere Electrical unit of measurement used to record the flow of electricity in a circuit. Generally referred to as amp or amps and measured with an ammeter.

Automatic advance A term used to describe process of making the spark occur earlier (advanced) as the engine speed increases. See centrifugal advance.

Ballast resistor Special wire or resistor which reduces the voltage applied to the coil in the ignition circuit. It is by- passed when the starter motor is in operation so as to provide a stronger spark for starting purposes.

Brush, distributor cap A small rod of carbon in the centre terminal housing of the distributor cap which is spring loaded into rubbing contact with the rotor arm.

Camshaft The second shaft of the engine which rotates at half crankshaft speed and is used to control the opening and closing of the valves. In most engines it also drives the distributor.

Capacitor Sometimes called a condenser, this is a non- conducting component that can store an electrical charge and release it when required to do so.

Capacitor discharge ignition An electronic ignition system in which a capacitor is charged up and then made to discharge through a transformer, to produce a very high energy but short- lived spark at the plug.

Centrifugal advance A method of advancing the spark, using springs and pivoted weights in the distributor.

Circuit In electrical terms a path or track along which electricity can flow.

Circuit diagram An illustration showing the layout of a number of circuits.

Coil As used in the ignition is made up of primary and secondary windings around a soft iron core ,and transforms the voltage supplied by the battery to that required by igniting the mixture.

Contact breaker A mechanically operated switch in the distributor which is used to interrupt the primary current.

Contactless ignition A version of electronic ignition in which the system is triggered by means other than the contact breaker.

Conventional ignition A term often used to describe ignition systems where the coil primary current is switched by the contact breakers.

Detonation A condition in the combustion chamber where part of the fuel/air mixture self detonates, causing a shock wave which produces a metallic tinkling sound known as pinking. Among other causes this can result from over-advanced ignition.

Digital ignition A form of electronic ignition, where the timing of the spark is controlled by a microcomputer. Ignition data is stored in the computers in the form of three dimensional maps, providing the optimum timing for all engine conditions.

Distributor A device used for directing the high tension current to the sparking plugs. In most applications it also houses the contact breaker capacitor and centrifugal advance mechanism.

Dwell meter A meter used to measure the dwell angle. In most cases it is one mode of a multi-meter instrument.

Dwell period The period of distributor cam movement, when the contact points are closed. This can be quoted in degrees and termed the dwell angle, or as a percentage and termed the dwell period.

Dynamic timing A phrase used to describe the method of checking the ignition timing with the engine running.

Electronic ignition Ignition systems employing electronics to switch the coil primary current.

Feeler gauge A thin strip of metal of a pre-determined thickness used for measuring purposes (contact-breaker). Non- metallic (plastic) gauges must be used for measuring the air gap in some electronic ignition systems.

Firing order The order in which the sparking plugs fire the mixture in a multi-cylinder engine. A typical in-line four cylinder firing order would be 1,3,4,2.

Four stroke principle A cycle of operations in an engine whereby the piston moves through four stroke to complete the cycle.

Generator Machine used to generate electricity. A DC generator is termed a dynamo and machine that (initially) produces an AC current is called an alternator.

Hall effect Triggering device used to initiate the ignition process. Named after the American E H Hall.

High tension Term used to describe that part of the ignition system which operates at very high voltages.

Ignition timing The time at which the spark occurs. If this should be late the ignition is said to be retarded, whereas advanced ignition means that the spark occurred earlier than it should be.

Low tension Term used to describe that part of the ignition system which operates at battery voltage or less.

Map ignition A term sometimes used for digital ignition systems.

Multi-meter An instrument capable of making a number of electrical measurements.

Ohm Electrical unit of resistance. Measured with an ohm- meter.

Ohms law Basic law of electrical theory which shows the relationship of electrical pressure (volts) resistance (ohms) and current flow (amps),

Pinking The common name for the metallic tinkling noise produced by either detonation or pre-ignition.

Pre-ignition Also known as pre-detonation, this is a condition where the fuel/air mixture in the combustion chamber is ignited before the spark occurs. Can produce similar symptoms as detonation.

Primary winding The winding in the coil which carries battery voltage or less.

Rotor arm A non-conductive rotor mounted on the distributor shaft with a metal electrode on its uppermost surface, which provides a path for the high tension current from the centre of the distributor cap to segments around its outer circum-ference.

Running-on Term used to describe the tendency for an engine to keep on firing after being switched off.

TAC ignition Short for Transistor Assisted Contact, this is a form of electronic ignition system which uses the contact breaker points to initiate the ignition process.

Secondary winding The winding in the coil which carries battery voltage.

Timing mark Mark or marks on either the flywheel or crankshaft pulley which are used in conjunction with marks or pointers on the engine to time the ignition.

Tracking Term used to describe the phenomenon where HT current finds its own path or track over an insulated surface.

Transistor A solid state electronic device which can be made to function as a remote controlled switch in much the same way as an electrical relay.

Two stroke principle A cycle of operation where the piston moves through two strokes to complete the cycle.

Vacuum Advance A method of making the spark occur earlier when the engine is lightly loaded.

Volt Electrical unit of pressure, sometimes referred to as potential difference or electro-motive force (emf). Measure with a voltmeter.

APPENDIX 3
SPECIALISTS & SUPPLIERS
FEATURED IN THIS BOOK

All of the products and specialists listed below have contributed in various ways to this book. All of the consumer products used are available through regular high street outlets or by mail order from specialist suppliers.

Autocar Equipment Ltd., 49-51 Tiverton Street, London, SE1 6NZ. Tel: 0171 403 4334
Lumentition electronic ignition aerials, security systems, in-car entertainment.

Robert Bosch Ltd., PO Box 98, Broadwater Park, North Orbital Road, Denham, Uxbridge, Middlesex, UB9 5HJ. Tel: 01895 838547
Car electronic systems, petrol injection systems, component manufacture and re-manufacture (alternators, starters), test equipment, diesel injection equipment.

Boyer Bramsden, Frindsbury House, Cox Lane, Detling, Maidstone, Kent, ME14 3HE. Tel: 01622 730939
Electronic ignition.

Champion, Arrowbrooke Road, Upton, Wirral, Merseyside, L49 0UQ. Tel: 0151 678 7070
Sparking plugs, wiper blades, ignition leads.

Draper Tools Ltd, Hursley Road, Chandlers Ford, Eastleigh, Hants, SO5 5YF. Tel: 01703 266355
Tools and electronic test equipment.

Ford Motor Co., Customer Services Division, Royal Oak Way South, Daventry, Northants, NN11 5NT. Tel: 01628 890505.

Gunson Ltd., Coppen Road, Dagenham, Essex, RM8 1NU. Tel: 0181 984 8855
DIY and professional electrical and electronic test equipment.

Hella Ltd., (Beru), Wildmere Industrial Estate, Banbury, Oxon, OX16 7JU. Tel: 01295 272233
Lighting accessories sparking plugs (Beru) electronic test equipment (Optilux).

Lucas Aftermarket Operations, Great Hampton Street, Birmingham, B18 6AU. Tel: 0121 236 5050
Car electronic systems, petrol injection systems, component

re-manufacturer (alternators, starters), test equipment, diesel injection equipment.

Maplin Electronics, P O Box 3, Rayleigh, Essex, SS6 8LR. Tel: 01702 552911
Electronic ignition kits, test equipment.

Newtronic Systems Ltd., Unit 3, Blackburn Technology Management Centre, Challenge Way, Blackburn, Lancs, BB1 1QB. Tel: 01254 680187
Piranha electronic ignition systems.

NGK Spark Plugs (UK) Ltd., 7-9 Garrick Industrial Centre, Hendon, London, NW9 6AQ. Tel: 0181 202 2151
Spark plugs, plug covers and technical ceramics (sensors).

Ring Automotive, Gelderd Road, Leeds, LS12 6NB. . Tel: 01532 791791
Lighting and accessories.

Sparkrite Ltd., Brenda Road, Hartlepool, Cleveland, TS25 2BQ. Tel: 01922 743676

Speedograph Richfield Ltd., 104 Rolleston Drive, Arnold, Nottingham, NG5 7JR. Tel: 01602 264235
Instruments and associated accessories.

Sykes Pickavant, Kilnhouse Lane, Lytham-St-Annes, Lancs, FY8 3DU. Tel: 01253 721291
Tools and electronic test equipment.

Time Instrument Manufacturers Ltd., 5 Alston Drive, Bradwell Abbey, Milton Keynes, MK13 9HA.
Instruments and associated accessories.

Vauxhall Motors Ltd., Griffin House, P O Box 3, Osborne Road, Luton, Bedfordshire, LU2 0SY. Tel: 01582 21122
See your local main dealer in Yellow Pages for Vauxhall parts.